Scotland, Darien and the Atlantic World, 1698–1700

Scotland, Darien and the Atlantic World, 1698–1700

Julie Orr

EDINBURGH
University Press

Edinburgh University Press is one of the leading university presses in the UK. We publish academic books and journals in our selected subject areas across the humanities and social sciences, combining cutting-edge scholarship with high editorial and production values to produce academic works of lasting importance. For more information visit our website: edinburghuniversitypress.com

© Julie Orr, 2018

Edinburgh University Press Ltd
The Tun – Holyrood Road
12 (2f) Jackson's Entry
Edinburgh EH8 8PJ

Typeset in 10.5/13 Adobe Sabon by
IDSUK (DataConnection) Ltd, and
printed and bound in Great Britain

A CIP record for this book is available from the British Library

ISBN 978 1 4744 2753 1 (hardback)
ISBN 978 1 4744 2754 8 (paperback)
ISBN 978 1 4744 2755 5 (webready PDF)
ISBN 978 1 4744 2756 2 (epub)

The right of Julie Orr to be identified as author of this work has been asserted in accordance with the Copyright, Designs and Patents Act 1988 and the Copyright and Related Rights Regulations 2003 (SI No. 2498).

Contents

Figures

Note on Dates

At the time of the events studied here, Spain had adopted the use of the Gregorian calendar. Scotland and England continued to utilise the Julian calendar, which resulted in dates ten days prior to those of the Spaniards. Dates contained in the following chapters are those cited by the individual document or author relevant to the event being discussed and have not been altered.

Acknowledgements

Three trips to Panama in the 1990s may have introduced me to that nation's rich history and environment, but only hinted at the range of experiences I would have pursuing the story of the Company of Scotland. From walking atop the old walls of Cartagena to months spent in Seville to a long-anticipated trip to Havana, the amazement and curiosity that compelled me to explore the story never diminished. Although I appreciated all I learned of the profound role of New Caledonia in the history of Scotland, I also saw its saga as a quintessential tale of the Americas. My initial view, supported by much of my early reading, indicated that the attempt to create the trading colony was unique in the sense that its ephemeral existence had a profound impact on its country of origin, but left the host territory virtually unscathed. Time and time again I learned I could not have been more wrong, my research continually revealing intricate, durable remnants of the Scots' failed effort within the entangled Atlantic World.

Along the way I had the unprecedented good fortune to spend a year at the University of Granada and to subsequently find my way to the University of Dundee and the guidance of Dr Christopher Storrs. As I completed my PhD he consistently shared my enthusiasm and provided support as I adapted to a new field of scholarship and a foreign system of higher education, simultaneously struggling to eliminate my American versions of both Spanish and English from writing and conversation. Appreciation is also due to Drs Christopher Whatley, Carlos Martínez Shaw and Arne Bialuschewski for their respective roles in reviewing my work and urging me on. It was an honour to work with them all.

Tribute is also due to those who participated in the original story of the expeditions. Despite the distance of over three centuries I thought of them often as I walked across the plaza following a day in the Archivo General de Indias, realising that Captain Pincarton had covered the same ground and would have recognised many of the structures surrounding me. Additional research in Simancas, Madrid, Boston, Jamaica, Maidstone, Edinburgh, Greenwich and Kew inevitably impressed on me the geographical extent of their story and the responsibility of expanding their legacies.

As the following chapters have evolved from academic work to book manuscript there are the related expressions of appreciation: for the kind permission of the Board of Trustees of the Chevening Estate to utilise excerpts from the Stanhope of Chevening manuscripts, to the Royal Bank of Scotland Archives for use of quotes from Company of Scotland directors' meetings, to the National Maritime Museum/Caird Library, Greenwich for material relating to Admiral Benbow's activities in the Caribbean, to the Massachusetts Historical Society for use of the Francis Russell Hart collection, to the National Library of Scotland for inclusion of numerous portions of the Darien Papers, and to Spain's Archivo General de Indias for the opportunity to use the superb work of seventeenth-century engineers. Special appreciation is warranted to Dr Melissa Lucas for her translations of seventeenth-century Danish documents.

Finally, my most significant gratitude goes to my daughter, Sydney Freeland, and my late cousin, Pam Clark. Their examples of courage, poise and determination under the most challenging of circumstances sustained me through my own far less demanding efforts, and to them I dedicate this work.

Julie Orr
Dolores, Colorado

Abbreviations

AGI	Archivo General de Indias, Seville
AGS	Archivo General de Simancas
AHN	Archivo Historico Nacional, Madrid
BL	British Library, London
CSP	Calendar of State Papers
HL	Huntington Library, San Marino, California
KHLC-Stanhope	Kent History and Library Centre, Maidstone, Stanhope of Chevening Manuscripts
MHS-Hart	Massachusetts Historical Society, Boston, Francis Russell Hart Collection
NA	National Archives, Kew
NRS	National Records of Scotland, Edinburgh
NLJ	National Library of Jamaica
NLS	National Library of Scotland, Edinburgh
NMM-Caird	National Maritime Museum/Caird Library, Greenwich
RBS Archives	Royal Bank of Scotland Archives, Edinburgh
UGSp	University of Glasgow, Special Collections
ULIHR	University of London, Institute of Historical Research

)

1

Introduction

The Spaniards, whom it highly concerns, will do their utmost to disturb us, but unless they be assisted by some other Nation, we have no great Reason to fear them; for the daily confluence from all parts, of great Shoals of People, the Strength of the Scituation of Fort St Andrew, the League with the Indians, and the frequent Defiles will render it an Enterprize too difficult for them. They made some feeble Attempts from St Maria, but we dispatching a few selectmen, under Command of Capt. Montgomery, met them in a Plantain Walk, quickly dispersed them, took over 100 Prisoners, and among the rest their Chief Commander Don Domingo de La Rada, who is as yet a Prisoner at Fort St Andrew, and will be continued there till we have a Good Account of the Spaniards treatment of Capt. Pinkarton . . . As we grow stronger, we shall endeavour to procure a part in the South Sea, from whence it's not above 6 weeks Sail to Japan, and some parts of China . . .[1]

SUCH INITIAL REPORTS FROM the Company of Scotland's first expedition to the coast of Panama to establish a trading colony were full of promise, but tragically saturated with unrequited hope. Spanish and allied forces would overwelm the sickly and starving New Caledonia in March 1700, Domingo de la Rada was actually an opportunistic trader who gave the Scots a hard lesson in survival in the Americas, Captain Robert Pincarton would be tried and convicted of piracy in Spain, and no Darien Scot would find a way across the Isthmus and on to Japan or China.

Over two and a half centuries later, writing of his recent archaeological surveys across Panama's Darien province, José María Cruxent would describe Spain's early abandonment of its local Caribbean coastline, with the result that other Europeans, motivated by New World riches and fortified by alliances with native populations, were drawn to the region. Most incursions, the Spanish-born Venezuelan explained, were essentially raiding parties and inconsequential to his scientific studies. The major exception was the 1698 arrival of the Scots and their intent to establish a permanent presence on the Isthmus. Cruxent had located their settlement of Fort Saint Andrew, easy to delineate due to its defensive canal excavated in coral rock and the presence of bricks, unique among sites he had examined across the area. Meticulously documented were the scattered ceramics, dated to the latter seventeenth century and identified as having been produced in the Lower Rhine for export to England and her colonies.[2]

Through his cataloguing of the anomalous infrastructure and dispersed fragments of the Company of Scotland settlement, the archaeologist provides a metaphor for the singular impacts of the Darien expeditions and their dispersed yet durable remnants on three continents. His accompanying reference to the allure of the strategic strip of land bridging the Atlantic and Pacific, enhanced by minimal Spanish development and proven opportunities for native support, addresses the high value of the property not only for the Scots, but also for the substantial cast of opposing interests determined to witness New Caledonia's failure.

Although the enterprise had a profound influence on diminished Scottish sovereignty and consolidation of parliamentary authority in Westminster resulting from the Treaty of Union of 1707, that justifiably well-examined aspect of the Company of Scotland should not be allowed to eclipse recognition of its implications and influence across a far broader geography. From New York and Jamaica, from Rome to Lima and across Spain, reactions were deliberate and dramatic. Testimony of Councillor and Captain Robert Pincarton before the judges of the Casa de la Contratación, payment of a *donativo* by churches across Mexico, conflicts between Jewish and English merchants in Jamaica, and confrontation with Danes on Crab Island all attest to the intensity and breadth of reverberations asserting themselves as the Company of Scotland implemented its dream of a flourishing trading enterprise. Economic implications were manifested not only in mercantile interest piqued across the Caribbean and up the coast of British North America, but also in Lisbon, where Spanish impoundment in Cartagena of slave ships belonging to Portugal's Cacheu Company and its English subcontractors resulted in lost revenues and frayed relations.[3]

Within the chaotic opportunism that characterised the Atlantic World at the close of the seventeenth century, the actions of the Company of Scotland provided enticing opportunities for alliance, redemption, intelligence-gathering and self-promotion. Juxtaposed against arbitration in Europe of the Partition Treaties and the anticipated death of Spain's King Carlos II, the Scots' offence to Madrid allowed Louis XIV ideal circumstances to proffer armed naval assistance and information, ingratiating France to the identical governor of Cartagena who had been so soundly humiliated three years prior during French raids on his city. The English also showed little hesitation in seeking advantage, deploying Admiral Benbow to the Caribbean with offers of support to Spanish governors along the coast. Convenient acquisition of intelligence from his squadron's calls along the Spanish Main not only provided updates to London on the activities of the Scots, but would also enhance the Royal Navy's knowledge of ports and defences during the forthcoming War of the Spanish Succession. Surviving their months within the colony, men such as the deserter Robert Allen and the eventual governor of Annapolis Royal Samuel Vetch would strive to seek personal advancement, marketing their individual experiences and acquired knowledge for position and financial reward.

Nor was the highest level of European diplomacy exempted from involvement in the short but turbulent history of New Caledonia. While the Spanish ambassador in London met with his Scottish spy and relayed the latest developments to Madrid, King William III was forced to initiate a campaign to assure Spain of his non-involvement and astonishing lack of awareness of his Scottish kingdom's initiatives. With no time to spare, the British monarch would finally heed the caution of his advisers, assigning the Hague's trusted envoy to Madrid to seek from the Spanish king a stay on the ordered execution of four Darien survivors convicted of piracy by the court of the Casa de la Contratación.

There were no less significant impacts for Spanish America. The threat imposed by the intent to create a permanent foreign enclave between the vital centres of Portobello and Cartagena, with its potential to interrupt the critical transport of Spanish wealth from the Pacific to the Atlantic, activated the intricate colonial complex of administrative and military resources that would effectively expel the Scots, even without the support of the armada mounted and dispatched from Cadiz. The native Cuna, in whose territories events unfolded and armed conflict was waged, would witness among the most immediate effects. Having cultivated relationships with a succession of European arrivals over the previous two centuries, their equally established history of discord with the Spanish, coupled with alarm over the Scots' attempt at permanent foreign occupation, provided a brutal reminder not just to Panama and Cartagena, but also to Lima and Madrid, of the absolute requirement to impose control over the highly coveted but porous Isthmus.

Inevitably, investigation into the broader implications of the Darien expeditions also reveals new and sometimes contradictory detail regarding individual participants, events that unfolded, and the way history has recorded them. From interrogations of deserters and prisoners to definitive identification of Walter Herries as a spy dealing directly with the Spanish Ambassador to testimony of the four men and one boy incarcerated in

Seville and reports of various Spanish officials' conversations with Admiral Benbow, new voices contribute their diverse Company of Scotland stories. Military composition of the enterprise, clear intent to trade illegally along the Spanish Main, the international crew, and initial censorship masking the degree of desertion all contribute to a broader understanding of what transpired and why. The contention of Casa de la Contratación judges that trade goods stowed on the *Dolphin* proved intent of the Company to participate in contraband trade directly contrasts with prevalent criticism and what has become accepted ridicule of the Scots' cargo. Reports submitted to Madrid by the governor of Cartagena verifying the accuracy of often denigrated accounts provided in pamphlets authored by the surgeon–spy Herries and dispatches from the Danish command sent to expel the Scots from Crab Island indicate the importance of re-evaluating the role of the Darien expeditions in creating and exacerbating tensions across an already entangled Atlantic World.

Any reassessment of the Company of Scotland must also acknowledge those who experienced the ordeal of New Caledonia. The lack of coordinated or consolidated departures from Darien by its surviving participants, including its deserters, has been a deterrent to thorough examination of the inadvertent diaspora they created. Though a small number of individuals did return to Scotland, contributions of the majority who settled in new communities scattered across the Americas would be notable. Colonel John Anderson's future in New Jersey, the acquisition of an estate on Jamaica by Colonel Guthrie and the addition of Archibald Stobo to the ministry in South Carolina are all significant, yet the unsung, undocumented lives of those who integrated into landscapes across Spanish and British America also deserve credit for their adaptation to completely unintended circumstances and itineraries far from the Panamanian coast where they anticipated a vibrant and promising future.

AMBITION AND ANXIETY

Accumulated evidence presented in the following pages supporting New Caledonia's broad wake across the Atlantic World exposes new complexities of a story that coincide with a fundamental premise shared by Scots and Spaniards in their respective hopes and fears regarding the Company of Scotland's potential. Although Scottish aspirations were not achieved and Spanish anxieties not realised, neither party had assumed the project's impact to be confined to a singular coastline, province, country or ocean. Both intruder and established colonial claimant considered the scope of the endeavour to be of immense expanse. In printed declarations widely and recklessly distributed from the barely established New

Caledonia in December 1698, the colony's governing council, seeking reinforcements for the fledgling settlement, enthusiastically declared the benefits of their chosen location,

> besides its being one of the most healthful, rich, and fruitful Countries upon Earth, hath the advantage of being a narrow ISTHMUS, seated in the heighth of the World, between two vast Oceans, which renders it more convenient than any other for being the common Store-house of the insearchable and immense Treasures of the Spacious South Seas, the door of Commerce to China and Japan, and, the Emporium and Staple for the Trade of both Indies.[4]

Spain's reciprocal concerns, prompting her to mobilise European and American resources to meet the threat, mirrored those of the Scots and voiced the additional element of religious protectionism. Responding to verification of the arrival and installation of intruders on the Isthmus, the Council of the Indies, peak of the administrative hierarchy overseeing Spain's overseas dominions, expressed the gravity of the situation through an advisory *consulta* to King Carlos II in May 1699:

> The Council represents to your majesty that with great regret and pain it hears not only confirmation that Scotch have obtained a foothold in Darien ... that which previously was menace only is today fact, and shortly these dominions will begin to experience violence, robbery, usurpation of provinces, in course of which the Catholic religion will perish, which is what will most deeply grieve your majesty's Catholic Heart. And although the nations will combat each other in those quarters, which may serve us as diversion yet, in the long run, all falls upon us, since their object is to seize those rich, far-extended kingdoms, whose treasure fertilizes, maintains, conserves these dominions, and although these nations be divided among themselves, ours must decline, for its commerce will fall off, and we will find ourselves lacking the substance which supports the body of this monarchy.[5]

Clearly, neither the Company of Scotland nor the Council of the Indies regarded the former's campaign to establish a trading entrepôt in Darien as an inconsequential colonial initiative symptomatic of the essentially unrestrained and pervasive illicit trading of the last decade of the seventeenth century. Both major protagonists acknowledged menace and opportunity, dosed with critical native alliances, defence of religious faith and major economic stakes. The perceived field of competition was not limited to a small peninsula of land extending into the Caribbean Sea demarcated by an excavation of coral rock, but instead extended across the Isthmus to the South Sea, down that coast to Peru, and across the Pacific to China and Japan.

THE CAUTIONARY TALE

The Scotland of the 1690s suffered crop failure and starvation, rising tariffs imposed on vital linen exports to England, resulting social unrest, and, following the 1697 termination of the Nine Years War, an influx of newly unemployed veterans of King William's Scottish troops.[6] Seeking to emerge from the troubled social and economic landscape, events upon which the following chapters are based, had their formal beginning in 1695 with sanction by the sovereign Scottish Parliament of the newly created Company of Scotland Trading to Africa and the Indies. Notably, required approval of King William, absent in the Low Countries, was instead provided by his high commissioner in Scotland, an action which later would be utilised by the monarch to defend ignorance of his Scottish kingdom's intent to intrude on Spanish territory.

Originally designed to be guided by a combined contingent of Scottish and English directors, the Company quickly succumbed to rivalries between London- and Scotland-based factions. As Scottish historian George Insh writes in his history of the Company, intentions of English interests focused on distinctly commercial success and conflicted with broader Scottish desires to facilitate their nation's long-desired but elusive participation in colonial development and emerging global commerce.[7] The chasm that developed between the competing sides provoked the Company's evolution into a distinctly Scottish joint-stock effort, based in Edinburgh and funded solely by Scottish subscribers. Along with the patriotic fuelling of economic support came the opportunity for the Scottish projecter and former Bank of England director William Paterson to finally witness the realisation of his long-held personal dream of a Darien-based trading entrepôt.[8]

Preparations for the implementation of the enterprise, facing a myriad of financial and political obstacles, continued in earnest during 1696 and 1697, with Company representatives being dispatched to Amsterdam and Hamburg to oversee the acquisition of appropriate vessels while trade goods and provisions to establish a colony were consolidated in Scotland. Markedly absent was serious study and debate regarding Spain's history on the Isthmus and the reaction that could legitimately be expected from an initiative by any foreign entity to establish a permanent presence in the strategic heart of her American colonial holdings. As presented in Chapter 5, Company of Scotland personnel would vehemently stand by their claims that they had sailed from Leith in July 1698 under sealed orders, ignorant of their final destination and unaware of the fatal affront they were about to impose on Spain and her empire.

The subsequent saga of New Caledonia encompasses successive abandonments of the site, missed arrivals of relief expeditions, issuance of proclamations ordered by King William prohibiting support or communication with the colony, the deliberate and forceful reaction of Spain and the involvement of a multitude of non-Company concerns. As presented in the following pages, challenges facing the colony also included desertion, poor and inadequate planning and supplies, and crippling internal strife. Permeating all was an ever-expanding list of fatalities: of the 1,200 individuals who sailed from Leith with the first expedition, forty-four died on the voyage to Darien, 300 at the site of the colony and 400 during the subsequent middle voyages between Darien and Jamaica and New York.[9]

The relative brevity of intermittent Scottish residence on the Isthmus, extending less than a year and a half from anchorage off Golden Island in November 1698 until final capitulation to allied Spanish forces in March 1700, did not, however, result in the immediate demise of its sponsoring company. Despite extreme capital and human losses incurred in its Darien initiative, the Company of Scotland Trading to Africa and the Indies had continued to dispatch ships to Africa and the East Indies. Meeting with their own series of questionable circumstances, these voyages added to growing discord with English trading concerns and culminated with the seizure in the Downs of the Company's *Annandale* in January 1704 and the retribution-fuelled capture and eventual hanging of crew from the *Worcester* by the Scots over the following months.

A semblance of resolution of the entire Darien affair would finally emerge among negotiations leading to 1707's Treaty of Union. As with other aspects of the intended establishment of New Caledonia, soothing economic losses would provide the basis for easing the initiative's acceptance. The Scots would acquire not only their long-sought free trade with England and colonial markets, but the unprecedented creation of the Equivalent would pay back, with interest, a broad spectrum of Company of Scotland investors. In return, Scotland would not only relinquish vital aspects of her sovereignty, but the Company of Scotland Trading to Africa and the Indies, along with dreams of a rich and thriving Scottish trading empire, would be dissolved.

Though the demise of New Caledonia had a profound impact on Scotland's future, it also imposed profound stresses upon the region it had sought to inhabit. Ignorant of the long-established history of entangled and virulent sociopolitics in the region to which they sailed, the Company exacerbated a myriad of existing conflicts. Having initiated the fortifications of Fort Saint Andrew and forged alliances with factions of resident

Cuna, the Scots literally constructed the strongest possible reminder to the Spanish of the vulnerability and attraction of the Darien region to outside invaders. Not only did the area have to cope with the responding influx of Spanish and associated forces and the trauma of actual combat, Scottish promises to defend their local allies against Spanish colonial authority were abruptly negated by the March 1700 capitulation, causing both immediate reprisals upon the native population and efforts to formulate longer term strategies to prevent future such occurrences.

EUROPEAN DISTRACTION, AMERICAN DISQUIET

As New Caledonia struggled to survive persistent setbacks, the greater European world was uniquely distracted by the implications of the anticipated death of Spain's childless King Carlos II and the potential French acquisition of the throne in Madrid. The gravity of the circumstances prompted Louis XIV and William III to initiate negotiation of the Partition Treaties, intended to prevent future armed conflict by diplomatically assigning Spain's heir and redistributing parcels of the Spanish Empire. This simultaneous occurrence of the Scottish presence in Darien and the delicate, secretive diplomatic drama being performed in Europe sheds considerable light on not only why the establishment of the colony was a distinctly unwelcome and threatening event, but also why history has not sought to explore the wider ramifications of the Scottish enterprise. As the First Partition Treaty, containing reasonable, long-desired assurances of maritime security, was ratified in October 1698, the initial Company of Scotland fleet was in the Caribbean, sailing to the mainland of Darien after having secured a pilot on the Danish island of St Thomas. In February 1699, as news spread of the death of Bavaria's electoral prince, Spain's negotiated heir, New Caledonia experienced the loss of the *Dolphin* and French and English naval emissaries were offering their support to the Spanish campaign to exterminate the colony. As word reached Madrid in March 1700 of the completion of the Second Partition Treaty, Spanish forces were receiving the capitulation of the weary final expedition survivors. In October of the same year, as a failing Carlos II seized the initiative and designated Philip, Duke of Anjou heir to the totality of his dominions, the quiet departure of five Darien survivors convicted of piracy was recorded in the prison log of Seville's Casa de la Contratación.[10]

Conditions in the Spanish America to which the Scots sailed were no less urgent than in the Europe they left behind, and dramatically expanded the cast to be impacted by their fatally flawed attempt to

Figure 1.1 New Caledonia's Spanish America, 1700. Illustration by Sydney Freeland.

establish a permanent presence across the Atlantic. The extent, complexity and interconnectedness of Spain's overseas dominions and their governance, already alarmed by recent internal unrest and hostile foreign incursions, dictated that New Caledonia would provoke a broad and powerful reaction. The offence of constructing a fortified settlement on the Isthmus became the highest priority of the king's principal representatives in the New World, the viceroy of Peru and the viceroy of New Spain.

Compounding matters for all concerned was the specific site chosen for New Caledonia, positioned between the principal Pacific administrative and ecclesiastical centre of Panama, with its Atlantic access at Portobello, and the major Caribbean port and slave-trading centre of Cartagena. The two cities, each under ultimate authority of the distant viceroy of Peru in Lima, fell within different provincial jurisdictions, or *audiencias*, both of which had established histories of over 140 years and had suffered devastating foreign raids well within living memory. Of vital consequence to the Scots, and reflecting the prominence of both urban centres in the maintenance of the entire Spanish Empire, Panama was administered by a *presidente-gobernador y capitán general* and Cartagena by a *gobernador* also designated as *maestro de campo general*, both men thus entrusted with consolidated military and civic authority.

Nor would American attention elicited by the Scottish enterprise be confined to Spanish-claimed territories. An international cast extending down the northern Atlantic seaboard and across the Caribbean, some authorised by monarchs and others operating outside any treaty or legal sanction, keenly watched, assessed and often participated in the Darien initiative, simultaneously wary and enticed by the entry of a new participant into a high-stakes world of commercial risk.

AN ATLANTIC WORLD OF EVIDENCE

The provocation of the Darien expeditions left a vast array of documentation and opinion, reflecting the varied participants impacted by events on the Isthmus. Although the purpose of this work is not to survey the full extent of historiography consulted, discovered and/or rejected, an important part of understanding New Caledonia entails acknowledging the diversity of the record as it moves across geography and language. Although limited here to English and Spanish sources, supplemented by translations of Danish documents, these chapters nonetheless expose ample new material and hint at the potential of yet additional voices waiting to be revealed.

Indicative of its critical role in the national history, the multitude of previously written material has been heavily skewed towards wide-ranging Scottish perspectives. Company of Scotland documents discovered in the basement of the Advocates Library in Edinburgh, and currently housed in the National Library of Scotland, breathe life and detail into events, decisions and controversies. In his introduction to the portion of the collection he chose to publish in *The Darien Papers*, editor John H.

Burton unapologetically describes the material as 'showing the unparalleled incapacity, producing endless blunders, of those who undertook the mighty task of establishing a new Colony for a people totally unacquainted with Colonial empire'.[11]

Other primary sources do not dispute Burton's comments. Two sets of contemporary works by expedition participants, understandably tinted by cultural and personal bias, provide textured descriptions of New Caledonia and records of events that enable comparison with other accounts. The first, Reverend Francis Borland's 1779 *The History of Darien 1700*, was written decades following his return to Scotland, but was based on the author's diaries.[12] The second is the frequently cited collection of pamphlets prepared by first expedition surgeon Walter Herries. His important role in the Company story, as controversial today as it was in 1700, was forged through actual experience in the colony, espionage and continued communication with survivors and officials, and is addressed in the following chapter. Pertaining to his credibility as a source, ample evidence is presented that the surgeon's testimony deserves higher regard than the scepticism and ridicule his writings have provoked, particularly due to independent corroboration in Spanish correspondence of details and accusations he recorded.

The task of preparing an initial comprehensive narrative history of the Company fell to George Pratt Insh in the early decades of the twentieth century. The Scottish historian's efforts, culminating in *The Company of Scotland Trading to Africa and the Indies* and its companion *Papers Relating to the Ships and Voyages of the Company of Scotland Trading to Africa and the Indies, 1696–1707* are deservedly utilised by virtually every later study. Insh's willingness to explore related events in North America, across Europe and as far distant as Company destinations in Africa and Asia indicate the story's expanding horizons, and the author is to be credited for his admitted reluctance to prepare his history without consulting Spanish sources. Acknowledging Frank Cundall's *The Darien Venture* and Francis Russell Hart's *The Disaster of Darien, The Story of the Scots Settlement and the Causes of its Failure, 1699–1701* for including material from Spain's Archive of the Indies, Insh contends that, while adding detail, the Spanish documents do not change the substance of historical events provided by Scottish and English records.[13] Unfortunately, that supposition eliminates recognition of the scale of preparations in both Spain and Spanish America to assure expulsion of the Scots, as well as broad and lasting impacts in the Americas. Despite these restrictions, Insh does provide an introduction to the integral participation of the native Cuna, describing divisions among them as well as the international commercial and diplomatic experience they possessed. The author also recognises the effective communication networks that existed across the region, including information the Scots received from both the pilot hired to take them to the coast and their initial indigenous contacts that they had been expected for a considerable time.[14]

Credit directed towards Francis Russell Hart is particularly well deserved. Trained as an engineer and having served as general manager of a railroad in Colombia, president of the United Fruit Company and eventually as consul of Colombia in Boston, he not only authored the volume Insh consulted, but his vastly unused collection of personal papers, housed in the Massachusetts Historical Society, includes numerous translated documents from Spain and the notable *Gazeta Extraordinaria del feliz successo: que las Armas Españolas invieron en el desalejamiento del Escoces que se avia fortificado en el Playon, Costa de Portovelo, Provincia del Darien en el Reyno de Tierra firme, á II de Abril de este presente año 1700*, an anonymously authored official account of the Darien campaign published in Lima shortly after the capitulation.[15]

Following the work of Insh and Hart by several decades, and uniformly cited by numerous historians, is a work deliberately deleted as a source in these pages. Despite its lack of footnotes, John Prebble's *Darien, The Scottish Dream of Empire* does reflect extensive research and has fulfilled an important role since its initial 1968 publication as *The Darien Disaster* by delivering the story to a wide audience. Its distribution and use, however, cannot eliminate its doubtful credibility as a historical source. Prebble's inclusion of some material, while contributing to his engaging narrative, fails to be substantiated by original documents. A notable example concerns the arrival of Cartagena's governor at the wreck of the *Dolphin* in an elaborate gold coach.[16] Not only is there no reference to the mode of transportation in either the governor's own correspondence or accounts of prisoners captured at the scene, recent devastating raids of the city by the French make it doubtful its humiliated leader would have at the time possessed such a carriage.

More recently, additional effort has been directed towards the wider implications of the Darien expeditions, several publications standing out for refocusing the lens of history. From Panama came the work of anthropologist Reina Torres de Araúz, who tragically succumbed to a lengthy illness after completing the first chapter of her intended full-length study of the Scots and Cuna. Based on observations expressed in her first instalment, she intended to analyse the Scots' presence within the lengthy and complex history of Darien, addressing the variety of previous Spanish initiatives to subdue the Cuna and suppress the extensive experience of interaction with foreigners, particularly English, which they possessed. Although the work was never completed, its introductory portion is invaluable in providing an understanding of the dynamic state of affairs into which the Scots naively inserted themselves.[17]

Exploration of the depth of the Spanish reaction and its role in the waning days of the reign of Carlos II falls to Christopher Storrs in his article 'Disaster at Darien (1698–1700)? The persistence of Spanish imperial power on the eve of the demise of the Spanish Habsburgs'. The author utilises records from both Spain's Archivo General de Indias in Seville and its Museo Naval in Madrid to illustrate the substantial and deliberate response to the Scottish intrusion, including military preparations on both sides of the Atlantic despite pressures of ending the Nine Years War and defending strategic North African outposts. Storrs also emphasises the instrumental role of a highly refined and experienced Spanish intelligence system, repeatedly illustrated in the following chapters, as well as diplomatic efforts across Europe to obtain financial support from the Vatican. Although the Navarette expedition eventually launched from Cadiz in June 1700 was not ultimately required to eliminate the Scots from Darien, its ten-ship, 4,800-man contingent speaks both to the value Spain placed on the Isthmus and the crown's ability to deploy forces across the Atlantic when a substantial threat was perceived.

Further exploring events from a Darien vantage point, including effective Cuna adaptation to centuries of Spanish, French, English and, suddenly, Scottish interaction, is Ignacio Gallup-Diaz's *The Door of the Seas and the Keys to the Universe*. The author reconstructs the multifaceted, unpredictable world into which the Scots were only the latest European arrival, providing the resident population with yet another opportunity to exercise their language skills, trade experience and political acumen. In effect, the Scots had sailed into a region recently rocked by political discord both within the structures of the Spanish colonial government and between the government and its presumed indigenous subjects. Not only did Panama's President Canillas, within whose jurisdiction New Caledonia fell, have to cope with recent murders of Franciscan missionaries, a bloody attack on a Spanish garrison and a troubling French presence, but a flotilla of Scots had now brazenly intruded, exhibiting every intent of constructing and inhabiting a permanent, armed settlement.

The continued opportunities presented by these European arrivals, and their consistent quests to identify assumed 'chiefs' with whom to treat, created, according to Gallup-Diaz, unique and innovative leadership opportunities for the native men of Darien. If the visitors wished political headmen, the indigenous population would be willing to create them for the benefit of both parties. These self-appointed Cuna leaders, designated as captains in the following pages in recognition of the status assigned to them by the Europeans with whom they dealt, were the same practised ambassadors who were neither surprised by the arrival of the Scots nor hesitant in establishing relations and pressing martial opportunities. One unintended consequence of the Scottish arrival was the exposure of a wider array of created Cuna leadership than the Spanish had previously assumed, a scenario that would continue to perplex and demand the resources of the Panamanian government long after the evacuation of New Caledonia.[18]

While the story has been deservedly expanded to Spain and her colonies, additional work on the Scottish perspective has not been ignored. Douglas Watt's *The Price of Scotland: Darien, Union and the Wealth of Nations* provides a comprehensive economic assessment, identifying the lack of novelty in choosing the Isthmus for trade and settlement, the degree of Spain's commitment to maintaining a presence in the region and the numerous reckless decisions made by Company directors that enabled the ensuing human and financial tragedy.

As indicated above and throughout these chapters, extensive records held in Spain's Archivo General de Indias are fundamental to both the saga of the Company of Scotland and any comprehensive investigation into its implications. As noted by the Spanish historian Joaquin Garcia Casares, the sheer quantity of pertinent correspondence, interrogations, reports and administrative documents held in the *legajos*, or bundles, signifies the acute importance of the Scottish incursion to Spain and her American dominions.[19] Nevertheless, a tendency has evolved confining research to what has become regarded as an established collection of Darien-related *legajos* within the vast holdings. Many of the significant new sources introduced here were discovered by searching material beyond that currently indexed as pertaining to Scots, Darien, New Caledonia or any of the principal individuals involved. Primary examples include the voluminous court record of the trial studied in Chapter 5, the related register of prisoners held by the Casa de la Contratación and documents pertaining to the imposition of the *donativo* discussed in Chapter 6. It is also vital to acknowledge that, although the site of the colony fell within the jurisdiction of Panama, officials from Cartagena, under the Audiencia de Santa Fé's authority, actually conducted the majority of direct contact with the Scots due to their city's position on the Caribbean coast. As the story of New Caledonia expands, despite a distance of over three centuries, the emphasis remains on how prudent the Company of Scotland would have been to fully consider the lands to which they sailed and the peoples upon whom they were about to impose their own tumultuous dream.

NOTES

1. Gentleman, *The History of Caledonia*, pp. 52–3.
2. Cruxent, 'Informe', pp. 12–14, 74–6.
3. Throughout this work, Cartagena refers to the Caribbean port, as opposed to its namesake on Spain's Mediterranean coast.
4. Entitled 'Caledonia: The Declaration of the Council Constituted by the Indian and African Company of Scotland, for the Government and Direction of their Colonies and Settlements in the Indies', the full document is included in this work as Appendix I.
5. MHS-Hart, Darien Item 13. The document is an English translation of the *consulta* found in AGI, Panamá 160.
6. The dire circumstances of the decade are described in Chapter 4, 'The 1690s: a nation in crisis' of Whatley, *The Scots and Union*, pp. 139–83.
7. Insh, *The Company*, p. 41.
8. Paterson had been promoting Darien's attributes since at least 1687. Watt, *The Price*, pp. 6–8.
9. Barbour, *A History of William Paterson*, p. 127, ft. 1.
10. AGI, Contratación 4887, *Entrada de Presos*. The trial of the men is the subject of Chapter 5.
11. Burton, *The Darien Papers*, p. xx.
12. Borland's diaries, containing important but generally overlooked supplemental material, are held by the University of Edinburgh, Centre for Research Collections as MS Laing 262, *Memorial or Diary of Mr Francis Borland, 1661–1722*.
13. Insh, *Historian's Odyssey*, pp. 203–4.
14. Insh, *The Company*, pp. 125–6.
15. *MHS Francis Russell Hart Collection, 1573–1936: Guide to the Collection (Massachusetts Historical Society)*, p. 1, last accessed 23 May 2011 and available at <http://www.masshist.org/findingaids/doc.cfm?fa=fa0161>.
16. Prebble, *Darien*, p. 178.
17. Torrez de Araúz, 'Nuevo Edimburgo', pp. 134–56.
18. Gallup-Diaz specifically addresses the presence of the Scots in Chapters 4 and 5, pp. 77–149.
19. García Casares, *Historia del Darién*, p. 252.

2

Unintended Itineraries I: Desertion, Opportunity and a Spy

These poor men who were design'd for Souldiers or Planters, finding themselves mistaken in their golden Hopes, and no appearance of any thing but felling huge Trees, and very shrimp allowance of Victuals (and those very bad) soon wearied of the Enterprize; and before they were a full month upon the place, several deserted, some by Land towards the Spaniard and others lurk'd in the Woods till they had an opportunity to transport themselves by water to Jamaica.[1]

As SURGEON WALTER HERRIES describes his early weeks in New Caledonia, he introduces both the causes of desertion and the impact it was to have on the Company of Scotland's colonial endeavour. The stories of those Darien participants who made the critical decision to voluntarily separate from the main body of colonists not only address the degree of desertion, acknowledged by the perpetrators themselves to the Spanish, but also add new dimensions to the understanding of New Caledonia's administration, participants, enemies and allies, including the international range of expedition members and predominance of military hierarchy. The chronicles relate how, devoid of familial resources and familiar environment to provide protection or sustenance, deserters implemented their change of circumstances and struggled to capitalise on limited and foreign resources to survive. While diminishing the labour force and skills of the colony they left behind, exacerbating strain on the remaining workforce, some of those choosing to desert were eventually able to effectively exploit their accumulated experience for self-promotion and monetary reward. The unintended and unacknowledged dispersal of these individuals not only undermined the goals of the Company of Scotland on the Isthmus, but their paths through New Caledonia would extend across the Caribbean into larger entanglements of the Atlantic World.

In addition to scattered personal accounts and official reports, the extensive and methodical catalogue of Spanish interrogations of deserters gives voice to sectors of the population who were either illiterate and thus unable to provide their own record or who felt inclined to maintain some semblance of anonymity. The records also provide a lens through which the effectiveness and intricacies of Spain's extensive intelligence network, vital to planning and execution of efforts to eradicate the Scottish presence, may be examined. Both administrative and military officials efficiently mobilised the support of translators, scribes and legal professionals to capitalise on the knowledge and vulnerability of their unanticipated guests. The resulting cast, from illiterate Irish soldiers serving in the Spanish military to the *capitán general y presidente* of Panama, the critical and often first-hand information they acquired, and its distribution throughout the vast structure of empire, all illustrate how Spain sought to protect her interests amid the chaotic and threatening conditions as the era of Habsburg rule reached its conclusion. This synergistic relationship between those who voluntarily departed New Caledonia and those who received them comprises a new perspective on the enterprise's dramatic failure.

EARLY, OFTEN AND UNACKNOWLEDGED

Desertion rapidly characterised the Darien effort, emerging as a problem prior to the initial expedition's departure from Scotland and continuing essentially unabated until eventual capitulation to the Spaniards in March 1700. Formally requesting a list of deserters as the fleet readied to depart Leith in July 1698, Company directors also ordered the apprehension of David Dalrymple, who had fled through a window after receiving his advance pay. Boatswain John Wilson was, at the same meeting, ordered to be prosecuted for mutiny and desertion.[2]

The initial desertion in the Americas, prior to the ships reaching their final destination, was that of Michael Pearson. In October, as the fleet prepared to sail following its stop at Crab Island, Commodore Robert Pennycook succinctly entered into his log 'we left one Michael Pearson behind, who ran away from the Tent to the Woods'. Whatever his intent, Pearson's action also provides an indication of how desertion was initially addressed. As noted by Scottish historian George Insh, acknowledgement of this and a series of impending desertions were distinctly absent from the version of events contained in the initial packet of correspondence

Figure 2.1 Route of Darien Fleet, September–November 1698. Source: James Barbour, *A History of William Paterson and the Darien Company, with Illustrations and Appendices*. Edinburgh: W. Blackwood and Sons, 1907, between pages 58 and 59.

sent from the fledgling colony. A comparison with the expedition's official journal, prepared by Hugh Rose, reveals that he merely edited and revised the log of the commodore, at the same time eliminating any reference to either Pearson's desertion or any of the others that had occurred.[3] The omissions helped assure news of unmitigated success, prompting celebrations in Edinburgh and enabling the Court of Directors to continue preparation for successive expeditions unmarred by the realities of conditions challenging the settlers and administration of the colony.

Desertions had, in fact, plagued New Caledonia within weeks of the fleet's November 1698 arrival. On the thirtieth of that month ten planters fled, along with a supply of arms stolen from the *Unicorn*. A council meeting convened that same afternoon dispatched a search party by boat which successfully located and returned the men, who were put in irons and provided with only bread and water. The morning of 16 December witnessed yet another group of seven planters desert. Despite both land and sea searches, and requests of assistance to local indigenous leaders, there is no indication of the group's return.[4]

Transport for at least part of this group may have been facilitated through a unique bounty programme designed by Governor Beeston of Jamaica to alleviate his island's chronic labour shortage. In a report from Secretary of State Vernon relaying the governor's initiative, King William was informed that Beeston had commissioned a sloop to sail to New Caledonia during those early months, promising her captain a reward of five pounds per individual Scot transported back to the island.[5]

Whether or not the bounty enticement was involved, at least two men were confirmed to have been carried to Jamaica by George Chine, a Scot captaining a small sloop under the command of the Englishman Richard Long. Long, whose presence in the region slightly predated the Scots, had sailed into New Caledonia in mid-November and spent several days hosting and being hosted by the colony's council. Although there was scepticism regarding his avowed mission to hunt Spanish wrecks, the Scots' general review of Long described a buffoon, often drunk and ridiculed by his own men. Aside from reciprocal hospitality and personal assessments, the English captain quickly created considerable animosity between himself and his hosts. A decade later he addressed the cause in a letter to the Duke of Hamilton, recounting that he had sailed his own ship to Jamaica and ordered Captain Chine to Old Providence. The latter defied orders, Long claimed, instead sailing back to New Caledonia to allow two vitally needed carpenters to board and, in return for ample payment in gold, accompany him to Jamaica.[6]

SURVIVAL AND OPPORTUNITY

Another early fugitive from the colony was Robert Allen, whose abilities and accumulated experience enabled him to survive the dual roles of deserter and prisoner and eventually thrive through his uniquely acquired knowledge of Spanish America. In 1708 Allen authored and submitted a memorial to the British secretary of state Charles Spencer documenting an impressive résumé. Although Allen does not identify himself as a deserter, he incriminates himself by conceding that he left the Scottish colony of Darien in December 1698 for Jamaica. From the island, he roamed widely throughout Spanish America working for merchants on trading voyages until 1701, when he found himself back in Darien exploring for logwood. As the lone survivor of a native attack, he lived for approximately eighteen months with a decidedly friendlier indigenous community until he received news of nine English sloops in the vicinity. Joining that combined force of 600 commissioned by the governor of Jamaica, and confirming his value to the project through the recruitment of sixty native allies, Allen and his comrades completed a successful raid on the town and mines of Cana. A second, smaller, attack on Antioquia proved far more hazardous. Finding their numbers reduced from 210 to 150, short on supplies and surrounded by hostile forces, the survivors requested quarter and safe conduct to Cartagena from their Spanish adversaries. Narrowly escaping execution, Allen was moved frequently over the following twelve months, witnessing the expanse of what was then Peru. Eventually imprisoned in Quito, he came to the attention of don Antonio de Ron Bernardo de Quiros, fiscal of the *audiencia* and surveyor general of the province. Continuing to exhibit a fortuitous talent to exploit his circumstances, Allen spent seven years as the official's secretary, gaining a unique understanding of the internal workings of Spanish colonial administration. As the men jointly departed Portobello in 1707 for Spain and don Antonio's prestigious appointment to the Council of the Indies, their ship was attacked by British naval forces under Admiral Wager. Witnessing the death of his mentor, Allen likely required minimal convincing by the admiral of the benefits to be derived from a return to England and employment in the expanding West Indies trade. Characteristically weighing his options, and having lost all his possessions, Allen declared it his duty to report to the secretary of state, politely writing that he found it necessary to accept offers to proceed to Holland for discussions with their West India Company, but conveniently adding he could be contacted through the merchant James Campbell.[7]

Although J. D. Alsop accompanies the publication of Allen's story with the comment that its sole corroboration is the account of the first, successful raid on the mines, the saga of the young deserter did leave a trail of additional evidence. Henry Barnham, in his unpublished *The Civil History of Jamaica to the Year 1722*, acknowledges Allen, identified as Irish, as serving as Admiral Wager's interpreter. Later in the same manuscript the author addresses Allen's fluid nationality, relating the young man's pleas to his Spanish captors that he was Irish and in their country involuntarily due to his status as servant to an Englishman.[8]

The deserter's good fortune continued upon his return to Europe, propelled by heightened interest in Spanish America during the War of the Spanish Succession and his preparation of a pamphlet entitled *An Essay on the Nature and Methods of Carrying on a Trade to the South Sea*. The publication, printed in London in 1712 and coinciding with negotiations to end the war, mirrored Allen's ability to survive with subsequent printings in 1762 and 1763 under titles reflecting contemporary political and economic concerns.[9] The author, emphasising his years residing in Spanish America, dedicated his work to Robert, Earl of Oxford. The acknowledgement is characteristic of Allen's tendency to attach his fortunes to influential individuals as the earl was Chancellor of the Exchequer and considered de facto prime minister, serving as a commissioner negotiating the 1707 Treaty of Union with Scotland and as secretary of state for the Northern Department. Having opened secret negotiations with Spain to end the war, he possessed a particular interest in trade and would eventually acquire a position as a governor of the South Sea Company.

Markedly absent in the original pamphlet and its two later editions is any reference to Darien, the Company of Scotland, or prior employment within Spain's colonial administration. What Allen does provide is a substantive primer on the workings of Spanish America, utilising, not surprisingly, the Audiencia of Quito as an example. The interests of his readers are specifically addressed by a discussion of means by which 'other European Nations, and in particular England, have always receiv'd some considerable Share of the Profits therof'. Following discussion of trade routes, including the transport of money being remitted to Spain and access to various mines of silver, gold and emeralds, the lucrative illegal trade between the Spanish colonies and Jamaica encompassing the occupation of New Caledonia is summarised:

> But that which most of all favour'd this Jamaica-Trade, was the galleons not coming from Old Spain, as had been usual for Nine or Ten Years together, viz. from the taking of Carthegena by Monsieur Ponti, Anno Domino 1697, until the Year 1706, for the Spaniards, during that interval of time, receiving few or no Supplies from Old-Spain, and at the same time many of them coming down with their Money and other commodities, under pretence of waiting for the arrival of the Galleons, they took their opportunities, supply'd themselves privately from our Vessels, and by such Means the Merchants and Factors at Jamaica, drove a very considerable Clandestine Trade ... the largest and most beneficial part of that Trade was carri'd on within the aforesaid Limits, on the Coast of Porto-Belo and Carthagena, those Places being the Ports from whence all the Kingdoms of Peru, Chili and New-Granada were supply'd, and whereof our Merchants had then a very considerable Share, to the very great advantage of their Mother Kingdom.

Allen continues, emphasising the value of English merchants' prior contracts with the Portuguese to supply the *asiento* with slaves (see Chapter 4) and the subsequent loss of that business to the French. In closing, the resurrected deserter writes of the benefits of assuring trade through both Spain and Jamaica and expresses his hopes for the encouragement of Parliament and the queen, characteristically hinting at more clandestine transfers of knowledge and the continuing value of his experience by adding that other of his proposals will not be made public, for they 'may require Secrecy in Execution'.[10]

SURGEON, DESERTER, AUTHOR AND SPY

December 1698 also witnessed the departure from New Caledonia of the man who would become the most vocal and infamous of deserters, ultimately presenting himself directly to the Spanish ambassador in London as a spy operating on behalf of King William III through Secretary of State Vernon. Unaware of their former surgeon's total portfolio, Company of Scotland directors would warn their councillors in the colony of his suspicious activities, alerting them to the fact that he had arrived back in Scotland with unofficial, unexplained correspondence from dubious sources.[11]

The man referred to was Walter Herries, a Scot from Dumbarton. His service in the Royal Navy from 1688 to 1695 had abruptly ended following a physical altercation with his commanding officer, resulting in both injuries to the surgeon and a court martial.[12] Relief came in the form of an offer of employment following discussion with Company of Scotland representatives in London in November 1696. The subsequent contract directed the surgeon to proceed to Amsterdam or Hamburg, then on to Scotland to depart on a trading mission to either of the Indies 'at the same time made tacitly to believe that I was to go to the East Indies and that the ships would sail next March at the farthest'. Although eventually labelled a deserter by the Company, Herries would defend himself through his own printed exposés by explaining he had been honourably discharged from New Caledonia and had a signed certificate proving his status.[13] Supporting his words with action, he would take the Company of Scotland before the Admiralty Court at London's Doctors' Commons and, like many other merchant mariners of his era, successfully recoup his wages.[14] Imposing a different and more permanent injury, Herries would also evolve into a highly effective and vocal critic of his former employer.

Departing the colony in the company of two emissaries tasked with delivering correspondence to Edinburgh, the surgeon sailed first to Jamaica and then on to Bristol, arriving there on 18 March 1699. After promising his companions that he would not write anything concerning the Company for two months, a trust he says he kept, he proceeded to London. Once he did begin to write, his virulent combination of literary skill, biting satire, first-hand experience with the Company and familiarity with the principal cast of personalities became apparent. In the ensuing production of competing pamphlets he claimed the lack of any man in the fleet who had been on the Spanish Main, the understanding by seamen that they would proceed on a trading mission and return to

Scotland following delivery of settlers to New Caledonia, and the inadequate quantity of provisions, illustrated by the description:

> Men sold their new shirts to the Indians for 20 or 24 plantains a piece, which would not serve a Man above three or four days, and our council were oblig'd to give strict Orders that no Man should sell his Cloaths, else I verily believe our Men had been naked in two months after our Landing.

Nor did Herries shy away from more inflammatory controversies involving the Company, writing of deliberate efforts to lure men from English and French Caribbean settlements to Darien and of the intent to initiate lucrative contraband trade with communities along the Spanish Main.[15]

The surgeon's accusations did not go uncontested. A campaign against him by the Company and its proponents culminated in a January 1701 warrant for his arrest, accompanied by a reward of 6,000 pounds Scots and indemnification for anyone harming the fugitive in the course of his capture. The blasphemous statements his writings were accused of containing resulted in a further order that the pamphlets themselves be burned by the Edinburgh hangman.[16]

Herries's campaign against the Company was not, however, confined to production of damnifying pamphlets or legal action to recoup wages. Evidence in British documents reveals both his complicity with English interests and his motivation for doing so. As early as June 1699 there emerged an unusual request for a pardon allowing his return to the Royal Navy. The following day the Admiralty Board considered the case, identified as originating with Secretary of State Vernon, but hesitated over its potential to undermine navy discipline. Unable to resolve their concerns, they included a request to the king for guidance. A response was forthcoming the following month through the secretary, resulting in the passage of an exceptional resolution pardoning the surgeon and halting all punitive action regarding his dispute with his former commander Captain Graydon.[17]

In return, the surgeon provided intelligence and attempted to influence opinion through a variety of means ranging from letters and pamphlets to active intervention with Company of Scotland personnel. Results of his efforts were submitted to the secretary of state, who in turn informed King William of relevant details. By June 1699 Secretary Vernon was reporting of initiatives on Jamaica to promote Scottish interests, information he had received from correspondence acquired by Herries.[18] In January 1700 the surgeon related his direct intervention to mitigate censorship of reports by individuals returning from Darien. 'Lest these gentlemen should have been biased by . . . agents of the Scotch company', the surgeon wrote, 'I took care that the material part of what they had said before several witnesses should be inserted in the public prints'. Herries was referring to Captain McLean, who had reportedly read his initial publication and verified its truthfulness, while others interviewed opted to maintain a discreet silence. Herries added that he was departing for the country where, in addition to tending to his pregnant wife, 'I design to answer the last scurrilous and rebellious pamphlet; I hope to the satisfaction of all sensible men, whether Scots or English'. Indicating the priority assigned to such activity, although not mentioning Herries by name, February 1700 correspondence from the attorney Trevor to Secretary Vernon reassured, 'I cannot find any evidence to charge any person with being the author of the libel in relation to the Scotch colony at Darien'.[19]

The full scope of Herries's activities, and the substantive threat to Scottish interests that he actually presented, is, however, not provided by British sources. Although the surgeon may have refrained from writing about the Company for the agreed two months, Spanish records verify that he was far from inactive during the immediate weeks following his return. Spain's ambassador to London, the Marquis of Canales, describes an April 1699 visit from Herries, disclosing not only his acknowledged role as a spy operating with full support from the secretary of state, but also his motive of a full pardon and reinstatement in the Royal Navy. Although historians have justifiably suspected collusion between the surgeon and Vernon, two manuscripts held in Spain's Archivo General de Simancas give a vivid account of how Herries actually provided critical and timely intelligence directly to the Spanish.[20]

In a May 1699 packet submitted to his monarch, Canales recounts a gentleman caller, initially identified as English, who had come seeking his secretary. The visitor refused to identify himself, explaining he had matters of the highest importance to discuss solely with the ambassador. Upon being allowed entry, the stranger claimed he could provide everything concerning the Scots in Darien, including their forces, ships and plans for relief under preparation both in Scotland and Hamburg. Explaining he understood the insult that Company of Scotland actions had afflicted upon Spain, the informant offered his services, adding that he and the ambassador could converse privately as they both spoke Latin.

During the initial three hours of the ensuing conversation Canales pressed his guest for his name and country without success. As the night wore on Walter Herries eventually identified himself, explaining he was a Scot who had participated in the first expedition to Darien and had returned during the month of January with Mr Hamilton, who had gone to Edinburgh to report to the Company regarding the positive state of the colony. Herries elaborated that he knew the calamities that could occur from the enterprise for the king of Britain. He offered to divulge all the secrets he knew, showing the ambassador a letter from Secretary Vernon verifying his role and identity. He also had come prepared with a small map of the Isthmus and demonstrated his authenticity by naming the vessels and captains of the Scottish fleet and the Council of New Caledonia as well as recounting stipulations of original Company patents.

The surgeon continued, confirming his familiarity with principal operatives in Edinburgh and relating that he had discussed the situation with Vernon, who had ordered him to interact with Scots instrumental in Darien affairs, especially the Duke of Hamilton and one Johnson, and to deliver resulting intelligence to him personally. It was for the good of both England and Spain that the Scottish endeavour should not succeed, Herries added, acknowledging problems created for English merchants involved in the transportation of slaves and for Spain's efforts to defend her American territories. Following six hours of conversation the men concluded the session, Herries saying he would require the secretary of state's permission before providing more information. He would return under cover of darkness, the need for secrecy being vital to protect himself from the Scots.

The subsequent visit did occur in the middle of the night, the ambassador being informed that permission had been granted by Vernon. The spy reported the disgust felt by his own king at action undertaken in Darien, particularly the deceitful way in which it had been perpetrated by the Parliament of Scotland and its potential to rupture the relationship between the two crowns. The reports Herries would make, he assured the ambassador, would not be frivolous and would help secure the peace between the reigns and in the Indies.

Verification that communication did continue is provided in a subsequent report sent to the Spanish king from the ambassador's residence in July 1699, relating further visits with the Scottish spy.[21] The value, detail and frequency of forthcoming intelligence, although not specifically attributed to Herries, is exemplified in another dispatch to Spain from Canales:

> The latest letters from Edinboro in Scotland assert that on the 19th of that month there cleared for Darien a convoy consisting of five vessels . . . which sent 300 gentlemen, young volunteers, and 1200 men and some women, to settle the country, 400 seamen, in addition to the ordinary crews of these vessels, with all sorts of subsistence, munitions, war material, and other

things necessary to offensive warfare and expansion into the region which they say they have taken under their protection. Further, that another convoy is making ready to clear before Christmas for, although they say they do not need further immediate relief, the wish to make themselves entirely safe against all enemies.[22]

Although having lacked verification of the surgeon's active espionage, suspicion regarding Herries's role in events, coupled with the virulent sarcasm of his writings, has impacted the credibility historians have assigned to his record. Insh describes the 'reckless assertion and corrosive satire' of the surgeon's work and labels it 'untrustworthy'. Watt, acknowledging the reliance historians have placed on Herries's writings, also issues a warning regarding their bias. Gallup-Diaz, while noting controversy surrounding the surgeon's publications, concedes the indisputable fact that Herries had first-hand knowledge of the colony.[23]

A review of the facts presented by Herries regarding the loss of the *Dolphin* and its corroboration with the Spanish record, discussed in Chapter 3, strongly suggests that more credit be given to the accuracy of the surgeon's accounts. His honest and direct presentation to the Spanish ambassador, clearly admitting his motive of Royal Navy reinstatement, provides further evidence of his truthfulness, no matter how unpalatable. Herries was an unapologetic and effective literary talent who made no attempt to conceal his disillusionment and outright disgust. While his qualitative assessment of individual personalities is certainly open to criticism, a differentiation between those opinions and the record he presents of events, independently confirmed by Spanish officials, constitutes a more historically accurate path to pursue. The surgeon's multiple roles as expedition participant, author and spy identify him as a key source who successfully manoeuvred the entangled tentacles of international concerns alarmed at the establishment of New Caledonia, providing him with unique opportunities to record events on two continents.

DESERTION ON VARYING FRONTS

While debate and intelligence echoed across the Atlantic, events continued to unfold at disparate points in the Americas. In April 1699 the problem of desertion finally forced itself into official Company correspondence. From New Caledonia the councillors were compelled to send home a representative with dispatches to enlighten Company directors on dramatic events with which they had to contend. A 'most villainous and treacherous design, that was lately carrying on, for running away with the *St Andrew*' was the provocation. Contributing to the councillors' anguish was the fact that declarations taken from conspirators revealed the plot had been known not only to one of the sea captains and others weeks prior, but the conspiracy had failed to be reported to the colony's governing body. While the identified perpetrators were reported to be in irons, the council expressed dismay: 'How such unnatural, and dangerous enterprises should be hatched among ourselves, and in such a place; and at a time, when we could reasonably dread of no manner of hurt, but from our professed Enemys.' One of the responses to the discovery of the intended mutiny was the passage later in the same month of *Rules and Ordinances for the Good Government of this Colony*. Although punishment for attempted desertion was designated as both whipping and a week of service for each day of absence, the failure to report any discussion or information regarding desertion was far more dire. Any man communicating or acquiring intelligence of rebellious discussion or activity was required to report immediately to a member of the council. Failure to do so carried a mandatory death sentence.[24]

In August reaction to the affair from exasperated Edinburgh directors was included in a response sent from Greenock. Ignorant of the ultimate irony that the entire colony had been deserted, they posed the question why any form of desertion should exist without severe punishment, particularly given expenses incurred 'in transporting them all and their effects, and that their transportation hinders so many more good men that would willingly have gone in their room'.[25]

On 20 June 1699, following a decision by their councillors, surviving members of the original expedition, succumbing to dissent, sickness, hunger and news of proclamations ordered by King William forbidding any assistance to them, had evacuated New Caledonia. Two of the Company's ships, *Caledonia* and *Unicorn*, eventually struggled into New York in early August, decimated by the loss of an estimated 300 men at sea.[26] The fact that salvation offered by resources in New York prompted a new wave of desertion could not have been surprising. While the absent Governor Bellomont corresponded with his lieutenant governor over strategies to deal with the Scots given the king's order, survivors drifted away into the population. As the remaining men comprehended their captain's intent to resupply and return to Darien for a rendezvous with relief ships from Scotland the number of fugitives increased, becoming so acute that on 22 September a memorial was presented to Lieutenant Governor Nanfan and the Council of New York pleading for assistance:

[S]ince our arrival in this Port Severall as well Saylors as Planters have run away and deserted the Company's service, and ships to which they belonged, by which and the great mortality which was among us, the ships are so disabled that scarce remains of what was in both so many as will be able to carry home one . . .[27]

Despite the desertions and proclamations, Captain Thomas Drummond stealthily managed to commandeer and man a vessel, leaving behind a frustrated and legitimately suspicious royal governor of New York. Setting their course back to the Isthmus the returning crew reached New Caledonia in time to witness arrival of the *Rising Sun* and her consort of three ships, and 1,200 would-be colonists on 30 November 1699.[28] Having been denied water and provisions on Montserrat by order of the king, and suffering an estimated 160 fatalities during their passage, the newcomers found their colony 'deserted and gone, their huts all burned, their Fort most part ruined, the ground which they had cleared adjoining to the Fort all overgrown with shrubs and weeds'. It was 'no wonder', continued Francis Borland, 'that our people were sadly discouraged upon their coming hither . . . Our party were not sent forth to settle a colony, but only to be a recruit and supply to a colony'. A council held shortly afterwards determined to send 500 of the men to Jamaica in order to conserve provisions, reduce the daily food allowance of those remaining and wait for further direction from Scotland. That decision, coupled with dashed expectations and the harsh realities of clearing jungle and rebuilding fortifications, prompted a major desertion within two weeks of the fleet's arrival. Borland recounts that nine men of the *Rising Sun* stole one of her boats and fled during the night. They were not pursued as their escape route could not be determined.[29]

The incident is also the first case for which we have both a Scottish and a Spanish version of events. Having firmly established and refined the value of gathering intelligence from deserters and prisoners of war, Spain would make extensive use of documented and widely distributed interrogations during the campaign to expel the Scots. The Count of la Monclova, viceroy of Peru, wrote to Carlos II reporting receipt of news from Panama of the Scots' return, enclosing depositions from the nine deserters, as well as two others who had opted to flee by land.[30] The detailed content of these declarations, along with their distribution to increasingly broader and more elevated levels of Spanish officials, provided a vital channel of uniform information with which to plan, implement and potentially alter operations.

The nine men that Borland and the viceroy wrote of had headed to Portobello, where they arrived safely and were brought forward for interrogation on 29 December 1699. Juan Bauptista, Nicholas Grillo, Simon Modesto and Juan Coda were the four individuals questioned, and exhibited the multinational composition of the expeditions. Two of the men were English, one Italian and one Greek. All are included on the pay list of the *Rising Sun*: 'John Baptista' listed as a yeoman, 'Nicholo Greilo', 'Simon Amodesto' and 'John Codd' as sailors. They related to their inquisitors their departure from Scotland three months earlier in the fleet of four ships, further describing the firepower of each vessel and the state of land defences currently being rehabilitated. Total manpower of soldiers and sailors had originally been 1,150 men, reduced by deaths to 1,000. They had understood they were coming to an established and functioning colony, but had found only two small vessels, one English and one Scottish, upon their arrival. They related what they had heard of ships from the original expedition, that one had returned to Scotland and another was in Jamaica. Their intelligence regarding enthusiasm in New Caledonia for a possible raid against Santa Marta no doubt raised some alarm but was likely countered by the accompanying revelation of a tentative plan to send the sick and one or two ships of men to Jamaica in order to conserve dwindling food supplies. Queried as to why they had chosen to escape, the men reported that they had been deceived and had no desire to take up arms against Spain as they shared the Catholic faith. As with other intelligence gathered from deserters and prisoners, the declarations were copied and sent to a network of officials across Spanish America, as well as to Madrid.[31]

Similar information was acquired from the additional pair of Scots who chose to desert, utilising a very different avenue of escape. Their interrogations were conducted by the president of Panama on 15 January 1700, and illustrate the standardisation, formality, organisation and thoroughness of the process. A team was mobilised to witness and document the procedure, accompanied by an Irish soldier serving in Spain's Windward or Barlovento fleet, who was summoned to act as translator. The first deponent was named as Juan Jadin, who gave his age as twenty-five and his birthplace as Monte, Scotland. He related he had come with the first expedition of five vessels and served on board *Caledonia* under the command of Captain Thomas Drummond. Their purpose had been to establish themselves in Darien and conduct trade with the Spanish. Jadin gave a detailed review of the design and structure of fortifications constructed by the first arrivals, as well as the placement and size of cannon and supplies of guns, grenades and ammunition. For sustenance, he

related, they had flour, meat and fish from Jamaica until the king's prohibition eliminated that trade. Because of the lack of provisions, high
mortality and illness, they had left for New England, where they received
notice of additional ships having left Scotland for New Caledonia. With
a crew of seventeen and a hold full of supplies, they re-embarked for the
colony, arriving after a month and a half. Two days later the squadron
of four ships arrived carrying 1,270 new colonists, including twelve captains, infantry and eight women. Questioned as to the cause and means
of his escape, Jadin simply said hunger had been his motive. Emphasising
the dire lack of provisions, he described his daily allocation of two small
biscuits and a little fish. He and his companion had not known how to
negotiate the jungle terrain so they had bartered linen for local Cuna to
guide them to the Spanish. They had been delivered to the *maestro de
campo* Luis Carrisoli, who had relayed them forward to Panama.

The second deponent, named as thirty-four year old Guillermo Estrafan, had also originally sailed on *Caledonia*. Although he couldn't provide the total number on the first expedition, he could clearly quantify
its military composition of twelve companies of forty-five men each. He
knew that for certain, he related, because he was a soldier in one. As
his companion had done, he detailed original fortifications and arms and
reiterated the intent to establish trade. Combined with high rates of death
and disease, he related the fear that there would eventually be insufficient survivors to man the ships. In response to why they had returned to
Darien, he corroborated Jadin's information and added that a new vessel
had been acquired in New England. The squadron that now lay at New
Caledonia included ships of sixty and thirty cannon and two merchant
vessels. The artillery had not yet been mounted, there was extensive damage to prior construction and there was much work but little food. He
verified they had departed voluntarily, hunger being the motive, and that
linen had been traded for guide services across the Isthmus to Real de
Santa Maria, from where they had sailed to Panama.[32]

INCREASED DESPERATION, DISCORD AND DESERTION

The pair who had successfully negotiated a crossing of the Isthmus did
mention the recent prior desertion of nine men in one of the Company's
boats, but did not refer to, and may not have known about, a more
serious but unsuccessful plot by some of their companions. Alexander
Campbell had been executed on 20 December 1699 following exposure
of his role in a plan to seize council members and sail away with two
Company ships.[33] The current Council of New Caledonia showed no

hesitation in reporting the intended mutiny to Company administrators in Edinburgh. Three days following the hanging of Campbell the harried governing body transmitted the news, noting: 'Wee have lame and partiall proofs against severall others, but not so legall as they should be. So we must have patience.' They also acknowledged rumours among the planters, exacerbated by the shortage of provisions, of a design 'saving the victuals for private advantage, and selling the men to be sent to Jamaica'. The earlier desertion of nine men, compounded by the loss of the eight-oar boat used in their escape, was also included in the report.[34]

There was a short-lived respite from the rapidly deteriorating conditions with the arrival on 11 February 1700 of Captain Campbell of Fonab with a sloop of provisions. Despite his successful leadership during a skirmish with a Spanish patrol (see Chapter 8), within two weeks the desperate conditions returned, as New Caledonia witnessed the presence outside their bay of a consolidating foreign fleet.

The forecasted arrival of Spanish forces, led by Governor don Juan Pimienta of Cartagena, facilitated a new rash of desertions. For the governor, these welcomed individuals would provide critical, timely intelligence of conditions in New Caledonia that enhanced strategic management of resources needed to successfully pressure the Scots towards capitulation. Settled aboard his flagship *San Juan Bautista*, Pimienta initiated his journal of the campaign. Within days three Scots were brought to him, declaring themselves to have deserted six weeks prior due to hunger. They quantified a force of 500 regulars in the Scottish settlement, prompting the governor to hold a council and subsequently send 200 foot soldiers ashore the same day, accompanied by the chief engineer, to establish an infantry camp. Having installed himself on land, obtained additional intelligence from both indigenous and French sources and dispatched his first message to the Scots, Pimienta lamented, 'Not a deserter has come in to this camp nor have we succeeded in taking any prisoner, although I have endeavoured, and much wished to do so, in order to acquire news of their strength and stores.'[35]

The governor's frustrations were quickly satisfied. Within a day deserters began to appear with the strategic information Pimienta sought to effectively further orchestrate his campaign:

> Now the enemy, either because they were afraid, or bored by the country, or wearied of their work, or vexed at the ill-treatment they received, were passing over to our side . . . Others hid from their men until they had the opportunity to come to us, and said that they would all come if they had not been frightened by their superiors who told them that

the Spaniards would give them no quarter. Senor Pimienta received them with great kindness, and sent them on board the ships with orders that they be treated well.[36]

The individual reports, though sometimes inconsistent, painted a bleak picture of a vulnerable foe. An officer reported only three months of short rations in the Scottish camp, endemic dysentery and a count of 300 veteran troops. A schooner had departed a little over a week earlier for Jamaica to obtain relief. A forward post had been established, implementing brass cannon covered in rawhide, to cover what was determined to be the only approach the Spanish could utilise. Armed fireships were being prepared and attempts were underway to reconnoitre the Spanish ships at night and set them afire. To illustrate the poor nourishment the Scots possessed, the deserter produced one of his meagre biscuits. Another deserter, when asked why there were not more desertions, reiterated the rumour being circulated that the Spaniards gave no quarter and that rewards for their sufferings would be forthcoming from Scotland. The same individual added that desertions would increase as soon as the Scots' own guards would permit them. There was also news of the Scottish command's reaction to Spanish ships not actually entering the port . . . 'unless they receive relief it is hunger which will compel them to surrender'.

An interrogation recorded by the notary of the *San Juan Bautista* on 25 March 1700 substantiated the acute lack of food and facilitated further refinement of Spanish strategies. The deponent was twenty-two-year-old John Fraser of Aberdeen. The Scots had enough supplies, he calculated, for six to seven months at a mere half pound of flour and a quarter pound of salt meat per day, plus any small quantities of fish they could catch, and some fruit provided by Cuna allies. Artillery had not been landed, but a scheme had been formulated where guns were mounted on one side of a ship, facing towards the port. The intent to use fireships was being successfully thwarted by the armed launches of the Spanish that patrolled the harbour mouth each night.[37]

Assisted by such precise and timely information, and further motivated by concerns over the status of his own forces' declining health and provisions, Pimienta was able to bring the engagement to a rapid conclusion. The final Articles of Capitulation were signed on 31 March 1700.

Having no knowledge of events since the previous December, recognition of the magnitude and continuing role of desertion finally received its due in Edinburgh. On 3 June 1700, two months following their expedition's formal capitulation to the Spanish, a proclamation was issued by the

Council-General of the Company of Scotland Trading to Africa and the Indies imposing the death penalty upon any resident of the colony who promoted, either in public or private, an act of desertion or surrender.[38]

Acknowledgement came far too late to stem the loss of men and resources upon which the fledgling colony was reliant. The extreme circumstances that provoked men to leave the settlement not only reflected fatal and unrelenting flaws in the management of New Caledonia, but also created a valuable flow of pragmatic information efficiently received, distributed and incorporated throughout Spanish America and across the Atlantic. The role of the deserters would be further recognised by its inclusion in the *Gazeta extraordinaria*, printed and distributed by Spain's viceroy in Lima following the capitulation.

Providing his own assessment of desertion and its causes, one of the Scottish ministers, writing from on board the *Rising Sun* in Caledonia Bay on Christmas Day 1699, laid the responsibility squarely on Company directors. His letter, which eventually reached the English secretary of state, declared:

> For it hath been our directors error first and last to send and entrust with their ships and concerns too many men who have no principle either of conscience or honour . . . too many knaves, too many fools, too many Lairds and lairds bairns that think it below them to work and finding themselves disappointed of their big Phantastick hopes of getting goupens of gold for the uptaking and never thinking of the necessities working and sweating for it. Felling trees, cutting down many groves, digging in the bowels of the earth, which now they find they must be put to with thrift and hunger. This makes many rue their voyage and long to be at home again . . .[39]

NOTES

1. Herries, *An Enquiry*, pp. 34–5.
2. RBS Archives, D/1/2, 20 July 1698.
3. Insh, *Papers*, pp. 272–3. Insh further notes Rose's deletion of the failure to locate reported logwood groves, anticipated to bring substantial economic rewards.
4. Ibid., pp. 90–3. Planters occupied the lower rung of a hierarchy created by the Company for its military participants, technically eliminating required approval by the Privy Council for troops raised in Scotland. Herries, *A Defence*, p. 31. At the hierarchy's higher end, captains became overseers, lieutenants became adjutants and ensigns became under-adjutants. RBS Archives, D/1/1, 403–9.

5. BL, ADD MS40774, f. 82r. Vernon to the king, 4 July 1699.
6. NRS, GD406/1/5437 and Insh, *Papers*, pp. 88–9.
7. Alsop, 'A Darien Epilogue', pp. 197–201.
8. BL, ADD MS12422, pp. 231, 251.
9. The 1762 version entitled *The Great Importance of the Havannah, Set Forth in an Essay on the Nature and Methods of Carrying on a Trade to the South Sea, and the Spanish West Indies* is used here.
10. Allen, *The Great Importance*, pp. 11–12, 23–4, 38.
11. NLS, Adv. MS 83.7.4, f. 185.
12. Bateson, *CSP, Domestic, 1699–1700*, p. 218.
13. Herries, *A Defence*, pp. 8–9 and Herries, *An Enquiry*, pp. 42–3.
14. Manuscripts at the National Library of Scotland identify payment made for clearing the Court of Admiralty ruling. Adv. MS 83.5.2, f. 175 and 83.8.8, f. 52.
15. Herries, *A Defence*, pp. 18, 30, 38, 46 and Herries, *An Enquiry*, pp. 35–6.
16. UGSp, Spencer f. 45, *Proclamation for Apprehending Walter Herries* and Insh, *The Company*, p. 235.
17. Bateson, *CSP, Domestic, 1699–1700*, p. 218 and NA, ADM3/15, minutes of the Admiralty Board for 3 June and 10 July 1699.
18. BL, ADD MS40774, f. 50v.
19. Bateson, *CSP, Domestic, 1699–1700*, pp. 345–6, 373–5. The attorney was likely Thomas Trevor, who served as Attorney General under William III.
20. AGS, Estado 4183, Marquis of Canales to Carlos II, 27 April and 11 May 1699.
21. Ibid., Marquis of Canales to Carlos II, 6 July 1699.
22. MHS-Hart, Darien Item 37, English translation of letter dated 31 August 1699 from the Marquis of Canales to Carlos II. Not all intelligence transmitted was correct, indicated by the Marquis's report that the Duke of Hamilton had been appointed governor in perpetuity of New Caledonia. AGS, Estado 4183, 11 August 1699.
23. Insh, *Historian's Odyssey*, pp. 171, 173–4, Watt, *The Price*, p. 19 and Gallup-Diaz, *The Door*, p. 112, ft. 100.
24. NLS, Adv. MS 83.7.4, ff. 171–4.
25. NLS, Adv. MS 83.7.4, f. 209r.
26. Borland, *The History*, p. 24.
27. Insh, *Papers*, p. 123.
28. Ironically, a Spaniard who had fled Cartagena following a murder served as Drummond's pilot. Renowned for his skill, the man would also guide the *Rising Sun* into Caledonia Bay. Being refused his proposal to continue assisting the Scots, he was next witnessed piloting the Spanish fleet under Governor Pimienta. NLS, Adv. MS 83.7.5, f. 207v.
29. Borland, *The History*, pp. 29–32.
30. AGI, Panamá 181, f. 640r.
31. AGI, Panamá 164, ff. 587r–97v and NLS, Adv. MS 83.7.4, ff. 103r–v.

32. AGI, Panamá 164, ff. 603v–19r. An English translation of correspondence including the interrogations is in Hart, *The Disaster*, App. XXX, pp. 340–52.
33. Hart, *The Disaster*, pp. 126–7.
34. Burton, *The Darien Papers*, pp. 212–13, 215.
35. Hart, *The Disaster*, App. XXXI, pp. 367, 402.
36. MHS-Hart, *Gazeta*-English, pp. 5–6.
37. Hart, *The Disaster*, App. XXXI, pp. 404–7 and 413–16.
38. NLS, Adv. MS 83.7.5, ff. 144r–v.
39. HL, MSBL9, *Copy of Mr Sheil's letter*.

3

Unintended Itineraries II: Prisoners

ALTHOUGH DESPERATE AND OFTEN just as hungry, ill and exhausted as the deserters, the prisoners examined in this chapter, by their very definition, were forced to deal with uniquely different circumstances. They had made no deliberate decision to depart from their comrades and often had no or minimal time to plan a strategy or consolidate any form of provisions. Nor could they choose their companions, a factor that could and did create the danger of exposing plans and identities, jeopardising both welfare and lives.

The vulnerability of the prisoners did not diminish their impact as reactions to the Scottish intrusion reverberated across the Atlantic. Some of those captured would find themselves transported back to Spain and the focus of the highest level of international diplomacy. Others would find themselves sources of intelligence instrumental to strategies implemented to expel their compatriots, and still others would face execution for establishing alliances with New Caledonia. Although the majority of captives were members of the Company of Scotland expeditions, they were by no means all Scots and this further demonstrates the multinational roster of participants. Fuelled by the mutual goals of intelligence-gathering and reprisal, and often caused by blatantly coincidental circumstances, prisoners were taken not only by the Spanish, but also by representatives of the colony. The exposure of conflicting records surrounding instances of capture and imprisonment also furthers the argument of how censorship and bias affected the understanding and deliberation of Company management and propelled its initiatives towards wholly unintended consequences from the courts of Europe to the coasts of Darien.

CAPTAIN ROBERT PINCARTON AND THE CREW OF
THE *DOLPHIN*

The first prisoners came to the Spanish without warning or design by literally grounding their vessel on the beach adjacent to the city of Cartagena on a Sunday afternoon in February 1699. The crew of thirty men and one boy provided not only a wealth of current information, but also a most welcome and strategic category of prisoner in the person of one of the colony's councillors. The abrupt appearance of the *Dolphin* immediately outside Cartagena's walls has largely been ignored by historians, but it is evident that the resulting rewards of material goods and intelligence suddenly available to the Spanish were substantial. The intended trading mission had been vehemently but unsuccessfully opposed by Councillor William Paterson on the basis that it would be reckless to send two highly valued, experienced sea captains with a crew of over two dozen seamen in a single vessel marginally able to handle current windward conditions. In addition, within the *Dolphin* would be a substantial portion of commercial assets, the loss of which would be a severe economic blow.[1] His warnings would be prophetic.

Governor of Cartagena don Diego de los Rios y Quesada reported his good fortune to his colleagues and superiors, relating that between three and four o'clock on that Sunday afternoon he had immediately responded to signals from the Santo Domingo guard-posts, where a ship had run up on to the beach. Although the vessel flew an English flag and her command introduced themselves as English, papers thrown overboard were recovered and translated; among them were correspondence from New Caledonia councillors to their superiors and printed copies of the Act creating the Company of Scotland. There was also intelligence acquired from the French passenger and an Italian serving among the crew. Particularly notable was the capture of Robert Pincarton, not only one of the colony's governing body, but also captain of the *Unicorn*, one of its principal vessels. With the information acquired from documents and interrogations, the governor was able to report to the general of the Barlovento fleet that the Scots had 700 to 900 men and three warships of poor construction, due to their original design as merchant vessels. New Caledonia was suffering from a lack of supplies and full of fear of an attack. Copies of the report were dispatched to Spain, both to the king and the Council of the Indies, being carried by one of the ships of the slave-trading *asiento*.[2]

Among the three accounts of the afternoon's events and the aftermath are depositions from Captain Pincarton and pilot James Graham, prepared for their employer upon their return to Scotland following their transportation to, trial and conviction of piracy in Seville. Editor John H. Burton, in a footnote to published versions of the accounts, notes both appear to be in Pincarton's handwriting and the contents' style and substance are remarkably uniform, an opinion verified by review of the original documents.[3] Pincarton writes that collision with a rock, so severe that baling and pumping were ineffective, required the run on to the shore. The subsequent arrival of the governor and his officers resulted in a canoe being dispatched for the imperilled men, who were duly ordered ashore. The initial plea for assistance to retrieve goods from the *Dolphin* received a positive response, but a brief consultation among the Spanish precipitated a rapid change of attitude; the crew were suddenly put under strong guard, marched to town and imprisoned. Pincarton, suffering a broken rib, found himself in irons and solitary confinement. Following his subsequent interrogation he was taken to the upper prison, where he was held for three months. Pleading for food and clothing, he was instructed to petition for liquidation of some of the cargo in order to provide for himself and his men. By that time some of the crew had died and he himself was 'in a starving condition'. His forthcoming request approved, allocations were made for daily meals and cloth retrieved from the stores provided clothing for both himself and Captain Malloch. Pincarton witnessed the cargo and fittings of the Company's ship being carried away and would recognise some of her guns remounted on his later transport to Havana. While the two officers were kept in a 'house of office for the guards', where they cleaned a place to sleep every night, the remainder of the crew was sent out daily to clean streets and work on the massive city walls, during which time they begged passers-by for charity. Upon receiving word that New Caledonia had been deserted, Pincarton petitioned the new governor for the group's release, but was denied with the explanation that he would instead be sent to Spain.

Graham's almost identical account does add that he was searched for papers and had his money confiscated. He also witnessed his personal effects, including books, instruments and clothes, carried away, being allowed to retain only 'one cap, one wescoat, one pair of drawers, one shift, one pair of shoes'.

Neither man elaborates on their interrogations in Cartagena, which constitute the second version of events. Initiated the morning following the beaching of the *Dolphin*, the Spaniards, having mobilised an efficient and experienced team, including an Irishman to serve as translator, began by considering the seized and translated documents. In addition to Company of Scotland papers, the French lieutenant, seeking return to his native country after being shipwrecked near New Caledonia, had judiciously prepared a written statement and submitted it to Spanish authorities. His effort would be productive, for he would be rewarded with a passport to embark for Curacao and on to France.[4]

John Malloch, captain of the *Dolphin,* was first to be interrogated and claimed that he was 'Diego Tamayson (Jamison?)', English and a thirty-eight-year-old Protestant from London. Cautioned by his captors to tell the truth or he would be manacled and held in solitary confinement, he maintained his English identity despite continued warnings and being informed that orders from New Caledonia to dispose of cargo along the coast of Caracas were in his interrogators' hands. Insisting he had sailed from Jamaica, he explained he knew little of the situation in Darien as he had been there only a short time to seek shelter from the winds. Asked about the whereabouts of Benbow, Malloch responded that he had heard in Jamaica that his squadron was in the area, but he had not seen the vice-admiral. The captain further indicated it had been in Jamaica that he had heard the Scots had their king's permission to settle in lands not held by any European monarch. Contradicting his earlier statements, he declared his sole purpose for being in New Caledonia had been to trade salted meat and wine he had brought from Madeira, assuring his dis-believing questioners he had not brought arms to the colonists. When asked if the governor of Jamaica had sent assistance to the Scots, and what else was said on that island concerning the colony, Malloch related that opinions varied and that most of the correspondence with the Scots had been through merchants.[5]

Having completed a frustrating, inconsistent interrogation with Jamison/Malloch, the next deponent was Captain Pincarton, who initially identified himself as 'Diego Robesson (Robertson?)', an Englishman from London. Presented with accumulated evidence to the contrary and the sanctity of his oath, the councillor of New Caledonia dropped his false identity, admitting he was the said Pincarton and a Scot from Prestonpons. He continued, pro-viding requested information regarding arms and personnel aboard each of the Scottish ships. He added that he was not fully aware of land force numbers, but that there were approximately 2,000 individuals, including eight or nine women, who had embarked from Scotland. So far there had been few deaths and general good health. A detailed explanation of for-tifications, including the construction of forty-five platforms for artillery, was described, as were the navigational challenges and ample capacity of the port itself. Five relief ships from Scotland were anticipated, none of them belonging to the English king. Pincarton was also asked about what he knew of Benbow's activities, to which he responded that he knew of him, but was unaware of his whereabouts and that he had not been at New Caledonia. He further explained that a Company messenger had been sent back to Scotland via Jamaica with pleas for supplies. The trade goods on the *Dolphin* such as shoes, slippers, wool and linen were to be traded for sugar and tobacco in Barbados, which were then to be transported to Scotland. With the exception of one Italian and one man from Holland, the thirty-man crew was from Scotland. Help had not been solicited from Jamaica and there had been no communication with that island's governor. Questioned regarding the indigenous population, Pincarton related they had established friendly relations and been assured by the native captains that their lands were not part of the Spanish king's domain. Although the Cuna had requested arms to fight Spaniards, the Scots had refused on the premise that they wished to maintain peace with all parties. Pincarton assured his interrogators that the Company of Scotland had no intention of expanding into other parts of the region. To the detriment of his colleague, he also identified his fellow prisoner as Captain John Malloch.[6]

Next to be interrogated was the Spanish-speaking Italian, Juan Bautista Acame. He declared himself to be a seaman who had originally sailed from Holland to Scotland on the *Unicorn* under Captain Pincarton. The mariner gave accounts of deserters, mortality, inadequate supplies and defensive measures, noting the latter were hampered by lack of appropriate construction materials. There had been searches for gold, but they had none in their possession. The French lieutenant that accompanied the *Dolphin* had been at the colony for about a month and a half and was attempting to return home after his ship had been lost. The sailor gave his age as twenty-seven, but did not know how to sign his declaration.[7]

With the assistance of a translator, the content of the paper provided by the French lieutenant was then introduced into the record. The author, who gave his name as Durinan, recounted his service under Captain Duvivier Thomas. At the behest of the king of France, they had been hunting pirates to assist security of Spanish dominions until they had lost their ship in Caledonia Bay. Identifying himself as an official of the marine guard of Rochefort, he provided a detailed description of what he had learned of the housing, defence and governance of the Scottish colony, as well as the presence there of a Dutch vessel. He reiterated that resident Cuna had assured the Scots they had never been conquered by the Spanish and that they had given the colonists permission to create a settlement.[8]

A seaman from Holland, for whom yet another translator was utilised, received particular attention. He identified himself as Esteban de Berga from Breda and of the reformed Calvinist faith. During his first session he denied having been at New Caledonia, with the result that he was manacled and placed in solitary confinement. After substitution of a German resident of Cartagena to serve as translator he was brought back before the inquisitors and was able to clarify that his city was under Swedish jurisdiction. After confessing to having sailed with the original fleet on the *Unicorn*, he transmitted what he knew of ships, men and arms at the colony.[9]

As interrogations continued into the week, twenty-three-year-old pilot James Graham was questioned, declaring they had been sailing to Barbados to trade for rum, sugar and tobacco to carry to Scotland. In response to an inquiry regarding the mission of the Dutch ship at New Caledonia, he replied it needed to be watered and careened. He elaborated that his role as pilot limited his knowledge of land activities to acquiring water and wood.[10] Thomas Bachah, a twenty-seven-year-old Scottish seaman, related he had not known their destination when he left Scotland, but was concerned solely with his salary for service on the *Unicorn*. He also admitted that Captain Pincarton had given the order as they ran aground that they should all deny having come from New Caledonia and maintain they were from Jamaica bound for Barbados.[11] Twenty-nine-year-old surgeon Andrew Livingston, who would escape his imprisonment and eventually return to New Caledonia via Jamaica, was asked for information similar to that demanded of his shipmates, but emphasised he could not be precise about current details as they had sailed fifteen days prior.[12]

The second interrogation of Captain 'Diego Tamayson/Jamison' resulted in the admission of his true identity as John Malloch and that he had sailed from New Caledonia. After giving intelligence regarding the defensive capacity of the colony, he verified Pincarton's order to present themselves as bound for Barbados and further confirmed the latter's elevated position within the colony.[13]

The consolidated information acquired from the ten documented interrogations was extraordinary for its quality, quantity and timeliness. The governor of Cartagena, with minimal effort and expense, had been able to capitalise on his enemy's misfortune to compile both a complete and current assessment of the situation at the colony and beyond, and readily disperse it to his superiors and compatriots.

An impressive amount of the same detail, supplemented with additional information, was also exposed through the pen of a source in England.

That author, the censured Walter Herries, would have undoubtedly appreciated the vindication of his own work that Spanish documents provide. In his 1701 pamphlet *An Enquiry into the Caledonian Project, with a Defence of England's Procedure (in Point of Equity) in Relation Thereunto, in a Friendly Letter from London, to a Member of the Scots African and Indian Company in Edinburgh, to Guard against Passion*, the surgeon–spy provides a third version of events in Cartagena. Based on claimed London conversations with Pincarton, Malloch and the surgeon Livingston shortly after their return and only three months prior to publication, Herries writes that the actual mission of the *Dolphin* was to trade along the Spanish Main in the vicinity of Riohacha and Santa Marta. The ship was then to seek Barbados or other English or French possessions where, under the pretence of needing water and wood, they were to conduct Company business and distribute the printed declarations intended to recruit additional settlers. Discovering heavy leakage in the ship, they instead turned back towards the colony. As they passed offshore of Cartagena they noticed another vessel, headed in her direction attempting to communicate, and collided with an unseen rock. Their sole option for survival a run ashore, the entire crew, recognising the danger they faced should they be revealed as Scots from New Caledonia, agreed to present themselves as Englishmen from Jamaica heading towards Barbados. Acknowledging that the Spanish well knew the identity of their councillors and captains, Malloch and Pincarton were to use the pseudonyms of 'James Jamison' and 'John Robertson', respectively. Incriminating documents were thrown overboard, while Pincarton's clerk John Neilson ('either designedly or negligently') kept a packet of letters to Edinburgh in his pocket. A Frenchman on board, after swearing to not betray the origin of the crew, was allowed to accompany the men ashore. As the English flag was flown from the *Dolphin* the immediate reception was welcoming, but 'upon suspicion (or some discovery of the French lieutenant)', Captains Pincarton and Malloch were each placed in solitary confinement. Interrogations began the following day, with Malloch maintaining his identity as 'James Jamison', even when faced with contrary evidence. The recovered documents, besides proclaiming the men's actual origin, included their intention to trade in Spanish-held dominions along the coast. Refusing to concede his contrived name or origin, Malloch was taken away and 'loaded with iron'. Pincarton was then sent for and initially declared himself as 'John Robertson'. Warned about the condition of his soul and informed about the letter submitted by their French passenger, he confessed his true identity and answered thoroughly questions regarding the circumstances at New Caledonia. He was then well treated, as opposed to Malloch, who was 'used like a dog'. Upon completion of his questioning

Pincarton sent for Livingston, directing him to notify the remainder of the men that the Spanish knew their identities and they need not maintain any pretence of being Englishmen. Based on full recognition of who the men were, their attempted false identities and colours, and the intent to blatently violate the Treaty of 1670 by trading directly with subjects of Spain, both the ship and her cargo were confiscated.[14]

The striking corroboration, including the identification of pseudonyms, between original Spanish reports and Herries's publication substantiates both versions of events, particularly when it is considered that the material was produced within a relatively short time frame on two continents, in two different languages, by two men who had never met. Herries also would have been well acquainted with the Scots involved, having served with them on the voyage to Darien and having abandoned the colony only weeks prior to the ill-fated departure of the *Dolphin*.

The entire saga of this first group of prisoners not only verifies the credibility of Herries as a source and the inclusion of non-Scottish participants, but, of greater importance, it acknowledges the goal of the Company of Scotland to establish illicit trade along the Spanish Main. Such a pretence underscores the complications the entire enterprise created for Scotland's king, the competition it presented to English, Portuguese, French and Dutch interests, and its flagrant violation of Spain's territorial claims and international treaties. Exemplifying the level of concern in London are reports reaching King William by June 1699, originating with Admiral Benbow and relayed through the secretary of state, providing notification of the capture of the *Dolphin*.[15]

PRISONERS OF THE INTRUDERS

While the drama unfolded in Cartagena, the Scots also acquired an unanticipated prisoner. Receiving intelligence of a nearby reconnaissance patrol of twenty-six Spaniards 'lying secure without guard or sentinel', a party of Scots and Cuna allies had surprised the sleeping camp. Abandoning provisions and scattering in the ensuing chaos, the Spanish and their own Cuna allies managed to kill two Scots and wound twelve.[16]

Among the men of the surprised patrol was Domingo de la Rada, who would quickly exhibit his survival skills, deftly manoeuvring across the entire range of Darien factions. The Spaniard would find himself a negotiating tool, but first he was interrogated on board the *St Andrew* on 10 February 1699. Referring to the Scots as 'English', he related orders from President Canillas of Panama deploying 230 men to Tubacanti. From that position a scouting party of twenty-five men had been sent forward to obtain prisoners and intelligence. The Cuna captain Pedro had promised that his men could obtain ten or twenty 'English', but, after being informed the Spanish did not have in their possession sufficient gold to pay for the services, negotiations broke down. The following morning, expecting to speak again with Pedro, the Spaniards were instead surprised by the force from New Caledonia. De la Rada found himself cut off from escape by the Cuna, immediately making the determination that approaching the Scots presented a more attractive option.[17]

An attempt was made to capitalise on de la Rada's capture by preparing a letter for Canillas, assuring him of the Scots' peaceful intentions and extending an offer to initiate diplomatic relations. The message was first relayed to the governor of Santa Maria, notifying him that they had the Spaniard in their custody and would continue to treat him 'with all kindness and civility until we have advice from you how to dispose of him'. *Maestro de campo* Luis Carrisoli produced the initial reply, both courteous and curt, writing that he had forwarded the Scots' correspondence and would wait for direction from his superior prior to making any judgement. As for de la Rada's future, he responded, 'I thank you for the offer, and leave it to your selves to dispose of him as you shall please'.[18]

As witnessed by his eventual deposition administered in Santa Maria by the same *maestro de campo*, de la Rada was well able to fend for himself. Three months following the Tubacanti skirmish he approached Carrisoli's home in the company of two Scotsmen and was recognised as one of the men who had participated in the surprised patrol. When he did not return it had been said he had gone into the Scottish camp. He had indeed been in New Caledonia and now returned with a valuable first-hand account of the colony and the gullibility of his Scottish captors. The thirty-eight-year-old described himself as a trader from Barbacoas who had accompanied the patrol. Witnessing his comrade wounded by an arrow, suffering from the flux, and finding himself cut off by Cuna fighters from whom he knew he would receive no quarter, he opted to turn himself over to the Scots. Near their settlement he had met two Frenchmen salvaging the wreck of their ship, who eventually took him to the Scottish vice-admiral, who in turn had released him on 4 May. He had been provided with a gun, two pistols and a supply of linen for his return journey, as well as his current two-man escort. The pair was intended to accompany him only part way, but de la Rada, 'through deceit and flattery', had delivered them to Carrisoli. The former prisoner explained his release had been contrived through his recognition of the Scots' desire to trade with the Spanish, their ample supply of textiles and their intense interest in procuring gold. He had proposed to act as their agent, promising to use his reputation and knowledge of the country to obtain the metal and return within a month to barter for their goods. He had further promised to notify others of possibilities available at New Caledonia and thus lay the foundation for even larger markets. While conscientiously emphasising this ruse was only to obtain his freedom and not to actually conduct illicit trade, de la Rada added he had even requested and received assurances from the colony's governing council of their continued protection as he proceeded with mutual commercial initiatives.

Characteristic of other interrogations completed by the Spanish, detailed intelligence regarding the status of New Caledonia was also compiled. Although he had not been allowed freedom to wander throughout the colony, the trader/prisoner had been befriended by one of the Scots and been told there were approximately 1,300 residents and a defensive moat filled with water. Continuing to exhibit his value, de la Rada updated his countrymen on the firepower of the Scottish fleet and the arrival of trading vessels from Jamaica with provisions. He claimed he had heard that Jamaicans, boasting Panama could easily be taken, had offered 7,000 men to help the Scots fight the Spaniards. The proposal had been denied by the colonists, unless they were to suffer an attack themselves. There were six to seven thousand additional Scots expected, including families, and their intention was to establish good relations with the Spanish. De la Rada expressed his opinion that, if adequate forces were not available to exterminate the colony, it would be prudent to leave them as they were. There was the possibility of attacking the intruders from the sea but it would be effective only if activated before the arrival of reinforcements, expected hourly from New England. He emphasised that he did not think the Scots would initiate an attack, but warned they had established alliances, both overt and covert, with local indigenous factions. The presence of five English ships off Portobello had been discussed openly in the colony. They were under the command of Admiral Benbow, but, contrary to Spanish belief, they were not there to assist the Scots. He did expect, though, that they would aid New Caledonia if it came under attack.

Carrisoli and his men later turned to de la Rada's captured escort. The first individual identified himself as George Drummond, a soldier from Edinburgh, who recounted his past service in one of the Irish companies of King James's Guard. The lieutenant explained the Company's licence from King William to settle in unoccupied territory and its intent to avoid war. Thoroughly questioned about details of the design and size of defences, he added that recovered cannon from the wrecked French vessel were being hauled up to and mounted at the fortifications. Contradicting de la Rada, he explained that Admiral Benbow's squadron belonged to the king of Britain and not to the Company, but was prepared to give the Scots assistance if needed. The only communication between New Caledonia and the admiral had taken place when the English fleet had met the ship sent to Cartagena to demand the *Dolphin* and her crew. Since Benbow had been in Portobello, two Scottish vessels had sailed there, but Drummond did not know their mission. The Jamaican vessels which had come to New Caledonia brought only food, as arms were not necessary – the Scots being amply supplied.

Perhaps attempting to deter the Spanish from aggressive action, the lieutenant gave the population of New Caledonia as an astounding 5,000 and then went on to describe the seven-councillor government, with Robert Pennycook at its head. He noted they had brought with them a large supply of trade goods such as clothing and textiles. One brigantine had been sent to Cartagena, which was the one lost, and one councillor had returned to Scotland to report to the directors. Six relief vessels were expected hourly from home, and they were anticipated to transport 'one of the most important personages in Scotland'. Families were also expected, but he did not know how many. Cuna were regular visitors to sell fruit, but no Spaniards or mulattoes had appeared. When asked about Africans, Drummond said they had brought none to sell nor to use in building their fortifications, nor did they anticipate any.

Turning to the events concerning de la Rada, Drummond said they had accompanied him because he had requested their command to provide an escort across the mountains for protection from indigenous groups. When they had intended to turn back at Tubacanti, they had been prevented from doing so by an order from President Canillas. He did not know the reason for de la Rada's release from New Caledonia, but he did understand a general policy to not arrest any Spaniard, instead allowing them freedom of movement. Verifying the military composition of the population, he explained that their squadron had twelve captains, all of whom had served in Flanders.[19]

A brief account of the skirmish that brought de la Rada into New Caledonia is also provided by Borland, who mentions the Spaniard as the sole prisoner acquired and that his two-man escort was never heard from again.[20] The second individual comprising the escort does, however, reappear. George Cowan's case was eventually presented before the directors in Edinburgh on 19 March 1700. Having accompanied de la

Rada with Drummond as ordered, he had been sent as a prisoner to Panama and eventually to Cartagena, where he had escaped on a trading vessel bound for Jamaica. From there he had found passage home and was rewarded with six pounds sterling. The Company acknowledged the strategic value of his experience 'traversing the most important places possessed by the Spaniards upon the Continent of America' and praised his offer of continued service, assigning him to the relief ship *Providence* headed back to New Caledonia.[21]

A variety of released prisoners, absent from the Scottish record, followed the first abandonment of the colony and initiated transmission of the dramatic news across the Caribbean and on to Europe. On 10 July 1699 Governor Beeston of Jamaica dispatched an urgent notice to Secretary of State Vernon. Although the governor had a packet of correspondence on board a vessel prepared to depart for England, that ship had been delayed and he was able to supplement his dispatches. Beeston related that a full desertion had taken place seventeen days earlier and, based on the Scots' lack of provisions, 'whither we cannot hear nor guess unless they are gon to disperse themselves amongst the Northern Plantations'. After offering circumstances he felt led to the desertion, he provided details of how he had obtained the information:

> The Master of the Vesell tells me that he met three Canoes . . . that came from Callidonia and had three Spaniards on them who had been Prisonors with the Scotch and Freed by them when they saild and also that those Canoes were laden with Iron Crows Shot and other Iron Tools the Scotch left behinde them which seems to Indicate that they went away in haste.[22]

Upon first word of the abandonment reaching London, the Spanish ambassador immediately wrote to Madrid, reporting the resulting clamour running through the English capital in response to the news, the validity of which he had confirmed by immediately seeking out the secretary of state.[23]

Released Spanish prisoners also carried the news to their own dominions. Shortly after arriving in Cartagena in July 1699, admiral of the Barlovento fleet Andrés de Pez, preoccupied with his own preparations to sail against the Scots, received surprising intelligence from seven arriving countrymen. They had been held prisoner at New Caledonia and deposed that the site had been deserted, its former inhabitants heading to New England. Writing to his monarch, de Pez provided a self-aggrandising interpretation of the Scots' departure:

The great anxiety occasioned them during the seven full months that this fleet remained in their vicinity, making war upon them both by sea and also by land, and by its having come to this port to assemble greater force, of which they were informed. This fear, added to certain lack of subsistence they suffered and sicknesses which came upon them, moved them to the aforesaid resolution.[24]

THE LINGUIST'S TALE

That the evacuees experienced no immunity from imprisonment or fear of the Spanish is illustrated by the case of Benjamin Spencer, the expedition's translator. William Paterson, who had also departed the colony on 20 June on board the *Unicorn*, recounted events to the directors upon his return to Scotland. By 25 July their solitary ship, suffering disease, insufficient crew and the death of her captain, had struggled into Cuba's Bay of Matanzas. Intending to replenish the water supply, a pinnance was sent into shore the following day. Seeking directions to a source to fill their barrels, they instead found themselves in the immediate vicinity of a Spanish fort. 'By some inadvertency' Spencer was captured as he stepped ashore. Although Spanish troops endeavoured to obtain the pinnance, the Scots were able to escape, dodging both gunshots and a small boat of pursuers. That evening they set sail without their linguist.[25]

As for Spencer, his version of what occurred would be well documented by his captors and their superiors. The depth and breadth of his depositions, enhanced by the translator's fluency in Spanish and resulting ability to converse directly with his inquisitors, provide a first-hand account of the initial expedition full of detail not recorded elsewhere. They also relate the harrowing story of the survivor abandoned on the beach, his torture and interrogations, and his transfer to Havana. Inadvertently, the documents also testify to the impact of the Scottish presence across the Caribbean and the magnitude of the geographic area that concerned itself with events at New Caledonia.

Spencer's words are included in the Spanish account of the encounter with the *Unicorn* submitted in a packet to Carlos II by Governor don Diego de Cordoba Lasso de la Vega of Havana on 25 September 1699, covering events initiated on 5 August.[26] On that day a large vessel had been spotted off Matanzas. A launch sent ashore bore a Spanish-speaking individual who conversed with the fort's Captain Serrano, identifying his ship as English, from Jamaica and headed to New England. Because they had lost their mast and required wood and water, they requested permission to land. As the captain extended his questioning the men remaining in the launch appeared to become agitated and departed, abandoning their Spanish-speaking comrade. Alarmed by that action and subsequent departure of the mother ship from view, the captain threatened torture (according to the governor, a threat not carried out) unless the prisoner fully explained his circumstances. Spencer then revealed his ship had been one of those at Darien, and that New Caledonia had now been abandoned. Recognising the critical nature of the news, a message was sent immediately to Havana, from where a command was issued to forward the prisoner to the governor.

After hearing the colony had been deserted due to high mortality, lack of expected relief from Scotland and the proclamation of the English king, Lasso de la Vega relayed Spencer's depositions to the viceroy of New Spain and General don Martin de Zavala, general of the Guardacosta, sending them via a dispatch boat that departed on 14 August. Zavala himself sailed into Havana on the 26th, followed in the first week of September by three vessels from Cartagena, each bringing verification of New Caledonia's abandonment.

In the hands of Havana officials, Spencer's interrogations intensified. They were initiated only a week following his arrival at Matanzas and began with the prisoner declaring himself a native of Holland. He recounted his original departure from Scotland, a census of ships and personnel, and the military organisation of the expedition. He stated clearly that there were Italians and Frenchmen among the men, as well as other foreigners. Five women had come with the expedition, but only one had survived Darien to depart the colony. Within a day after sailing they could see smoke and flames at the settlement, recognising that houses and other buildings were being burned, as the fort was not constructed of combustible materials.

Spencer was required to provide a chronological description of the arrival and settlement at New Caledonia. During initial clearing and construction Cuna individuals had brought notice of an imminent Spanish offensive. In response, 160 men were sent under command of James Montgomery to the camp of one of their native allies, eventually engaging in the Tubacanti skirmish. The Spaniards had withdrawn hastily due to the far greater number of their enemy, abandoning supplies of bread and cheese. In return for the unexpected provisions, the hungry Scots left a musket as they turned back to their colony.

Addressing further questions regarding circumstances and intentions beyond the immediate vicinity of New Caledonia, Spencer said he did not know whether or not their departure was known in Cartagena, but he did know they knew of it in Santa Maria. There had been no trade with that town, but it was only a journey of a day and a half from their settlement and the Scots knew it was adjacent to the gold mine called Cana. Trade with the Cuna was minor, basically food materials. There had been no discussion of crossing to Panama, as they had been occupied establishing their settlement, at which no one remained. A French ship, apparently spying on their activities, had been sent by Admiral Du Casse. Evidence of its intent had been acquired from a letter contained in a bottle discovered on a vessel taken along the coast. In that document Du Casse, governor of Petit-Goave, offered to assist the governor of Portobello in dislodging the Scots.

Returning to events at the colony, Spencer explained that a failure of promised relief ships from Scotland had created serious confusion and was only understood when news of King William's proclamation order was received. At that point 'they resolved to abandon their scheme to settle, because they could not maintain it'. The four ships that had sailed away had become separated, and Spencer's vessel had entered Matanzas Bay not understanding where it was. As Spencer had been speaking to the Spanish guard ashore, his shipmates, remaining in the launch, had become frightened by the sight of Spanish guns and the sound of shooting as they rowed away from shore.

Spencer also provided information regarding the Scots' reaction to the imprisonment of Captain Pincarton and the taking of the *Dolphin* in Cartagena. After the return of the men had been refused, the decision had been made to attempt to capture 'persons of esteem' to negotiate an exchange.

The interrogation then led into a discussion of authority for their settlement, which Spencer claimed had come from the king of Britain. He recalled the stipulation to settle in lands unoccupied by any European monarch and that permission of any native population was to be secured. The indigenous people were to be exempt from taxation for a period of twenty-one years.

Questioning then turned to ships that had visited New Caledonia, providing the Spaniards with a localised census not only of vessels in the immediate vicinity, but also those communicating and potentially collaborating with the colony. Spencer responded that he had seen five English ships and several French vessels. One of the latter had come to trade along the coast, and this was the one that was wrecked as it was leaving the bay. It was from that ship that some gold and considerable amounts of silver had been salvaged. Commodore Pennycook had a portion of the treasure in his possession, prompting discord with the French captain. Eventually an agreement was reached, giving the Scots one eighth of the gold and silver saved, but the argument did not end and arms were eventually raised over the allocation.

Gold had also been obtained from the native *cacique* Diego as compensation for the hospitality of the Scots and 'in recognition of a perpetual league and alliance'. Having an estimated value of 300 pounds sterling, it had been presented following an incident involving a launch belonging to the colony being retained by Diego's people. Some additional gold had also been acquired from nose and ear jewellery worn by Cuna men and women.

Goods originally brought to New Caledonia were intended for trade with both the English and Spanish, and included many types of linen. In one of the few references to slavery in the Darien record, Spencer said there were also wrought iron implements, arms of all kinds, and various tin, iron and copper plates, as well as cups and goblets designed for barter with kings along the Guinea coast in return for Africans. Some of these original stores were still on board the *Unicorn*, which, according to what he had heard his captain say, was headed to New England to secure provisions. The ship was leaking badly and they estimated they had only a month's worth of supplies. Spencer had heard no word about returning to Darien.

As the interrogation wore on, the governor returned to the subject of fortifications at New Caledonia. He was told there had been no engineer at the colony. A captain who had served in Flanders was in charge of construction and the intent was to expand the fort when reinforcements arrived from Scotland. At the present time it was more of a battery than a regular castle.

Tension appeared to intensify between captor and prisoner as the governor indicated scepticism regarding some of Spencer's responses, particularly his explanation as to the presence of the Scots at Matanzas. Mention was made of the content of documents seized at Cartagena, which had previously been provided to Havana. Spencer found himself remanded in jail and ordered to be 'pressed' regarding the circumstances of Darien's abandonment and his arrival in Cuba. Overtly threatened with torture, the translator repeated that the survivors, approximately 500 individuals, had departed in their four remaining ships, leaving behind four or five Frenchmen. Recounting again events at Matanzas, he pled 'and this is the truth and God fail him if it is not, and may his soul burn endlessly in hell if he is lying'. He was taken to a torture chamber where he was stripped, placed on 'the horse', and again commanded to tell the truth.[27] At that point the governor, 'seeing how heavily this illness bore upon him', suspended the proceedings.

Contributing to Spencer's difficulties were the first dispatches from Captain Serrano relating the linquist's initial claim that the *Unicorn* was English. It had only been under threat of torture that the translator had admitted otherwise. The status of Spencer's religion also surfaced, identifying him as a Jew, which would have a bearing on his trial in Seville the following year. The statement that he 'was sick of the horse' before he left Matanzas appears to indicate, contrary to the governor's claim, that he had also been tortured earlier. Serrano did relate that they had suspected the *Unicorn* of being pirate, and Spencer's request for wood, water and repair had been regarded as a ruse.

As word drifted into Havana verifying abandonment of New Caledonia, Spencer's testimony gained credibility. His surprise and relief at discovering himself reunited with Captain Pincarton and his three companions from Cartagena must have been profound, and the exchange of information regarding what had happened to each of them, as well as the grand design of the Company of Scotland, must have been related numerous times.[28]

For the captors, news of the Scots' departure must have seemed no less sensational. Systems of communication, faced with the considerable impediments of the time, had functioned well. Word had crisscrossed the Caribbean and had been forwarded to Spain, compiling a vast amount of information. Advantages presented by unanticipated events had been exploited by the established system of intelligence-gathering, information provided by deserters and prisoners assisting Spanish officials in mounting what would become an effective land and sea operation. Consistent evidence of the Company of Scotland's military character and its intent to participate in the thriving world of contraband trade alerted the diverse web of legal and illicit commerce to the validity of the threat and underscored the need for prompt and definitive action.

Although examined more thoroughly in Chapter 8, any review of the array of prisoners involved in the attempted establishment of New Caledonia would be incomplete without addressing the crucial role of the local indigenous population. The *Memoirs of Mr William Veitch and George Brysson* relate an effort to intervene on their behalf during negotiations leading to the Scottish capitulation:

> Some of the Indian chiefs who had been most friendly to the colony, were taken from the side of the Scottish ships and made prisoners. The ministers, pitying the poor natives, drew up a petition in their favour and sent it to the Spanish.[29]

The request being denied, we are reliant on Walter Herries for the punishment imposed. Unlike the trials, interrogations, dispersal and release of other prisoners, and indicative of policies aimed at preventing further alliances with foreigners and assuring control over the Cuna, native prisoners who had fought alongside the Scots at Tubacanti were, the surgeon wrote, 'impaild alive'.[30]

NOTES

1. Burton, *The Darien Papers*, p. 183. Douglas Watt addresses the significance of the lost cargo, estimating it at 18 per cent of trading assets. Watt, *The Price*, p. 154.
2. The governor's report, including interrogations and translations of seized documents, is in AGI, Panamá 215, ff. 193v–265r.
3. Burton, *The Darien Papers*, pp.102–4. The originals are at NLS, Adv. MS 83.7.5, f. 160 initiating Pincarton's and f. 158 Graham's.
4. AGI, Panamá 215, ff. 255r–6v.
5. AGI, Panamá 215, ff. 199v–208r. Benbow, the subject of the next chapter, had sailed from Cartagena only days prior to the *Dolphin*'s sudden arrival.
6. Ibid., ff. 208r–15v.
7. Ibid., ff. 216r–18v. A 'Joan Baptista triconia' is listed as originally sailing on the *Unicorn*. Adv. MS 83.7.4, f. 93v.
8. AGI, Panamá 215, ff. 220v–5v. The lieutenant had been aboard the *Maurepas*, which had broken apart on rocks attempting to leave New Caledonia, eliciting a rescue by the Scots.
9. Ibid., ff. 226r–7r and 236v–7v. 'Stephen Deberg' is included as a sailor on the *Unicorn*'s pay list. NLS, Adv. MS 83.7.4, f. 94v.
10. AGI, Panamá 215, ff. 227r–9r. Graham had originally sailed as first mate on the *Dolphin*. NLS, Adv. MS 83.7.4, f. 100r.
11. AGI, Panamá 215, ff. 229v–31v.
12. Ibid., ff. 232r–3v. and Burton, *The Darien Papers*, p. 298. The surgeon's escape was not unique. The 1705 investigations, or *residencias*, of the administrations of Governors Rios and Pimienta cited lax prison security, resulting in numerous escapes. AGI, Escribania de Cámara 1192.
13. AGI, Panamá 215, ff. 233v–5r.
14. Herries, *An Enquiry*, pp. 44–7. Regarding the high quality of transatlantic intelligence even prior to initial landfall in Darien, the journal of first expedition participant, Dr Wallace, contains a November 1698 entry noting that the Scots' identities were well known in Madeira and St Thomas and that the Spanish in Portobello possessed listings of the names of their councillors and ships' captains. Insh, *Papers*, pp. 76–7.
15. BL, ADD MS40774, f. 41v.
16. Burton, *The Darien Papers*, pp. 84–6.

17. NLS, Adv. MS 83.7.4, f. 136r.
18. NLS, Adv. MS 83.7.4, ff. 140r, 149–50.
19. Utilised here are English translations of the interrogations in MHS-Hart, Darien Item 32. Originals are in AGI, Panamá 160 and AGI, Panamá 109, the latter contained in a packet forwarded to Madrid from Panama on 9 May 1699.
20. Borland, *The History*, pp. 21–2.
21. RBS Archives, D/1/2 and NLS, Adv. MS 83.7.5, ff. 147r–8r. The mission of the *Providence* was negated by the capitulation.
22. NA, CO137/4, ff. 135r–v.
23. AGS, Estado 3971, Marques de Canales to Madrid, date illegible but referring to letter written by Governor Beeston 10/20 June 1699.
24. Hart, *The Disaster*, App. XXII, pp. 306–8.
25. NLS, Adv. MS 83.7.5, f. 39.
26. An English translation of the majority of the original, used here, exists as MHS-Hart, Darien Item 48. Copies of the Spanish original are found in AGI, Panamá 161 and AGI, Panamá 181, the latter starting with f. 177r.
27. 'The horse' consisted of a wooden frame having a sharp ridge on which the accused was forced to sit astride.
28. The men's Havana reunion and subsequent Seville trial is the subject of Chapter 5.
29. M'Crie, *Memoirs*, p. 65.
30. Herries, *An Enquiry*, p. 40.

4

Admirals, Governors and Slave Traders

DISPATCHED TO THE CHAOS of the Caribbean by King William III, Admiral John Benbow would fulfil his written orders while tenaciously maintaining the confidentiality of supplemental directions given to him by his sovereign.[1] Glimpses into that secrecy through offers of assistance to Spanish officials and the logs of the fleet's vessels expose deliberate surveillance of events surrounding New Caledonia and complicity to assure its demise. Examination of Benbow's reports and actual communications submitted by governors and generals in Cartagena and Portobello further our understanding of the scope of interactions and initiatives among Portuguese, Dutch and French interests, as well as English and Spanish. No major party was remotely interested in witnessing the success of a new competitor in the region, ensuring that there was no means by which New Caledonia would survive, much less flourish.

The opportune need to respond to the Company of Scotland intrusion was not restricted to the elimination of its fledgling settlement, but also provided convenient cover for intelligence-gathering and rehearsals for future deployment. Benbow and his entire fleet would return to England with acquired knowledge and practical Caribbean experience that would soon prove its worth. As uncertainty, speculation and intrigue prevailed over the anticipated death of Spain's king and the lack of an heir, the Scottish initiative inadvertently provided the snarl of intertwined interests with an invaluable tutorial in the personalities, places, vulnerabilities and capacities of both potential enemies and supposed allies.

Previous efforts undertaken from London to undermine implementation of the Scots' venture were enumerated by England's Secretary of State Vernon in a March 1699 letter to Ambassador Alexander Stanhope in Spain. First, he related, Parliament had taken action to thwart proposed London subscriptions. William III had then dismissed his secretaries in

Scotland over the affair and further intervened to suppress proposals in Hamburg. Once the Scots had 'settled themselves', effectively revived their plans with Scottish capital and successfully sailed their fleet as far as St Thomas, the king went further, issuing orders to the respective governors of his plantations to provide 'no correspondence or succour'. 'His majesty', Vernon summarised, 'has of himself done all the Spaniards could have desired of him.' The secretary concluded the letter with orders to the ambassador to 'take care to make this matter rightly understood'.[2]

From the opposite shores of the Atlantic more pragmatic concerns demanded attention. Speaking for his fellow royal administrators struggling to maintain viable Caribbean plantations, Governor Beeston of Jamaica wrote to London verifying the arrival of the Scots and declaring that success on the Isthmus, fuelled by the 'irresistible noise of gold (of which there is great plenty in those parts)', could jeopardise his island's precarious existence.[3] His anxieties over the recruitment of volunteers to join the Scots would be substantiated by Darien surgeon-turned-critic (and spy) Walter Herries. In his 1701 pamphlet, the man who possessed first-hand experience of New Caledonia wrote of declarations printed in Boston that were to be clandestinely and widely spread to entice men to come to the settlement, offering privileges equal to those of the original colonists. Jamaica, being the closest colony, would be the first destination to receive the documents.[4]

From London Bishop Gilbert Burnet would reiterate the enticing lure of gold and Spanish plunder, further recognising New Caledonia's provocative proximity to vital ports at Portobello, Panama and Cartagena, the intense Spanish alarm it caused and the resulting offers of French support it elicited. Perhaps the Bishop's most inflammatory claim, however, stated that the king's strongest motive for opposing the Scottish endeavour

> flowed neither from a regard to the interests of England, nor to the Treaties with Spain, but from a Care of the Dutch, who from Curacao drove a coasting trade, among the Spanish plantations, with great advantage; which, they said, the Scotch colony, of once well settled, would draw wholly from them.[5]

Directly impacted was yet another monarchy and its international array of slave-trading partners. At the time the Scots chose to proceed with their effort for commercial advancement, the *asiento*, providing a monopoly over delivery of slaves to Spain's American dominions, was held by Portugal's Cacheu Company. The Portuguese had initially established themselves in 1693 by providing 4,000 slaves under a subcontract with a Spanish company.[6] Three years later they had secured the *asiento* for themselves for a period of six years and eight months, committing to deliver 30,000 Africans of acceptable quality and age, and counting Portugal's King Pedro among investors realising considerable profits.[7] Stipulating delivery of slaves to Cartagena, Havana and other designated ports, the lucrative contract recognised the need for an optimum number of transport vessels, allowing subcontracts with English ships from London and Jamaica and Dutch ships from the Low Countries and Curacao.[8]

As extensive as the financial rewards of the slave trade were, associated benefits were readily available for added exploitation. Beyond the sanctioned commerce in human flesh lay a well-developed network of accompanying contraband trade and proven profits, facilitated by the fact that slaves did not have to be registered or taxed by Spain's Casa de la Contratación. The convenient presence on board of both free labour and contraband goods provided resources for enterprising merchants, coordinating with Spanish accomplices, to create bundles carried by slaves to an established isolated location prior to a ship's formal entry into port. The jettisoned contraband would then be guarded until eventual movement into secure storage under cover of night.[9] The advantageous condition of legal entry into Spanish ports, coupled with a functioning parallel system of illegal trade, created a dedicated cast of profiteers wary of new competitors and fiercely protective of their substantial revenues.

Despite inevitable friction with the *asiento* and its associated illegal activities, officials in both Spain and her colonies recognised the vital communication its traffic sustained. The slave trade's liberal movements across the Atlantic and within the Caribbean, assignment of factors in major ports, use of international crews, and transportation of colonial officials and religious personnel created an invaluable stream of intelligence. From Jamaica it had been the Cacheu Company's representative who had written to Spain in February 1699, providing notice of the arrival of four Scottish vessels.[10] In another case, don Juan de Castro y Gallego, returning to Madrid from royal service in Chile, had sailed from Havana to Lisbon on a Company vessel and produced testimony regarding not only what he had experienced in his own position, but also information about the Scots and English that he had acquired from other passengers.[11]

MISSION TO THE CARIBBEAN: ADMIRAL JOHN BENBOW

In March 1698, months prior to departure from Leith of the first Company of Scotland expedition, then Rear Admiral John Benbow, his career ascending following success against the French and convoy escort service, found

himself called before the Admiralty to be informed of the king's resolution to assign him his initial command of a West Indies squadron. Despite
chronic funding shortages, preparations would be pushed forward, assisted
by persistent reports from the Caribbean of commerce being thwarted by
the Spanish.[12] Formal written orders, notably vague and frustratingly brief,
were finally issued in November 1698, the same month the Scots arrived in
Darien. Benbow was directed

> to visit his Majesty's respective islands to windward (of Jamaica) taking
> particular care that the ships under your command be from time to time
> so employed as may most conduce to the safety of his Majesty's islands
> and plantations, and the trade in those parts, until such time you shall
> receive further orders.[13]

The brevity and lack of clarity of the directive did not go unnoticed, an
anticipated scenario relayed to the king. Secretary of State Vernon reported
the Lord Justices 'can't tell what to make of Benbow's Expedition' while
expressing his greater personal concern that 'when they become to be
known among the Scotch as that can't now long be defer'd I am rather
apprehensive'.[14]

Sailing away from the speculation, the fleet departed from Portsmouth
on 29 November, making initial landfall in Barbados, where Benbow
was informed by infuriated officials of Spanish injustices. Ignoring stipulations of the *asiento* contract strictly forbidding interference with movements of slave-trading vessels, the governor of Cartagena had seized two
English ships, declaring his purpose to be requiring the vessels for the
upcoming campaign to oust the Scots from Darien.[15]

Contemporary tensions, the impact of the seizures, relief of merchants
involved in the slave trade at the arrival of the admiral's fleet, and the
ensuing complications were relayed to London by Josiah Heathcote, the
Royal African Company's factor in Jamaica. In a March 1699 report
he complained further of offences committed by the Spaniards, adding
that Benbow was sailing to confront officials along the Spanish Main,
accompanied by several merchants. Heathcote emphasised losses to his
king caused by 'Roguery of the officials Real', specifying the 'impudence'
of payments to 'the Master out 22 or 23 and Sold Each Negroe before
their faces for 200'.

The factor also informed the Board of Trade of another worrisome
impact of the current circumstances, the flight of the meagre Jamaican
labour force to the Scots, exacerbated by the presence of Benbow's fleet.
Despite the king's command and the failure to gain the required support

of the governor, the factor claimed that the admiral had been impress-
ing men, frightening 'away all our seamen and Ordinary people to the
Scotch or any Place Else where they think they can be Easie'.[16]

The impressments had understandably also alarmed Governor Beeston,
who quickly mounted his own campaign to counter the admiral's activities
and tactics. Late in January, he reported to Secretary of State Vernon, two
of Benbow's ships had arrived and reported that their commander had
parted from them at Nevis. He had apparently sailed in the company of
a slave-trading vessel to the coast of the Spanish Main without explaining his intentions to the remainder of his fleet, which he had directed to
Jamaica.[17] News of the ultimate destination particularly piqued Beeston as
he was currently engaged in delicate diplomatic correspondence with the
president of Panama, the admiral of the Barlovento Fleet and the governor
of Portobello, seeking to assure them of King William's total lack of complicity or support for the Company of Scotland.[18]

The governor's concern was not misplaced. Logs of the master and
lieutenant of Benbow's flagship *Gloucester* chart the progress of a mission steadily increasing in diplomatic complexity. As Beeston dispatched
his complaints to London, the admiral was in the midst of a strained dialogue with the governor of Cartagena, don Diego de los Rios y Quesada.
Benbow had anchored outside his city in late January, pleading the need
for water. The governor had initially refused the visitors access into port,
instead relaying to them the requested water by two Portuguese boats.
In response, Benbow implemented a campaign of diplomacy and threat
to obtain the release of the detained English merchant ships, with the
eventual result that all the vessels were cleared to depart on 3 February.[19]

A distinctly different interpretation of interactions between Cartagena's governor and the visiting naval command, complicated by simultaneous French proposals, is covered in the former's report to Carlos II
and dramatically expands the reasons for the English presence. Rios first
recounted the heavy demands upon his position, providing a self-appraisal
that he was handling his responsibilities admirably. In the midst of trying
to organise action against the Scots and control contraband trade, the
governor had received an offer of assistance against the Scots from French
captain Jean Rache. Within days of vetting the validity of that offer, and
sending Rache in the company of the Barlovento fleet to gain Darien
intelligence, two additional arrivals had caught the governor by surprise.
The pair of vessels had immediately posted English colours and sent in a
launch with a letter from one Admiral Benbow. The visitor reported concern over the site and intent of the Scottish settlement, declaring that his
total fleet was 'ready for any eventuality should the Scotch commit any

evil'. They were also hunting for pirates, Benbow elaborated, which were reported to be operating off the coast of Hispaniola. He was so concerned about getting accurate information, he declared, that he had come alone so as not to alarm local jurisdictions. He requested water, explaining that it had been fifty days since their departure from England and there had been no previous opportunity to replenish their supply. They would, he assured the governor, be departing for Jamaica once the task was completed. The captain assigned to relay communications ashore volunteered that their squadron was under direction from King William to 'gather up the Scotch', adding that additional ships of the fleet were standing at Nevis and off the coast near Santo Domingo.

Rios was particularly wary that the English visitors were seeking intelligence on how much the Spanish knew of Scottish initiatives, and that they might actually comprise the relief fleet he had heard was expected from Scotland. Exercising prudence, he dispatched a contingent of officials to meet with the admiral on his flagship and provide a first-hand evaluation of the situation. The embassy was received cordially and given surprising news:

> The Englishman stated that it was by command of his king to inform himself of the governor concerning the place and position where the Scotch had landed and were founding a settlement, in order to advise his majesty and later to return to execute them all for having come without the authorization of their king, who was in Flanders when they left, and who, as soon as he learned of it, sent this admiral after them with the purpose stated, to which end he had in Jamaica as many as ten ships, and a supply of bombs.

The Spaniards remained sceptical as the English continued to press their case, emphasising peace and amity between their sovereigns. The representatives from Cartagena were given gifts of cloth and departed on amiable terms 'talking among themselves of how to return the courtesy shown, but cautiously'.

Governor Rios responded cordially to Benbow, expressing appreciation for the offer of assistance and the cloth sent to him for a coat. He provided information regarding the Scots and assured the admiral that he was confident the English would remove the intruders immediately, adding that the dominions of Spanish America were pursuing their own measures to assure elimination of the Darien colony. Negotiations over watering the *Gloucester* continued, with the governor claiming he needed his king's permission to allow the English access and Benbow countering that, in order to save the lives of those under his command, he may have to force his way in. A compromise was finally negotiated with an offer from Rios to send men to obtain the empty barrels and return them to the English replenished. An acceptable arrangement was also forged to allow the small *asiento* vessel accompanying the admiral into port to unload its cargo of slaves and obtain its own water supply.

There remained the issue of the detained slave transports. The governor had been pressured for their release as early as 15 January by the local representative of the Portuguese concession, who requested that his company's ships be allowed to clear for Lisbon, along with the pair of English ships for their home port. It was claimed the vessels had been held for a month, causing substantial delay and expense, without formulation of any firm plans for operations against the Scots. Settlement was eventually reached with the governor acknowledging the stipulation of the Slave Trade Concession prohibiting detention of its vessels, graciously expressing his desire to avoid financial losses for all concerned.

In spite of consistently finding himself in receipt of assurances that the 'sole object of their coming was to remove the Scotch, who, they said, had come hither without order of their king', Governor Rios was no doubt relieved to witness the English depart on 12 February. The parade of surprising offers to assist in eliminating the colony at Darien, however, continued the following day as word came of an additional proposal from the French Governor and Admiral Du Casse of Petit-Goave, offering 'munitions, firearms, and all the assistance possible' to expel 'this evil people from these parts'.[20]

No doubt gratified by his initial success, Benbow sailed for Jamaica, from where he filed a report to London dated 3 March 1699. The document, forwarded by Secretary of State Vernon to the king, informed his superiors he had found the Spaniards in Cartagena very disposed towards the French and very 'jealous of us on the Scotch account'. He included the latest intelligence on New Caledonia, including the dramatic news that the *Dolphin* and her crew were being held in Cartagena and an initial armed skirmish had occurred between the Spanish and Scots in Darien. He was sailing the following day for Portobello, he wrote, to gain a better account of the situation and to demand additional English-owned trade goods, men and ships seized by the Barlovento fleet. Vernon included his own assessment, noting to his king:

The Spaniards are very little sensible of the declarations that you did not approve of the Scotch, since they make no end of the seizing of our ships. Benbow is taking a course that will either make them very civil or very angry.[21]

CARIBBEAN EVENTS, EUROPEAN DEBATE

As William pressed his case to assure the Spanish monarch of his lack of complicity in the Scottish effort, increasing expressions of concern from English and Portuguese slave-trading interests demanded a response. Following Benbow's report from Jamaica, Secretary of State Vernon wrote to Ambassador Stanhope in Madrid, informing him of additional English ships detained in Portobello. He related that merchants involved with the *asiento* had paid him a visit 'to complain that some of their ships there and the Negros [were] taken away from them without paying for them'. Included in his letter was a deposition taken during March 1699 illustrating the tactics and consequences behind the complaints. John Chapman and John Noale had been chief mate and gunner, respectively, of the *Good Will*, sailing with a prescribed cargo of slaves from Guinea. They had arrived in Cartagena on 27 September and delivered their human merchandise to the Portuguese as stipulated. Preparing to depart for England, they were consistently denied permission to clear and their rudder was ordered unhung by the admiral of the Barlovento fleet, incapacitating their ship. This was followed by a visit from the governor, who 'took away all small arms, locked up the great cabin, powder room and hatches and ordered the Captain and two doctors on shore . . . at their own expense'. After two days the men had been allowed to return to the ship, discovering that powder, provisions, iron bars and two sets of sails had been seized. The explanation given by the Spaniards was that the Spanish and French were to 'join against the English, then that the reason was because the Scotch had landed on Golden Island'. They were to be held prisoner, the men were informed, until word was received from Spain regarding their future. An escape attempt to Jamaica, fully supported by their captain, had succeeded in an English vessel sailing under the Dutch flag. The secretary added a footnote to Stanhope, directing him to 'make people there (Madrid) sensible'.[22]

Stanhope was not caught by surprise. He had previously initiated a campaign to assure the Spanish court of his monarch's innocence and frustration, writing to Vernon to assure him that England's position would be conveyed to all relevant authorities. The effectiveness of his efforts was transmitted two weeks later, when the ambassador reported:

> I have, either by myself or friends, published so effectually his Majesty's disowning the Scotch design in the West Indies, that I am sure not a man in Madrid, that ever heard of the former, but has been informed that his Majesty not only disowns it, but has done all that is possible to disappoint it.[23]

In July Vernon forwarded a copy of the proclamation issued by Governor Beeston of Jamaica prohibiting assistance to and communication with the Scots, instructing the ambassador to submit it to the Spanish court. By early August Stanhope was able to report that the Spaniards had publicised the substance of the document by printing it in their gazette and that other diplomats had assured him the Spanish did indeed 'comprehend William III's sincerity'.[24]

The situation in Lisbon was no less perplexing. London's ambassador to Portugal, Paul Methuen, had initially written to his equal in Madrid saying he didn't consider the Spanish threat to the 'American Scots' as substantial, identifying the greater concern their own 'King's disowning them, must of necessity rout them, and I fancy it may be likely to make them turn pirate'. Within weeks, however, he was expressing an increased degree of alarm. Addressing his own efforts in the Portuguese capital, Methuen described fears pertaining to the Scottish presence in Darien and potential consequences for the contract between Madrid and the Cacheu Company, particularly relating to the transport of slaves via English vessels. Affirming the Portuguese enterprise's dependence on London-based subcontractors, the ambassador echoed his Madrid colleague's assurances that he had effectively persuaded Lisbon contacts 'that his Mgsty has entirely disowned everything the Scotch had done as contrary to his intention and command'.

Successive correspondence, however, reflected continuing confusion and growing doubts over future collaboration between the English and Portuguese companies. On 16 June Methuen expressed disbelief at a report that sickness was decimating the Scots, adding that *asiento* representatives were 'pressing hard at the Spanish Court to assure the freedom of English ships'. Within a week he forwarded a contrary message following arrival of a Cacheu Company vessel in Lisbon reporting the strong position of the Scots. As the alarm increased over potential economic consequences, Methuen pragmatically stated in September: 'I know not how the Portuguese will come off of the security they have given in England to be answerable for all damages, or whether their agreement with the English can go on.'[25]

PORTOBELLO

Continuing his mission, Benbow had proceeded to Portobello. On the way he also conducted his initial documented conversation with the Scots. On 17 March the log of the *Gloucester* recorded the presence of two small vessels from 'Caledonia'. They reported they had been at

Cartagena to demand the *Dolphin* and her crew. The Spanish governor, however, had refused. The Scots, 'after giving the Admiral an account', sailed for New Caledonia.[26]

Within a week of the dialogue Benbow's fleet anchored off Portobello, where they received a less than enthusiastic reception from the governor. Master Thompson of the *Gloucester* recorded that an introduction had been relayed into port, eliciting dissatisfaction at their close proximity and warning that the Barlovento fleet was present in the harbour. The governor had good reason for caution. Unknown to the English, Admiral don Andrés de Pez was absent, conferring in Panama on plans to eradicate the Scots and had left his fleet manned 'with only seamen, ship's boys, and some officers, in small number'.[27]

Subsequent developments at Portobello are provided by both English and Spanish reports to their respective authorities and reflect the tension created by the Scottish presence in the region. In his communication to the Lords of the Admiralty, Benbow expressed his frustration at the continuing belief that England's interests were inseparable from those of Scotland:

> I used all the arguments I could to persuade them to the contrary but to little progress being denied the privilege of their ports to water, all the country in an alarm, letters passed almost every day wherein I insisted to have the goods, men and vessels that belonged to my prince and subjects, which at last they did consent that if I would go from befor their port my demands should be sent after me, for my lying there was very nervous to them.[28]

Circumstances were exacerbated by an incident documented by one of Benbow's captains on 28 March, when a sloop was brought in by the English fleet. She had come from Cartagena, transporting 'ab.103 negros several passengers and goods with three fryars, in the evening cleared the sloop but detained the fryars'.[29] The detention and suspicions it was perceived to substantiate were included in a letter from the governor of Portobello to his counterpart Beeston in Jamaica. The Spaniard expressed his frustration with the Scots, Benbow and claims that New Caledonia had been initiated without King William's knowledge and sanction. The Scots would not have dared to 'undertake so bold an enterprise', he wrote, without the support of their king. Suspicions had only increased over the forty-four days of Benbow's presence outside the harbour and the seizure of church personnel. Although the English admiral claimed he had come to seek his own country's vessels, it could not be believed 'that a squadron of such strength and cost should come upon a matter of so small importance since the expense of the Admirall's Fleet must in 15 days amount to more than he asked for'.[30]

Missing from official correspondence concerning Portobello, but noted in the logs of two of the English ships, was a brief reappearance of the Scots. On 9 April two sails were spotted which were subsequently identified as being from New Caledonia. They had appeared at night and departed the following morning, but not before the captain of the *Germoon* had occasion to log 'Rear Admiral with Scotch vessels'.[31]

The stalemate between Benbow and Portobello's governor continued until the arrival of the *Maidstone* on 20 April. With her came urgent news in the form of the proclamations prohibiting any assistance to the Scots by citizens of English dominions. Copies were rapidly transmitted to shore and produced a marked change of attitude. Benbow abruptly found himself treated 'very civilly', adding that a French ship had sailed into port, offering its services against New Caledonia. As Benbow notified his Spanish hosts that he was preparing to sail, he wrote that they now seemed hesitant to let him go 'for fear the Scotch should invade them'. Citing pressing orders of his own but acknowledging the request for defensive support, the admiral ordered Captain Pickard to take command of the *Soldado*, *Falmouth* and *Lynn* and remain behind, while 'the *Maidstone* I sent to cruise the Gulph of Darien for ten days then to return to Jamaica'.

The orders prepared for Captain Pickard specifically addressed interaction with the Scots and clear intent to provide assistance against New Caledonia should it be requested by the Spanish. Dated 28 April 1699 they instructed the reduced fleet to maintain communication with the Spanish,

> unless it be their request that you stay to protect them from the Scotch, if so then you are to remain there, taking care you use no violence against the Scotch, without they are the first aggressors, and send one of the ships to Jamaica to advise of the matter . . . if the Spaniards . . . nor think well of ye proposal in assisting them, you are to depart that place.[32]

Not surprisingly, Spanish accounts from Portobello project a different perspective and continuing distrust of the lingering English. Admiral of the Barlovento fleet, Andrés de Pez, had returned from consultations in Panama regarding the Scots to discover a message on his flagship from the English admiral. The Spaniard sent a vessel after Benbow, who had sailed that afternoon after leaving the three ships behind 'under pretext of embarrassing the Scotch in any unbecoming design they might seek to execute against us'. De Pez believed that the actual purpose of the small squadron was 'just the contrary, his object being to hamper operations which from here might be undertaken against said Scotch, by so standing watch over any movement we might make'. In his report to Carlos II, the Spanish admiral included copies of both the letter from his English counterpart and his subsequent reply. Benbow had written of his irritation with the Portobello governor's claim that nothing could be done about releasing a detained English merchant as the prisoner was in de Pez's custody, at the same time complaining that the governor was deliberately obstructing communication between the two admirals. De Pez found himself challenged to provide an explanation for the continued detention. 'I await your honor's reply,' Benbow wrote, 'if your honor wish to make one or not, in order to advise the King, my master . . . Since your honor wishes to be arbiter the world over, detaining his vassals and goods without any shadow of justice.'

De Pez replied in kind, noting he had just returned to his flagship and received his correspondence. Listing the concerns Benbow had communicated, the Spaniard wrote that he was entrusted with protecting the dominions of his sovereign not only against enemies, but also against illicit traders. In the course of fulfilling these responsibilities he had captured the brigantine of one Juan Fleuet off Havana. Fleuet, recognised as English, had been found in possession of treasure salvaged from a sunken ship, 'a grave offense . . . not permissible even to Spaniards'. The case had been forwarded to the Council of the Indies in Spain, where it would be judiciously administered in 'the procedure to conclude matters of this sort, and which will satisfy your honor'. Regarding the detained English merchant, de Pez assigned blame squarely on the Scots:

> News that the Scotch had settled in these dominions under patents issued by the British King was the reason of his arrest, it being plain that had no such news arrived he would by now be in his own country, a free man. It is equally clear that my course is justified, for if vassals of the British king, having no right to do so, proceed as though possessed of absolute authority to intrude upon and settle his majesty's territory, thereby occasioning expense to his royal treasury, how much greater justification have I to hold his British majesty's vassals' property . . .

The Spanish admiral continued, recounting the numerous times he had offered assistance to English vessels, clarifying that he was making the point 'not that the English nation may be grateful to me, but that the gallantry of Spaniards and Englishmen may be known'. He then returned to the case of Fleuet, noting the hospitality the Captain had received when aboard the Spanish flagship:

> If it is true that he has complained, this is to the discredit of the English nation, for he has lied barefacedly, and he should be punished. I am deeply grieved by the insolence, with which he has defamed the credit of Spaniards.

Returning to the question of the Scots, de Pez acknowledged Benbow's claim that New Caledonia had been occupied contrary to King William's wishes, adding it was at odds with letters and patents he had seen. Nevertheless,

> accepting as more reliable the statements contained in your honor's communications, and realizing that a gentleman of your honor's qualities and employment could not by any means fall short of the truth, I have forthwith extended to your honor my entire confident relief. I could never persuade myself that his British majesty could employ duplicity and issue patents as they claim, for in this instance to do so would involve implications unworthy of utterance against such majesty as his, therefore I am persuaded that the Scotch claim to possess a patent is false.

In closing, and further testifying to the negative impact the establishment of New Caledonia maintained upon English commerce, Benbow was provided the sole assurance that 'as soon as I know that the Scotch have left these dominions' the English merchant and his goods would be liberated.[33]

Adding to Benbow's frustrations while at Portobello was the defection of his translator, an Irishman named Juan Fernandez who had accompanied the fleet from Jamaica. Attributing his decision to his Catholic faith, the clerk made his declaration before local officials on 15 May, substantiating Benbow's claim that the mission to Portobello had been to secure the return of English ships and relating communication with the Scots off Cartagena following their unsuccessful attempt to liberate the men and goods of the *Dolphin*. Fernandez explained that Benbow had gone to Jamaica to take on water after having experienced some success in trading merchandise he had carried. He further expressed his belief that the admiral had been given an order to negotiate with the Scots but that a new directive from the British king banning assistance had been received.[34]

Failing to experience satisfaction of his demands, Benbow proceeded to Jamaica, leaving behind Captain Pickard and the reduced squadron to cope with both Spaniards and Scots, as stipulated in his orders. On 10 May the remaining ships stood off Portobello, their crews increasingly decimated by disease. A log entry the following week records two-thirds of the ships' company was sick, and within a few days 'men dying'. By the end of the month the small English fleet was anchored off Cartagena, where they witnessed the arrival from Cadiz of the city's new governor, don Juan Pimienta, accompanied by three ships and orders to eliminate the Scots. The royal administrator was saluted by the English squadron's guns, returning the same.[35]

LIFE, DEATH AND PURSUIT OF MERCANTILE INTERESTS

Upon arrival in Jamaica, Benbow again instituted impressments to replenish his diminishing crew, augmenting the history of friction between himself and the governor. In a letter to the secretary of state, Beeston acknowledged high mortality affecting the fleet, but complained that the admiral's efforts were causing local seamen and their families to desert the island, severely undermining the governor's ability to 'Exercise His Majtys Authority' and protect the island's citizens from 'the Injurys and Insults they receive'.[36]

Into the strife sailed survivors from the Company of Scotland, verifying the first expedition's abandonment of New Caledonia and precipitating additional interactions with the admiral. Captain Colin Campbell, following the death of Commodore Pennycook and 'most of our Sea Officers, and a hundred and thirty or fourty of our men', had brought the desperate *St Andrew* into Jamaica. He requested assistance from Governor Beeston, 'butt he could by no means suffer me to dispose of any goods for supplying my men, altho' they should starve'. He turned to Benbow, asking for men to bring the ship from its anchorage to the security of Port Royal, but was again refused any support. Campbell's dire circumstances were vented in his report to Edinburgh, which declared the probability of the men mutinying, 'for they have nott a weeke's bread, and besides, they expect to have their wages here'.[37]

The presence of Benbow's fleet, coupled with arrival of desperate Scottish survivors, would appear to indicate the opportunity of a labour supply to satisfy impressments. A comparison of the pay lists for the admiral's ships and those of Company of Scotland vessels, however, does not give an indication that there existed any wholesale effort to take on men from New Caledonia, at least not under their actual names. Benbow's pay lists do reflect recruits and impressments, not only in Jamaica, but also during stops in Cartagena and Portobello. The sole indication of Darien survivors transferring to the English fleet involves William and David Strachan, who came aboard the *Maidstone* at Port Royal, Jamaica, on 12 February 1700. William was likely the deserter 'Guillermo Estrafan' who had been interrogated by the president of Panama the previous month. He had identified himself as having served on the *Caledonia*, but neither he nor the like-named David are listed on that vessel's rolls. It is, however, possible that they were not originally seamen but landmen and had endured the pragmatic and challenging naval training their circumstances demanded.[38]

Some of the survivors who arrived with the *St Andrew* did, however, openly replenish British military ranks. William Hutchinson had arrived in New Caledonia with a relief expedition to find the colony abandoned and witnessed the burning of the *Olive Branch* and her vital store of provisions.[39] Evaluating the remaining food supply and realising the shortfall, his group had sailed for Jamaica. They discovered the *St Andrew* there, expecting it to go to sea within two weeks. The infirmity and mortality among her crew, however, made it obvious to Hutchinson that the ship would have to remain in port until the Company made alternative arrangements. Hutchinson had himself been severely ill but was now recovered and had been approached by a Colonel Knight regarding potential service commanding forces at Port Royal. His first priority would remain the Company of Scotland, Hutchinson wrote to the directors in Edinburgh, assuring them he had accepted the position only after consultations with fellow surviving officers present in Port Royal.[40]

The news of Benbow's mission to the Caribbean, and the potential threat it posed for New Caledonia, had not failed to reach Scotland. As relief ships were being dispatched there was speculation about the admiral's orders and whereabouts. George Hume, who had invested 500 pounds in the venture the initial day of subscriptions, wrote in his diary of the uncertainty:

> We hope that if Jameson and Stark continued their course and were not interrupted (as some say they are by Bambo) we have 9 months provisions aboard and knowing there were recruits soon to follow would continue in their places . . . there is talk as if Bambo should all ready have taken possession.[41]

As events in the Caribbean ricocheted from the first abandonment of New Caledonia in June 1699 to the arrival of the second expedition in November of that year to the final March 1700 capitulation to the

Spanish, the region continued to maintain its high level of competitive trade, legal and otherwise. Captain Pickard, commanding Benbow's reduced squadron remaining near Portobello, would succumb to the lure of contraband profit and eventually be court-martialled following a petition instigated by his own men. Among the list of accusations was that he had overstayed his ordered departure following sixteen days, and instead 'stay'd there as many more by the persuasion of his Clerke as I heard from himself to relate to sell merchant goods'. He would be acquitted of the majority of the charges but fined for allowing the sale of rum 'out of the Steeridge for days together, which made the Men Drunk and disorderly'.[42]

The factor of the Royal African Company, Josiah Heathcote, appeared in Portobello in October, reporting his alarm at the presence offshore of eleven French and Dutch ships. Furthermore, in the port he had discovered an imposing vessel of sixty guns, 'loaded with goods', that represented a new French trading company. Expressing his concern, he warned that the situation 'doth oblige the Jamaica merchants to conserve themselves for to preserve that trade which decays everday'.[43]

Benbow's remaining ships continued their patrols through the tension, the *Lynn* standing off Portobello from 16 September to 3 October, then sailing to Cartagena. On 22 October she was anchored at Santa Marta, where she was fired upon three times. After sending in a boat to demand the reason, they were told it was because they were thought to be Scots.[44]

There was also at least one more direct interface between Benbow and representatives of the Company of Scotland. When the relief vessel *Margaret of Dundee* reached St Thomas her command sought, as directed, to obtain all information available concerning the fate of the colony. Among the news they received, including the blockade of New Caledonia by the Spanish, was that Benbow and the Company's Captain Thomas Drummond had simultaneously been in the Danish port in October. Drummond was headed back to Darien with supplies acquired in New York and had maintained 'good correspondence' with the English admiral, dining with him and 'being very intimate'.[45]

The final departure of Benbow from the Caribbean in February 1700 indicates his awareness that the Spanish offensive against New Caledonia, combined with the vulnerabilities of the colony, would be effective and his appointed vessels would be adequate to provide any requested support as well as continuing intelligence. Sometime after the middle of the month Captain Allan of the *Maidstone* filed a report to the Admiralty, expressing appreciation for his new commission and notifying them that he had returned from 'enquiring after the Scotch Settlement'. His assessment concluded 'they every Day doe the Spaniards some damage'.[46] The Spanish fleet under Governor Pimienta had indeed arrived off New Caledonia as the remnant English squadron remained in the vicinity. According to eye-witness Reverend Francis Borland,

> an English Sloop came into our harbour, pretending to be from Jamaica, but was really a spy from the Spaniards, as afterwards we understood, they had gone from us to the Spaniards, and were in their company, when some few days after this, the Spaniards arrived upon our coast with their Fleet. Likewise about the same time, there were about nine French-men that dropt in among us, in a small Periago with Tortoises to sell to our chief men, that were able and willing to buy the same: and these also afterwards were found to be among our enemies; for there was a mixture of several nations serving in the Spanish fleet that came against us.[47]

Despite international complicity, recorded negotiations of the Articles of Capitulation undertaken at New Caledonia during March 1700 give no indication of any other than Spanish and Company of Scotland participation. While the Scots prepared for the ultimate abandonment of their Darien enterprise, the distressed survivors finally had a surprising and pragmatic opportunity for a small piece of the lucrative trade that had prompted their dream. An informal market sprang up between the formerly opposing forces. The men,

> with the allowance of the General, came and traded with our people, buy-ing several of their commodities, which our men were very willing to sell to them: and by this means some of our people came to be provided with money to bear their charges, when they arrived at another port, which proved a favorable providence to many of them.[48]

As the remaining seaworthy Scottish ships struggled out of the bay, the varied factions that had sought their removal returned to other assorted missions, equipped with an expanded understanding of allies and adver-saries. Upon his return to Cartagena, Pimienta faced an onslaught of new accusations from the Cacheu Company regarding interference with the *asiento*. Whatever her precise location during the final days of New Caledonia, the *Germoon* was in Jamaica on the first day of April. Cap-tain Boye filed his report to the Admiralty, notifying them he was fitted with a full complement of men and six weeks' provisions. He requested a continuance 'in these parts, being well acquainted with ye Country

& my men all Seasoned to it'. They would return to the Spanish Main, logging their presence in the vicinity of Portobello and the nearby San Blas Islands through June.[49] From his vantage point in Jamaica, Governor Beeston addressed his own appreciation, not only pertaining to resolution of the Scottish problem, but also regarding the absence of challenges to his authority: 'Now the ships of war are gone all in quiet and amity.'[50]

On the opposite side of the Atlantic obvious expressions of relief followed both the first abandonment and final capitulation. In response to the failure of the initial Scottish expedition, Ambassador Methuen reported from Lisbon of 'very joyful' receipt of the news at court, based on the 'great hindrance the settlement was to . . . furnishing the West Indies with negroes by our means'.[51] To the English secretary of embassy in Paris, Alexander Stanhope wrote from Madrid to say the Spanish court was 'extremely pleased with the advice of the Scots' removal from Darien'. He acknowledged offers of French assistance, adding, 'I assure you it was very lustily promised, and would have certainly have been accepted, if the news has staid a little longer.' He reiterated the French position in a second communication, emphasising to his secretary of state the fortunate timing of the news, for the king of Spain had been anticipated to 'declare that very day his acceptance or refusal to accept French help to rout the Scots . . . France to furnish 40 Men of War and 1200 land men'.[52] As a most uncomfortable series of events came to a close, King William III could experience some sense of relief over conflicts caused by his northern subjects, about whom he wrote to the Pensionary Heinsius prior to hearing of the capitulation:

> I am sorry to be obliged to tell you that affairs go on very badly in the Scotch Parliament. People there are like fools, on the subject of their colony of Darien, which they will not tolerate in England: this causes me great annoyance. What vexes me in particular is that this affair retards my departure for Holland, for which I long more than ever. I shall become ill, if I have to remain here longer.[53]

The Caribbean would experience only a brief respite before the long-anticipated death of the king of Spain in November 1700 and ensuing struggles over his succession. Survivors from New Caledonia would face continued perils as they struggled towards any source of security, whether it be labour in Jamaica, a new life in North American colonies, or even transport to Spain following shipwreck. Admiral Benbow, now well versed in managing a fleet in the West Indies, had

successfully completed a delicate mission that simultaneously moni-
tored Scottish failure, eased the concerns of English, Portuguese and
Dutch merchants, and provided a salve to Spain's deep irritation over
Darien.

NOTES

1. Bassett, 'English naval policy', p. 122.
2. KHLC-Stanhope, U1590, 053/8.
3. Cundall, *The Darien Venture*, p. 36.
4. Herries, *An Enquiry*, p. 26. For a full transcription of the declaration, see Appendix I.
5. Burnet, *History, Vol. II*, pp. 216–17, 235.
6. Brooks, *Eurafricans*, p. 192.
7. Francis, *The Methuens*, pp. 18, 101.
8. Palacios Preciado, *La Trata*, p. 52.
9. Nettels, 'England and the Spanish–American trade', p.15.
10. AGS, Estado 4183, *consulta* of the Council of the Indies, May 1699.
11. AGI, Panamá 181, declaration of don Juan de Castro y Gallego, 26 June 1699.
12. Bassett, *The Caribbean*, pp. 410–11.
13. NA, ADM2/25, f. 178.
14. BL, ADD MS40774, f. 51r.
15. Campbell, *Lives of the Admirals, Vol. 3*, p. 236.
16. NA, CO137/4/107.
17. Bateson, *CSP, Domestic, 1699–1700*, p. 187.
18. HL, MSBL10, *Copies of Severall Letters from the Governors of the Spanish West Indies to Sir Wm Beeston, with His Answers to Them.*
19. NA, ADM52/39 contains *An Account of the Proceedings of His Majesties Shipp Glouster*, completed by Master Robert Thompson. The flagship's lieutenant logs are at NMM-Caird, ADM/L/G/47.
20. MHS-Hart, Darien Item 8, English translation of AGI, Panamá 160, ff. 148–74.
21. NMM-Caird, PLA/23, f. 3r. and BL, ADD MS 40774, f. 41v.
22. KHLC-Stanhope, U1590, 053/8, 16 May 1699.
23. Stanhope, *Spain*, pp. 129, 136.
24. KHLC-Stanhope, U1590, 022/2 and 033/15.
25. KHLC-Stanhope, U1590, 029/5. Methuen's concerns were proved prophetic in November 1701 when he received a memorial from English merchants in Lisbon indicating that their losses in Cartagena had not been reimbursed. NA, SP89/18, f. 44r.
26. NA, ADM52/39. Despite the brevity of Benbow's recorded communications with the Scots, New Caledonia was aware and speculative of his proximity. Reverend Alexander Shields, writing from the colony in February 1700, informed Edinburgh directors of 'advice that Admiral Bembo was gone to

Portobel to demand prisoners, and was intending to come hither also, which was very supporting to us'. Burton, *The Darien Papers*, p. 250.

27. NA, ADM52/39, entry for 23 March 1699 and Hart, *The Disaster*, App. XIX, p. 296.
28. NMM-Caird, PLA/23, f. 9r.
29. NA, ADM51/341, captain's log of the *Falmouth*.
30. HL, MSBL10, *Copy of the Governor of Porto Bello's Letter to Me. Received June the First 1699.*
31. NA, ADM51/389, captain's log of the *Germoon* and ADM52/39, master's log of the *Gloucester*. The latter records the shallop and sloop departed 'plying to windward'.
32. NMM-Caird, PLA/23, ff. 9r–v. and 79r.
33. MHS-Hart, Darien Item 18, English translation of letter from Andrés de Pez to Carlos II, 10 June 1699.
34. AGI, Panamá 109, testimony taken by the general of Portobello, 15 May 1699.
35. NA, ADM51/341/Part III, captain's log of the *Falmouth*, entries for 17 and 19–20 May 1699 and ADM51/3892, captain's log of the *Lynn*, entry for 29 May 1699.
36. NA, CO137/4, f. 382r.
37. Burton, *The Darien Papers*, pp. 150–1.
38. Company of Scotland pay lists for marine personnel are in NLS, Adv. MS 83.7.4, starting with f. 88r. Those for Benbow's fleet are: NA, ADM33/204 for *Germoon*, ADM33/206 for *Lynn* and *Maidstone* and ADM33/207 for *Gloucester*. Muster books for *Saudados Prize* are in ADM36/3378.
39. Although the fire's accepted cause was a reckless seaman, a witness stated the loss of the vessel and critical stores was 'through wicked negligence . . . while (Captain) Jameson and his Mate were cutting one anothers throats for a whore'. HL, MSBL9, *Copy of Mr Sheil's Letter*, 25 December 1699.
40. UGSp, MS1685, letter from Port Royal, 24 October 1699.
41. NRS, GD1/649/2, typed transcript of Diary of George Home of Kimmerghame, Vol. 2. 1697–1699, entry for 13 Oct 1699 and Burton, *The Darien Papers*, p. 374.
42. NA, ADM1/5261, ff. 223r–6r.
43. NA, CO137/5, f. 8.
44. NA, ADM51/3892, log of the *Lynn*, 14 September – 22 October 1699.
45. Burton, *The Darien Papers*, pp. 311, 337.
46. NA, ADM1/1435. Allan to Admiralty Office, date illegible but referring to a 16 February communication.
47. Borland, *The History*, p. 59.
48. Ibid., p. 68. Borland's account contrasts with the *Gazeta extraordinaria*. Likely included to indicate compliance with policies regarding contraband trade, the document maintains that 'He (Pimienta) ordered that none of his men should purchase any cloth or any jewelry from the enemy, under penalty'. MHS-Hart, *Gazeta*-English, p. 13.

49. NA, ADM1/1462 and ADM51/389, captain's log of the *Germoon*, entries for 26 and 29 June 1700.
50. NA, CO137/5, f. 51, Beeston to Board of Trade, 20 April 1700.
51. KLHC-Stanhope, U1590, 29/5, Methuen to Stanhope, November 1699.
52. Stanhope, *Spain*, p. 151 and KLHC-Stanhope, U1590, 022/5, Stanhope to Jersey, October 1699.
53. Grimblot, *Letters*, p. 415.

5

The Long Reach of Spanish Justice

REACTION TO THE COMPANY of Scotland's Darien intrusion was not confined to military campaigns undertaken from both Spain and her American dominions nor political and economic discord within Britain nor diplomatic wrangling pertaining to detention of ships involved in the *asiento* trade. The decision to involve Spain's justice system through the Casa de la Contratación was a manifestation of New Caledonia in the administrative heart of Spain's empire. The development was supported by the highest level of government in Madrid and instigated through established interfaces with governors in the Americas and support of naval personnel tasked with the transport of prisoners. While the resulting convictions and death sentences intensified the web of existing tensions, they also activated a coterie of English and Dutch diplomats working in Madrid, Brussels, Cadiz and Seville to fulfil anxious directives from London, extending the influence of New Caledonia far beyond Caribbean shores directly into the highest echelons of international diplomacy.

The examination of legal proceedings presented in this chapter is possible solely due to discovery of the trial record and associated correspondence in the Archivo General de Indias.[1] Not only does the material illustrate the elevated priority Spain attributed to the Scottish incursion, but it starkly reveals a trio of judges determined to pursue financial redress from the Company of Scotland, its management and investors. The file also provides a rich example of the Casa's legal function and its process against international defendants, while testimonies of the five detainees enhance the understanding of those who struggled to establish and maintain an ill-conceived and faltering New Caledonia.

THE CASA DE LA CONTRATACIÓN, THE TREATY OF MADRID AND FIVE DEFENDANTS

By October 1699, as word reached Madrid's powerful Council of State (Consejo de Estado) via London that a second expedition from Scotland had sailed with additional arms, supplies and colonists, discussion turned to pursuit of judicial means as well as military force to eradicate the foreigners. The council members, sceptical of the sincerity of King William's efforts to castigate his subjects, agreed that the gravity of the matter required application of all solutions legal and possible.[2]

Pursuit of legal recourse in matters relating to Spain's American dominions rested with the Council of the Indies (Consejo de Indias) and its administrative institution, Seville's Casa de la Contratación. Initially established in 1503 and receiving its first set of ordinances and a designated university-trained judge by 1510, the Casa's legal authority exercised jurisdiction over both civil and criminal cases pertaining to trade and navigation. With a reach extending over all individuals violating laws designed to protect Spain's monopoly over her vast American territories, the court received defendants from any portion of the king's dominions and was subject to review solely by the Council of the Indies. 'Strangers', succinctly prohibited to trade in the Indies without direct approval of the king, were subject to confiscation of their goods, proceeds to be distributed in equal measure to the monarch, judges and any informer. All cases considered would be given both a hearing and a rehearing, options for punishment in criminal convictions encompassing 'loss of life, loss of limb, exposing to public shame . . . and other corporal punishment'.[3]

Specifically addressing prosecution of King William's subjects at the end of the seventeenth century, remarkable for its delineation of offences committed by the Darien initiative, was the Treaty of Madrid. Concluded in 1670 between the Crowns of Great Britain and Spain it was the latest attempt to assure 'composing of differences, restraining of depradations, and the establishing of Peace in America'. Towards those ambitious ends, the two monarchs were entrusted to monitor the behaviour of their subjects jeopardising the peace, assisted by mandatory revocation of commissions and letters of marque that had previously sanctioned reprisals and taking of prizes. Offenders were subject to criminal punishment, as well as required to provide 'restitution and Satisfaction for the Losses to the Parties damnified'. Essential for the treaty's approval had been the stipulation conceding lands possessed in the Americas, tacitly formalising British occupation of Jamaica and the vital Caribbean foothold the island represented. The lure of illicit trade, a continuing and perverse condition facilitated by an easily abused safe haven provision, remained expressly forbidden. 'The subjects of Great Britain', the treaty declared, 'shall not sail unto, and Trade in, the Havens and Places which the Catholique King holdeth in the said Indies.'[4]

Not surprisingly, the Scots' arrival and settlement on the Isthmus was regarded by Spain as a direct assault on her sovereignty and treaty stipulations. The February 1699 acquisition of prisoners, trade goods and incriminating documents from the *Dolphin* provided a wealth of evidence as well as a lucrative collection of potential defendants. Arrival in Cartagena the following month of an embassy from New Caledonia demanding return of the ship, cargo and crew, coupled with threats of reprisals, prompted a Council of War, irrefutable denial on all counts by the governor and the decision to transport a contingent of prisoners to Seville to 'give account to Your Majesty'. Four individuals, Captain Robert Pincarton, Captain John Malloch, pilot James Graham and the boy David Wilson were to be remanded, with the remaining surviving men to be distributed to supplement crews of Spanish warships currently in port.[5]

From his prison cell, Pincarton had received word of the first abandonment of the colony in June and petitioned the new governor to either free his men and himself or allow them to depart for one of the English islands. In response, Pimienta told him the former governor had left such a negative report that release was impossible and he would instead be conveyed to Spain. As promised, the three men and one boy were dispatched in September to Havana aboard an advice boat, recently fitted with the *Dolphin*'s guns, to initiate the long journey back across the Atlantic. Upon arrival in Cuba they found themselves again detained and in irons.[6] While in Havana, they also experienced the unanticipated reunion with their former translator, Benjamin Spencer.

The consolidated group of five defendants would next be incorporated into the homebound Guardacosta fleet of General don Martin de Aranguren Zavala. Zavala, with his flagship *San Ignacio* and her two escorts, had arrived from Veracruz intending to proceed to Cartagena and on to expel the Scots from Darien. As word arrived in Havana verifying abandonment of New Caledonia, the relevance of the orders was reassessed, Zavala opting to take advantage of the new circumstances and sailing for Spain with his cargo of defendants on 12 October 1699.[7]

Two days out of Havana contact with an unidentified ship from Jamaica enquiring about Pincarton would concern the Casa de la Contratación sufficiently that the incident would find its way into the

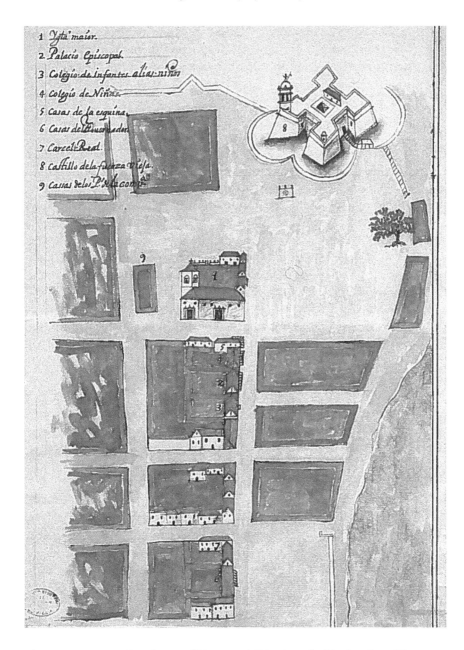

1 Ygla' maior.
2 Palacio Episcopal.
3 Colegio de Infantes alias niños
4 colegio de Niñas
5 Casas de la esquina,
6 Casas del Gouernador
7 Carcel Real.
8 castillo de la fuerza vieja.
9 Casas de los Pl. da comp

Figure 5.1 Fuerza Vieja Sector of Havana, 1691. Note the king's prison (7), adjacent to the governor's palace at the bottom of the map. Source: Spain. Ministry of Culture. General Archives of Indies, AGI, MP Santo_Domingo 96.

subsequent trial. The prisoners, held aboard the *San Ignacio* some distance from the communicating vessels, reported they could identify the ship's English construction, but had no knowledge of the content of or motivation for the dialogue. John Malloch did state he recognised the ship from the river in London and that it appeared to be that of Captain David Breholt.[8]

Evidence indicates that Malloch's identification was correct, and Breholt's actual mission, had it been revealed, would have elicited a strong reaction from the Spanish fleet. The *Carlisle* had recently been active across the Caribbean, documented in Montserrat in August prior to joining a chase after a pirate off St Thomas. Admiral Benbow acknowledged the vessel's primary mission in a log entry, noting he had sailed with her from Jamaica 'in order to countenance Captain Brahoult who was going also on a wreck which was cast away two years since off the Havana with great treasure'.[9] Although no documentation defines the relationship with the prisoners, Breholt's bold approach indicates he knew Pincarton and the other men through their mercantile careers and/or he had heard of their plight while in Jamaica. It is likely pertinent that Pincarton himself had experience of recovering Spanish treasure, having served as boatswain for Sir William Phips during his enriching 1686–7 expedition to the Caribbean.[10]

Apparently without additional unusual events, the homecoming fleet sailed into Cadiz in mid-December, the five New Caledonia veterans once again placed in irons.[11] Officials of the Casa did not immediately acknowledge their arrival, however, apparently distracted by the activities of General Zavala. The commanding officer aroused suspicion and was subjected to his own imprisonment when he failed to complete entry documents or allow the requisite inspection. Compounding matters were multiple accounts of French and English launches ferrying unidentified cargo from the *San Ignacio* on a moonless night. Zavala responded with disdain, declaring his rank and status elevated him above the Casa's jurisdiction and adding that the launches were benignly bringing foreign officers wishing to express congratulations on his successful sail, an action for which he was compelled to provide appropriate hospitality.[12]

Despite diverted Spanish officials, the prisoners soon came to the attention of the port's English consul, Martin Westcombe, who took up their cause with the Marquis of Narros, president of the Casa de la Contratación, pleading that the men had not been 'found in the exercise of any thing that was prohibited, but were only sailing to the parts of the dominion of the King of Great Brittain with marchandizes of their own manufacture'. The consul cited the prisoners' service on the *San Ignacio*, informing the marquis of their 'being the most forward on all occasions of danger that offer'd in the whole course of the voyage'. The initial diplomatic effort elicited only an oral reply, relaying that no resolution would be forthcoming without the king's order.[13] Nevertheless, involvement of Westcombe and his deputy, a Scot named James Chalmers, instituted continuing efforts to mitigate the prisoners' conditions and seek their release. Resulting benefits included receipt of fifty pounds from the Company for the men's subsistence, along with documents intended to convince the Spanish court of their innocence.[14]

The seemingly positive steps failed, however, to halt the prescribed examination by the Casa's judicial arm in Seville. At the end of March the men, still accompanied by young David Wilson, were again put in irons and loaded into a small open boat for the trip up the Guadalquivir River, where the case against them awaited and their arrival in custody of boat owner Diego Gomes was documented in the log of the Casa's prison.[15] The long reach of Spanish justice had retrieved the Scottish dream of a Darien-based trading empire and presented it before the formidable, highly experienced tribunal of the Casa de la Contratación.

ADJUDICATING FAILED DREAMS

The trial took place throughout April and May, exacerbated by the receipt of news of the second expedition's arrival at New Caledonia.[16] The proceedings would be punctuated by short recesses: translation services were secured from Benjamin Pitis, a Catholic Englishman living in the city, and Joseph Moreno, appointed as legal guardian for eleven-year-old David Wilson and twenty-three-year-old James Graham due to their minority ages, was given time to prepare the defence of his clients.[17] Once the initial examination of Benjamin Spencer was completed, presiding judge Manuel de la Chica ordered that the prisoners be restricted to separate quarters and prevented from communication with each other and outsiders. Each detainee was brought twice before the tribunal and outside witnesses were also solicited, notably Captain don Bartolome Antonio Garrote, aboard whose advice boat the prisoners had been transported from Cartagena to Havana.[18]

The fundamental importance of the trial record, however, rests in the lines of questioning undertaken during the dual examinations. These subjects of interrogation, here identified as 1. Intent to Invade Dominions of his Catholic Majesty; 2. A Question of Trade; and 3. Indicting the

Company of Scotland, indicate Spain's assessment of the colony's most aggregious offences. They also illustrate the efficacy of intelligence gathered and transferred across continents and institutions to reach inclusion among the judges' points of inquiry. Lastly, they explore the intent of the Spanish justice system to seek recompense from the Company of Scotland and its principals, a lingering consequence previously omitted from analyses of the Darien expeditions.

1. Intent to Invade Dominions of His Catholic Majesty

The trio of judges confronting the five defendants was incredulous, particularly since Spain had learned as early as 1697 from its resident in Hamburg that two ships departing for Scotland were intended for an expedition to Darien, that the men before them could not have known their destination or grasped its critical geographical position within their king's American dominions. Why, they questioned Spencer, would anyone sail without knowing their destination? What would happen in the case of separation due to storms or accident? The interrogators could not comprehend how the translator, in light of his testimony that he had previously worked in customs enforcement in London, could not have been aware of where the expedition was intending to sail.[19]

When it came to the professional seamen, the disbelief was just as acute. In response to Pincarton's account of sailing under a series of closed orders to be opened only upon reaching specific destinations, de la Chica and his colleagues refused to accept that a captain claiming over sixteen years of experience and serving on the Council of New Caledonia could not have been privy to where the fleet was headed. Reiterating ignorance of any objective within dominions of the Spanish king, Malloch claimed that, prior to departure, some said they were going to Africa and others that they would sail to the Amazon, which appeared to be within Portuguese territory.[20]

Asked specifically about their understanding of the prohibition against sailing to Spanish territories without express permission, the men claimed a lack of awareness of the law until they had become prisoners in Cartagena and learned otherwise from Spaniards. Pincarton related efforts to investigate settlements along the coast near New Caledonia Bay, but those explorations discovered solely natives and a few Frenchmen, none of whom identified the area as under Spanish control. Pincarton, Malloch and Graham all testified their sole interest in the expedition was their salaries, the former emphasising his responsibilities to wife and family. Malloch admitted he had recognised from maps the proximity of their colony to Panama, Cartagena and Portobello, but local indigenous informants had assured them they were not within lands of the Spanish Crown.[21]

Repeating much of the content of interrogations compiled from diverse foreign and domestic sources in Cartagena, Havana and Portobello, details of the military force and organisation of expedition personnel was acquired from each prisoner. In addition to an inventory of ships, fire-power and constructed land defences, the presence of an engineer was a particular concern. Spencer explained that although the expedition did not include a professional engineer, Captain Thomas Drummond, who had served the English king for many years in Flanders, had gained knowledge of fortifications and been charged with overseeing construction activity at Fort Saint Andrew. In response to questions of manpower, the existence of companies of infantry on board the ships, the names of their captains, and the ample complement of arms were all detailed. Pincarton stated to the sceptical judges that the substantial quantity of 100 cannon had not been intended for offensive action against the subjects of the Spanish king, but constituted a defence 'against pirates, Indians or Spaniards that came like enemies'.[22]

Throughout the entire trial there was not a single reference to the 'planter' moniker established by the Company of Scotland to profess a non-militant motive for its enterprise. Spencer did, however, shed light on the five women who accompanied the fleet, relating that the forty-year-old wife of William Paterson, their daughter of fourteen or fifteen years, and their maid of approximately thirty all died in Darien. The two other women, wives of sergeants, had survived to depart the colony with their husbands.[23]

Exemplifying acquisition and review of intelligence from American officials, reprisals committed by representatives from New Caledonia following the governor of Cartagena's refusal to relinquish prisoners also became a point of scrutiny. The judges asked Spencer why two armed sloops had been dispatched with orders to go along the coast from Portobello to Cartagena to seize friars or persons of importance to negotiate for the held Scots. Failing to locate such individuals, a pair of small vessels carrying corn, hens, sugarcane and beans had been cap-tured and the goods transported back to the settlement. Following a reminder of the severity of the crime, Spencer claimed he didn't take part, as he was neither a soldier nor an official.[24]

Expressing particular alarm following confirmation of the November 1699 arrival in Darien of the second Scottish fleet, the Casa tribunal probed into further movements of the first expedition's survivors. Spencer, who had retained a presence in the colony longer than his fellow prisoners, could speak first-hand to the intent and conditions of the initial abandonment. They had been seeking refuge in Boston, he related, to resupply and return to Scotland. The decision to abandon the site had resulted from their scant supplies and absence of any word of the relief convoy anticipated from Scotland. They had simply lost hope, particularly after hearing of King William's order prohibiting them any form of assistance. New Caledonia's structures, including 130 of wood and cane, two or three others built to sell rum, beer and other commodities, and the fort had been abandoned as they were in response to word of forces mobilising against the colony and the inability to defend themselves, fully one half of the population suffering from illness.[25]

Despite continual and prolonged imprisonment, the detainees reported receipt of information regarding the whereabouts of some of the expedition's original ships. While in Cadiz they had been told by fellow prisoners from England that the St Andrew was in Jamaica, the Caledonia in Scotland and the Unicorn in New England. Pincarton added he had heard it had been published in newspapers that a second group had actually returned to Darien.[26]

2. A Question of Trade

At the end of the seventeenth century Spain could neither adequately supply her overseas dominions nor effectively halt contraband trade and related foreign incursions. In particular, the Caribbean coastal provinces of Riohacha, Santa Marta and Cartagena had emerged as the most prominent sites within the empire for accessing the enticing illegal commerce.[27] Considering Treaty of Madrid prohibitions forbidding British subjects from trading along the Spanish Main and the unequivocal Company of Scotland effort to construct an unprecedented permanent base on the Isthmus, the Casa judges were acutely interested in exploring the enterprises's commercial aspirations.

Not surprisingly, the general story presented by the Scots regarding the Dolphin's specific mission and New Caledonia's broader trading initiatives painted an innocent picture of struggles to maintain expedition participants and denials of contraband activity. Pincarton declared that their linen and wool was destined for Baruada in exchange for much-needed provisions. Should they fail to secure the required goods, the Dolphin was to proceed to Scotland to give account of their perilous circumstances. In response to questions about plans to establish sugar and tobacco operations, he denied any such intentions, but Graham divulged that he had heard such projects were under consideration. The pilot also related he hadn't witnessed any commerce during his brief months at Darien other than limited barter of shirts and old coats to the native population in return for bananas and other produce. The men did admit that a Dutch ship had entered their bay seeking refuge from the Barlovento fleet, one or two vessels had come from Jamaica to fish for turtle, a French ship was obtaining wood and water, and yet another arrival from New England had brought supplies of wheat and salted fish.[28] Clearly, New Caledonia was attracting an array of international interest.

Testimony given by Captain Garrote presented a contrasting portrait. The Seville resident informed the tribunal he had received orders from the governor of Cartagena to transport four prisoners to Havana and forward a request to the governor there that his passengers remain confined pending transport to Spain. He recounted it had been public knowledge that the Scots were frustrated by their failure to instigate trade with coastal areas near Santa Maria and Panama. Furthermore, Garrote had heard from other *Dolphin* crew members while in Cartagena that Pincarton occupied a high position within the Company and had expended up to 80,000 pesos for preparation of a squadron intended to pursue trade with Tierra Firme and Peru from New Caledonia. Towards that end the Scots were to dispatch small ships to the Darien River and penetrate markets in the inland cities of Popayan and Antioquia. The incriminating account was corroborated by Captain Philipe del Real, who had served with Garrote. The mariner, who resided across the river in Triana, verified his acquaintance with the defendants. Not specifying his source, he said he had learned during the transit from Cartagena to Havana that establishment of the Darien fort was to facilitate trade with New Granada, Tierra Firme and Peru, but that the Scots had been motivated to abandon the site due to its harmful climate.[29]

As the defendants were brought forth for their second round of questioning, they were probed both on the damning information acquired from Spanish naval personnel and further on the pursuit of contraband trade. The latter was substantiated, the judges noted, by appropriateness for the Spanish West Indies of trade goods the *Dolphin* was transporting. Although the tribunal was primarily investigating the commercial goals of the Scots, their auxiliary evaluation regarding suitability of the cargo is in marked contrast to the general criticism and even ridicule assigned to the product inventory throughout Darien historiography. Given the cumulative concern shown by the Casa, which for two centuries had administered Spanish America's governance and commerce, reappraisal of the intensity of criticism levelled at the Company's cargo is warranted.[30]

Spencer, for example, was required to explain why, since the linens, wigs, lumber, staves for making pipes and woollens on board the *Dolphin* were commodities regularly traded to the West Indies and not to Africa or Asia, he could not have determined where the fleet was destined, particularly with his customs experience. He responded that the expectation of the Scots had been to trade with English, Dutch and French, but not with Spanish. He flatly denied knowing anything about trade with Panama or Santa Maria, only that the *Dolphin* had been ordered to Baruada. Textiles they were transporting were intended for Jamaica, the Baruadas and Montserrat, all territories of the English king. In response to Garrote's allegations, the linguist repeated that he knew nothing of plans to trade with Spaniards.[31]

As Pincarton was recalled he was given a review of the grave consequences for breaches of the treaty between the Spanish and English kings. He was also reminded that his dual positions of vice admiral and councillor made him privy to the highest levels of decision-making. Apprised of Captain Garrote's testimony, he was asked to explain his impressive 80,000-peso investment in the Company, particularly when he claimed ignorance of the fleet's destination. Emphatically denying the allegation, Pincarton claimed he had no funds other than his salary, especially since he had lost two successive ships to France during the recent war, suffering imprisonment and confiscation of his goods on both occasions. Now, with the *Dolphin* in Cartagena, he had again lost everything. Furthermore, he had not even heard of the places known as Antioquia and Popayan until this very hour. He claimed complete ignorance of any motivation to trade with Santa Maria or Panama, insisting they were bound for Baruada when forced to run on to Cartagena's beach.[32]

Malloch and Graham were also confronted with Garrote's accusations. The former flatly denied having said ten words to the Spaniard during the passage from Cartagena to Havana and claimed the major portion of merchandise they transported was for the squadron itself, with wigs, woollens and shoes to be utilised as trade goods with English islands. Graham's response was to explain the goods they carried could be used everywhere and were to be sold on English and Dutch islands.[33]

3. Indicting the Company of Scotland

Accusations of illegal trade had not been admitted to by any of the prisoners, but the Casa was well versed on the larger organisation behind those accused. In turning its attention to the hierarchy and authority of the Company of Scotland Trading to Africa and the Indies, the judicial body initiated an effort to secure redress far beyond persecution of the five operatives before them. The judges' acknowledgement of Pincarton's role as vice admiral and councillor identified him as the highest ranking among the defendants and allegations levelled by Captain Garrote indicated a position of greater influence than the prisoner would admit. While the Scots' actual activities and orders would remain a point of contention, it was well recognised there were more elevated personages and an extended association of financial backers supporting New Caledonia. With accumulated documents and intelligence in hand, the judges sought to gain additional evidence against the parent organisation.

Questioning regarding the Company of Scotland corporate structure was understandably largely directed at Pincarton, who admitted early in his testimony he had heard from his wife that King William was being actively solicited to secure the men's release. Asked for specific names and numbers of those who created the Company, the vice admiral replied he only knew the major part of the nobility of the Kingdom of Scotland was involved. A less elusive response was forthcoming from Graham, who identified the Duke of Hamilton, Lord Panmure and the Marquis of Tweeddale as among those instrumental in Company affairs, although he too related broad participation among Scottish nobility. Widespread support was echoed by Spencer who, when asked to relate the number and status of investors, responded that there were between 150 and 200, including some women. He couldn't recall their names, but they ranged from dukes, marquises and counts to merchants and tradesmen, all from Scotland.[34]

During the second round of testimony the judges returned to identifying principals who had established and financed the corporation. Pincarton explained that none of them present in Seville had been party to forming the Company, nor did any of them hold any financial interest in it. He knew the governor of Cartagena had in his possession a document, printed in English, which listed all subscribers and amounts invested, as well as a copy of the patent from the king of Britain sanctioning the enterprise.[35]

Signalling Spanish acceptance of the credibility of King William's claims of ignorance of the Scots' intent to establish themselves in Darien, Pincarton was reminded the Company's activities were not only an offence against the Spanish Crown, but also against their own king. Why, the vice admiral was asked, had they continued the occupation of their colony and construction of homes and fortifications when William had forbidden any form of assistance or interaction with them? To this accusation Pincarton could justifiably respond that they were unaware of any such proclamation when they left Scotland. Perhaps the news had been one of the motivations for abandoning New Caledonia, but he could not say as he had been a prisoner in Cartagena at that time.[36]

The remaining prisoners were also questioned about the founders of the Company and Pincarton's status. Malloch reiterated that none of his comrades before the Casa, including Pincarton, were among the names on the list he had read of individuals establishing the corporation. In rebuttal to the charge that Pincarton had invested 80,000 pesos, Malloch declared it totally false, for he had known the vice admiral for many years and knew his personal fortune had never reached 2,000 pesos in all his life. Graham testified he had never heard of any of his companions taking part in the Company's creation, nor Pincarton investing even a *maravedi*. As for the proclamation from their own king, the pilot said he too only heard of it during imprisonment in Cartagena.[37]

The weeks of questioning finally came to a conclusion with the second deposition of David Wilson, still accompanied by court-appointed advocate Joseph Moreno, on 15 May 1700. The eleven-year-old was pressed about what he may have heard from his father or others about the designs of the Company of Scotland. Sounding confused and anxious, the orphaned boy simply said he didn't know and had heard nothing about the matters.[38]

DEATH SENTENCE, AGONISING DELAY, LINGERING THREAT

It could have been no surprise given the content and tone of court proceedings when, at the end of June, the sentence from the Casa de la Contratación confirmed all negative predictions. For their crime of having gone from Scotland 'With a Squadron consisting of Five Ships of Warr, bringing with Them divers Goods into America, and a Colony therein called Darien, and building there Houses and Forts, and doing other things contained in The Libell' the men were found guilty. Pincarton, Malloch, Graham and Spencer were condemned to death, David Wilson excepted and liberated on account of his age, but prohibited from returning to Spain's dominions in the Americas. Time and manner of the four executions were to be determined. All goods belonging to the men, as well as the *Dolphin* and her cargo, were to be confiscated. The sentence was to be immediately dispatched to Governor Pimienta in order that proceeds from the sale of the ship and freight could be forwarded to Spain as expeditiously as possible.

The judgement also addressed the broader scope of culpability, holding the Duke of Hamilton, Lord Panmure, the Marquis of Tweeddale and others guilty of the formation and administration of the Company. Included were those who provided financial backing, as well as participants and officers of the expeditions. The findings of the court were to be transmitted to the appropriate official at the English embassy, to be forwarded to the British king for his 'exemplary punishments upon the Said Delinquents'. The Casa further directed that accounts be compiled of all expenses incurred by Spain 'on occasion of this Embarcation, as well in fitting out a Squadron to go to Darien, and the golden Coast to retake it' in order to pursue compensation. Governor Pimienta, who as yet unknown to the Casa had secured the capitulation of the second expedition, was to be issued a reprimand for not proceeding with punishment of the men while they remained in Cartagena.[39]

The situation in Seville had been closely monitored from Edinburgh, sustained by correspondence initiated in Cadiz and continuing during the trial. The prisoners wrote of their fear of the outcome from their Casa cells in April, stating 'Our declarations are taken, and their determinations is by some dubious, by most thought it will be hard, and we fear the event'.[40] The defendants' families had mounted their own campaign, with Henry Graham of Brackness, Glasgow merchant Robert Malloch and Mrs Pincarton preparing a 'Humble Petition' to the king's High Commissioner and Parliament on behalf of the men. They claimed their family members had been detained 'for no other reason, but for their being found imploy'd in the Service of the said company and their Colony' and implored the recipients to take up the issue with the king on the basis that such support would promote others to join future Company endeavours.[41]

Indications of the eventuality and scope of the sentence precipitated a new intensity of concern, the Court of Directors submitting fifty pounds to assist the prisoners and forwarding requested documents, simultaneously beginning to address their own legal vulnerabilities through an appeal that 'by any means an Extract of the Process against them be required and obtained if possible to be transmitted hither'. Plagued by a chronic inability to attract a quorum despite charged circumstances, the directors finally considered the Casa's formal sentence on 20 August 1700. Among their decisions was that the now-convicted Marquis of Tweeddale lead an embassy to the secretary of state for Scotland, Lord

Seafield, to ascertain the status of a promised letter from King William soliciting the prisoners' freedom.[42]

While the Company laboured to conduct business, international diplomatic efforts to secure release of the men and prevent the executions had been implemented at the highest level. King William had belatedly responded to warnings of mounting discord in Scotland and the need for intercession. The *Edinburgh Gazette* of 11 to 15 July 1700 had contributed to growing public outrage through coverage of letters from the condemned prisoners, part of a stream of articles keeping its readership informed of events. Combined social unrest over the proclamation prohibiting assistance to the Darien expeditions and the precarious position of the men in Seville had prompted the treasurer-deputy in Edinburgh to write the king's confidential minister, William Carstares, expressing the ominous opinion 'You may be assured this does not a little blow the coal here'.[43]

Lord Seafield also struck the alarm, appealing to his fellow Scot Carstares to intervene with their monarch. News of the men's death sentence provoked the warning 'if they suffer death, it will certainly much increase the ferment in Scotland'. He further advised, 'When you speak of this matter to the King, do it with great concern, and I am hopeful his letters may yet come in time.' Writing directly to the king, Seafield tactfully reminded his sovereign of previous promises to solicit the men's freedom and the urgency a death sentence implied. The secretary for Scotland continued, writing that he had consulted, as directed, with Secretary of State Vernon, who had promised to write to Spain on the prisoners' behalf and also to 'yor Mty for further orders'. The following day Seafield wrote again, forwarding numerous entreaties for intervention, including one from the father of condemned John Malloch and another from the Company of Scotland declaring a letter from the king would save the men's lives. Seafield repeated his fear that the action may come too late, simultaneously requesting his monarch's pardon for 'trobling you so often for the same thing'.[44]

In Spain, King William's consular corps, hampered by the current absence of a British ambassador in Madrid, had not ceased efforts on the prisoners' behalf. From Seville in early July Consul Godschall informed Secretary of State Vernon that he had prepared and submitted an appeal, emphasising the need for the previously promised letter from the king and cautioning 'they will suffer if they have not the Pious interposicion of His Mjty'. Consul Westcombe added his own concerns from Cadiz later in the month, verifying receipt of information that the case had been forwarded to the king and adding that Pincarton and his men remained incarcerated. Even the British resident in Brussels, Jacob Aceré Marmande, was solicited to utilise his position in the Spanish Low Countries to approach ministers, urging them to advocate with Madrid while reminding them 'an execution may be long kept in remembrance'.[45]

The combined campaign finally elicited action by King William from his court at Loo on 22 July 1700. In a letter to his 'Most serene and potent Prince, very dear brother and cousin . . . His Most Serene and Potent Prince Charles the Second' the king of Britain wrote:

> We doubt not that your Majesty has heard what has recently happened to our Scottish subjects, how by agreement with your Majesty's governor of Carthagena they left the country of Darien, how a short time before one of their ships sailing thence for other parts of America was cast ashore in the neighbourhood of Carthagena and was wrecked, and how those on board, when they repaired to the above-mentioned city to seek help, were seized and thrown into prison, were afterwards transported to Spain and were there condemned to death, and have now appealed to your Majesty's supreme court at Cadiz for redress. Such is your Majesty's renowned and known clemency to all men that we most heartily commend to it those our subjects who have been thus condemned for their designs and attempts against your sovereignty, and have already endured such grievous suffering. We believe that, when the condition of these men is known and considered, your Majesty will not hold them unworthy of that clemency. Therefore we have given instructions to our minister, M. Schonenberg, to explain fully to your Majesty their circumstances, and the weighty reasons why their release and restoration to liberty may be hoped for. We persuade ourselves that there will be easy access for his advocacy, and that as all our subjects are now withdrawn from those countries, nothing more remains of that unpleasant enterprise than that those unhappy prisoners may enjoy your Royal clemency and compassion. Such an act so worthy of your Majesty's noble and magnanimous disposition we well look upon as a singular proof of your Majesty's goodwill towards us, and we will make suitable return as often as opportunity may arise.

King William had capitalised on the fortuitous recent capitulation at New Caledonia and the resulting scouring of the Isthmus of a Scottish presence. The available expertise of the trusted Franciscus van Schonenberg, envoy from Holland to Spain, provided diplomatic stature and experience in Madrid to assure appropriate delivery of the request. Secretary of War Blathwayt had successfully solicited the assistance of the Dutchman, who was entreated to intervene on the understanding he knew 'how these things come about' and, equally crucial, the 'stir in the world' the intrusion of Darien had created.

While Schonenberg's expertise was tested in Madrid, the consular corps was kept apprised of and included in diplomatic developments. Consul Westcombe was requested to provide the prisoners, at his Majesty's pleasure, with 'all the assistance and succour you can . . . by furnishing them with necessarys and endeavouring their release in the best manner' while coordinating directly with the Dutch envoy 'to bring the matter to resolution'.[46]

The concerted diplomatic activity forthcoming from Edinburgh, Loo, Brussels, Madrid, Cadiz and Seville, coupled with extraordinarily fortunate timing and communication of Pimienta's successful operation at New Caledonia, resulted in an order from Carlos II dated 17 September 1700. Following consultation with his Council of War for the Indies, the king upheld the seriousness of the crimes and sentence imposed, but remanded the prisoners to the British sovereign for assured and appropriate justice. The four men and David Wilson were officially relinquished to the custody of Consul Godschall in Seville on 1 October 1700. Informed by the diplomat that they were considered prisoners at large pending further direction from King William, they were granted permission to proceed to Cadiz where Consul Westcombe told them 'he had no order about us, and that we might go what way we pleased'. By 31 October the four condemned men, accompanied by the eleven-year-old, were in London where Pincarton signed a receipt for five pounds from Company representative Hugh Fraser for transportation expenses to Scotland. An expenditure of thirty shillings was issued to James Graham to purchase clothing for David Wilson.[47]

Although the rush of international diplomacy had superficially completed a successful course, there existed residual concern over future implications of the Casa's convictions. The prisoners had been released from incarceration based on King William's promised custody and dispensation of justice. There had been no pardon or dismissal of charges. Forces behind the Company of Scotland found themselves in a vague and vulnerable legal position, tried and convicted of violating an international treaty, yet receiving no definitive word pertaining to potential future accountability. Anxiety was evident over what legal process, if any, might be forthcoming.

Word had originally been received in Edinburgh via a June letter from Pincarton and the other condemned men of not only their own sentence, but of inclusion of the Duke of Hamilton, Marquis of Tweeddale, Earl of Panmure 'and whom others of that company' in the guilty verdict. The Casa had stated the various individuals' 'estates should be confiscated, to make reparations and satisfaction for equipping of a fleet to the Indies, and for all other damages, and their persons to be seized'. Notice of this 'droll passage' was submitted to Lord Seafield on 1 August, along with a message that the alarming letter had been seen in possession of one of the Company directors. Later in the same month Seafield arrived in Edinburgh and could assess the situation for himself, after which he wrote to Carstares giving his estimation of various factions in the Scottish Parliament:

> What connects and unites the opposing party is that resolve concerning Caledonia; and the argument they use is, that, if the right of Caledonia be not declared, the directors themselves are not safe from being prosecute; for they have got information that the King of Spain will apply to the King, that it may be so.

The findings of the Casa de la Contratación had clearly caught the attention of Company of Scotland management and investors, prompting them to seek protection for themselves and their estates. Seafield remained in Scotland, attempting to resolve the conflicts expected to infest the upcoming session of Parliament, yet thwarted by the cloud of the Spanish sentence. Writing again to Carstares in September he reiterated his concerns, expressing his opinion that some remedy for assuring 'security of the managers and directors of the company' be provided, but admitting he was unsure of its specifics.

He also included a word of caution: 'Should they carry a vote upon us in this, it is like it might unite them in other particulars . . . you may let his Majesty know what I have written.'[48]

A defensive campaign was also waged from within the Company of Scotland. On 7 November letters were read before the directors from both Consul Westcombe and Pincarton. While they awaited the arrival of their vice admiral in Edinburgh, it was decided to express gratitude to the Cadiz diplomat, at the same time again requesting he procure and send the process pertaining to their convictions.[49] Failure to return home with the documents was one of five concerns Pincarton and Graham were required to explain in a January 1701 deposition submitted to Company directors. They wrote that the Seville consul had told them that obtaining copies of the record would be costly. When the men had pressed the issue, assuring Godschall funds would be forthcoming from Edinburgh, they were further advised:

> He could not understand for what end we required it; and that, in regard it might give jealousy and raise ill blood, he would not appear in it, without a special order from the King his master, or from the English Secretary of State.[50]

The eventual homecoming of the prisoners, finally reunited with their families, in no way resolved the threat of wider prosecution. Finding its way into the centre of contentious politics both within Scotland and between Scotland and the king, the Company of Scotland's 'right to Caledonia' failed to acquire any royal sanction.[51] Repetitive, unrequited pleas from Scotland testify to the vulnerability, whether perceived or actual, the Company and its associates detected. Although the degree to which the liability was exploited, particularly during negotiations toward the Treaty of Union of 1707, cannot be defined from available records, it remains a viable possibility.[52] As for Spain, her commitment to pursue redress for Scotland's ill-fated attempt to establish a permanent presence in Darien provides eloquent testimony to the gravity she assigned the incursion. The Casa's judicial reach literally extended across the Atlantic, not only to transport Company operatives back to Europe and place them before the trio of judges, but also to create a reciprocal intrusion into the affairs of the country tenuously seeking its own dreams of entrepreneurial glory.

NOTES

1. The file, Contratación 5726A, *Ramo* 2, is comprised of over 700 handwritten pages of testimony, orders and correspondence.
2. AGS, Estado 4183, minutes of Consejo de Estado, 8 October 1699.
3. Veitia Linage, *The Spanish Rule*, pp. 36, 85, 123.
4. NA, SP113/6, Item 27 – Treaty of Madrid with Spain, July 1670.
5. AGI, Santa Fé 79, testimony of Governor Pimienta, prepared in August 1699.
6. Burton, *The Darien Papers*, p.103.
7. Hart, *The Disaster*, App. XXIX, pp. 338–9.
8. AGI, Contratación 5726A, *Ramo* 2, ff.182v–3r, 213r–14r, 236r–v, and 255v–6v.
9. Headlam, *CSP, Colonial, 1699*. Items 880ii, p. 480 and 907, p. 503.
10. Pincarton's earlier experience salvaging Spanish treasure is noted by Herries, *A Defence*, p. 36 and verified by Pincarton's signature for debts against his wages for brandy in the Phips expedition accounts. BL, Sloane MS 50, f. 41r, 42v(2).
11. Burton, *The Darien Papers*, p. 103.
12. AGI, Indiferente 2015, report of Marquis of Narros, 18 January 1700.
13. NA, SP94/212, memorial from Consul Westcombe to the Marquis of Narros, 16 January 1700 and Grant, *Seafield Correspondence*, p. 292.
14. RBS Archives, D/1/2, 3 and 20 February 1700.
15. Burton, *The Darien Papers*, p. 103 and AGI, Contratación 4887, *Entrada de Presos*.
16. AHN, Estado 702/20 and AGI, Panamá 165, ff. 575r, and 583r–6r.

17. AGI, Contratación 5726A, *Ramo* 2, ff. 50r–1r and 110r–13v. The age of majority was twenty-five. Wilson testified his father, the *Dolphin*'s boatswain, had died in a Cartagena hospital and he had no mother or anyone to look after him in his own country. Ibid., ff. 134r–8r, 263r.

18. Ibid., ff. 49r and 150r–8v.

19. AGI, Panamá 159, f. 658r and AGI, Contratación 5726A, *Ramo* 2, ff. 32v and 172r–v.

20. AGI, Contratación 5726A, ff. 53r–7v, 218v.

21. Ibid., ff. 57r–61r, 207r and 222r–v.

22. Ibid., ff. 193r–5r.

23. Ibid., ff. 17v–18r.

24. Ibid., ff. 181r–2v. For the *Articles of Agreement* pertaining to the reprisals, see Appendix II.

25. Ibid., ff. 25v, 42v–7r.

26. Ibid., ff. 48r, 80r.

27. Grahn, *The Political Economy*, pp. 20, 23.

28. AGI, Contratación 5726A, *Ramo* 2, ff. 71v–7v, 81r–v, 98r, and 124r–9r. 'Baruada' may refer to the island of Barbuda, today part of the country of Antigua and Barbuda, or Barbados, the latter cited in numerous English language documents.

29. Ibid., ff. 152v–4v and 159r–61r. 80,000 pesos was the sum paid in 1702 to acquire the position of treasurer of the mint for the Viceroyalty of Peru. Haring, *The Spanish Empire*, p. 271.

30. For an example of the assessment of trade goods see Fry, *The Scottish Empire*, p. 29. Watt presents a broader appraisal in *The Price of Scotland* by noting the persistent notion of inappropriate cargo, countering with data verifying the small percentage of total goods ridiculed products comprised (pp.122–3).

31. AGI, Contratación 5726A, *Ramo* 2, ff. 172r–80r.

32. Ibid., ff. 188v–91v, 204v–9v.

33. Ibid., ff. 226v–8r and 248v.

34. Ibid., ff. 80r–1r, 132v and 34v–5r.

35. Ibid., ff. 203v–4r. The documents had been submitted to the governor in March 1699 as part of the unsuccessful embassy to recover the men and goods of the *Dolphin*. NLS, Adv. MS 83.7.4, ff. 157–8.

36. AGI, Contratación 5726A, *Ramo* 2, ff. 210r–13r.

37. Ibid., ff. 228v–31r and 249r–55v.

38. Ibid., ff. 257r–66v.

39. NA, SP94/212, *Translation of the Sentence against the Scotsmen Taken at Carthagena*.

40. Grant, *Seafield Correspondence*, p. 288.

41. NRS, PA7/17/1/23.

42. RBS, D/1/2, 9 July, 16 July and 20 August 1700. The prisoners' account was established through R. Anderson, a San Lucar merchant. NLS, MS70, f. 210.

43. NLS, RY.II.b8, f. 36 and McCormick, *State-Papers*, p. 554.

44. McCormick, *State-Papers*, pp. 558–9 and Grant, *Seafield Correspondence*, pp. 304–5.
45. NA, SP94/212, 6 and 30 July 1700 and SP32/12, ff. 52–3.
46. Grant, *Seafield Correspondence*, pp. 306–9.
47. AGI, Contratación 5726A, *Ramo* 2, f. 329r, Burton, *The Darien Papers*, pp. 110–12, NLS, Adv. MS 83.8.5, f. 177 and RBS Archives, D/1/2, 7 November and 21 December 1700.
48. McCormick, *State-Papers*, pp. 532–3, 586, 629, 650–1.
49. RBS Archives, D/1/2, 7 November 1700.
50. Burton, *The Darien Papers*, pp. 110–12.
51. McCormick, *State-Papers*, pp. 679–80, 684–90, 702.
52. See Devine, *The Scottish Nation*, pp. 12–16 for the scope of inducements deployed to assure approval of the Treaty of Union.

6

The View from Spanish America

On the 14th of July of the current year 1700 common joy came even before dawn, the public rejoicing in the city of Lima being aroused by the merry peal of the bells. This was commenced at the Cathedral at half past one in the morning, and was followed by other churches and chapels, and by religious institutions. The joyful sound was so unseasonable and so untimely that it led people to believe that without doubt it portended good news to the city and to the country on the day of St Bonaventure, news that might dispel the fear that reigned in their minds lest there should be a repetition within the same year of the earthquake that last year, on the same day and with a slight difference in the time of day, had violently laid the city in ruins. Soon the news spread of the success that the army of His Majesty had in the dislodgement of the Scotch.[1]

THE CELEBRATORY REACTION UNDERTAKEN in Lima to the final departure of the Scots, far distant geographically from the site of New Caledonia, was one of many responses across the Americas provoked by the Company of Scotland's attempt at colonisation. From New York and New Jersey to Jamaica and the Caribbean and throughout Spanish America there were numerous and highly varied unintended consequences resulting from the enterprise. Although the vast majority of scholarly effort has been directed at exploring events in Europe, this chapter and the two following will, respectively, establish the substantive legacy of the Company of Scotland across the broad swathe of the Americas and, more specifically, within the region of Darien. Although New Caledonia would not survive, it would produce both short- and long-term consequences disproportionate to its longevity and the size of its land base. While Scotland would experience sociopolitical convulsions leading to 1707's Treaty of Union and the formation of the United Kingdom following failure of the Darien expeditions, the Americas would witness their own panorama of demographic, cultural and economic impacts as the region struggled to maintain a semblance of peace and economic viability.

Examination of these consequences on the Atlantic's colonial world also provides additional context for the critical concerns expressed by the judges of the Casa de la Contratación during the trial examined in the previous chapter. Not only was the attempt to establish a colony on the Isthmus perpetrated at a time of palpable fear within Spanish America resulting from foreign raids and local unrest, but it also incorporated the unprecedented merging of two vital factors. In addition to New Caledonia's conception as a permanent and armed community, its designated location placed it squarely within the most strategic and valued geography bridging the Pacific and Atlantic Oceans. Implementation of the Company of Scotland's ambitions to establish and maintain international commerce from a fortified location upon the mainland dominions of the Spanish king constituted the gravest of threats to an already precarious order, offering a simultaneous opportunity to both old enemies and new allies. There was also the inseparable matter of religion, which would prompt comment from as far away as Boston and Rome and provoke the Papacy to impose financial responsibilities on Catholic institutions from Mexico City to Lima for over a decade.

Impacts of the Scottish expeditions to Panama were, therefore, not limited to the royal courts of Spain or England, or to mercantile houses from Edinburgh to Lisbon, or to Seville's halls of justice. The Company of Scotland's short-lived attempt at permanent colonisation in the heart of Spanish America reverberated across both American continents, imposing a myriad of stresses and change into the lives of highly varied societies and institutions.

A HISTORY OF OFFENCES

The Scots had unwisely inserted their own expectations into a volatile landscape characterised not only by a history of raiding, but also currently experiencing, as discussed in earlier chapters, a thriving and highly competitive contraband trade penetrating the coasts of the mainland. Initiation of the settlement at New Caledonia not only added a new, untried cast member to the international high-stakes game of illegal commerce, but it also directly impacted local populations. It was the permanent residents who faced immediate threats and disruption to themselves, their families and their financial resources. Royal officials throughout Spanish America were also well aware that their own appointments and thus their careers could be assigned, revoked, tested or extended depending on orders issued and performances delivered in response to circumstances as dire as intrusion of a foreign force intending occupation.

Nowhere were such causes more pronounced than in the case of Cartagena, where memory of communal and personal vulnerability and loss was still acute. It had only been in 1697, the year prior to arrival of the Scots in Darien, that a joint contingent of French navy and corsairs had appeared with a fleet exceeding sixteen ships, 5,000 men and 538 cannon, constituting nothing less than the largest invasion force yet mobilised in the West Indies. Pushing its way into the city's heavily defended harbour, the combined land and sea operation unleashed upon the port an initial round of treasure looting, only to be followed by a second wave of plunder when the buccaneer faction, ironically commanded by the same Du Casse who would later offer Cartagena's governor assistance against the Scots, returned to compensate itself for what it considered unsatisfactory division of the spoils.[2] Among other indignities, Cartagena suffered a hole torn in its cathedral and the flight of much of its population, many of whom drowned or died of hunger as they fled their city. Of those who elected to stay, some were subject to torture as homes and convents were sacked. Among the worst atrocities, committed by aggressors who declared themselves practitioners of the same devout Catholic faith as their victims, was the murder of a friar attempting to prevent the despoiling of a golden crown adorning a statue of the Virgin. The degree of financial loss and fear of future depredations had been so pronounced that a substantial part of the citizenry and commerce of Cartagena had relocated inland to Mompox, where life and economic resources were considered more secure.[3]

The scourge presaged major changes for the city, whose strategic location and expansive, sheltered bay had made it the primary trading centre of the Caribbean coast. It had, since its founding in 1533, established itself as the initial entry point for convoys coming from Spain, as well as ships of the *asiento* trade in slaves, concurrently evolving into the dominant military, governmental and ecclesiastical centre of the region. Although the Treaty of 1670 provided a level of assurance that English perpetrated raids such as those of Hawkins in 1568 and Drake in 1586 would no longer occur, there was no equivalent agreement with the French, allowing the population to be terrorised for weeks until spared from permanent occupation by the onset of yellow fever among the unseasoned invading navy.[4]

Cartagena had certainly suffered most recently, but other locations had experienced their own episodes of terror at the hands of foreign invaders. Between 1655 and 1671 eighteen cities, four towns and over thirty-five settlements had been sacked, these totals only encompassing locations along the exposed, easily accessible Spanish American coast of the Caribbean and Gulf of Mexico. Many communities had been subjected to multiple depredations, while locations in Cuba, Hispaniola and Central America suffered at even greater frequencies. After 1671 expeditions against Portobello, Campeche and Cartagena were mounted, with that year's January capture and sacking of Panama by Henry Morgan, who had departed Jamaica only a month after the signing of the Treaty of Madrid, the most rewarding and renowned.[5]

Regardless of treaties negotiated, the periodic presence of the Barlovento fleet and development of the Guardacosta, augmented after 1674 with *piraguas* specifically designed to monitor coastal and riverine waters, the danger did not cease.[6] As the French raid on Cartagena exemplified, malevolent foreigners came in a variety of categories and guises and could operate with or without a sovereign's sanction, under a variety of financial schemes and regardless of professing a common religion. The Scots were only the most recent in a long line of interlopers attempting to share in the financial rewards of the Americas, but their novel intent to establish a permanent presence in a strategic region recently subjected to a devastating raid raised the alarm to the highest level.

DISSEMINATING THE ALARM, PREPARING THE DEFENCE

In sharp contrast to the pealing of bells portending news of victory in Lima, a flurry of frantic dispatches ricocheted across Spanish America and on to Spain in response to reports of the initial appearance in the Caribbean, and eventual arrival at Darien, of the Scottish fleet. In a remarkably comprehensive report sent from Caracas only weeks prior to the anchoring of the first expedition, Governor Francisco de Berroteran reported to the Count of Adanero, president of the Council of the Indies, of notice he had received via the Dutch trading entrepôt of Curacao. The correspondence relayed the presence of a fleet of six vessels, identified as English but transporting 1,200 Scots, bound for the vicinity of Darien. The convoy 'united thither all nationalities and qualities of persons, to make the settlement more populous'. The group's intent was to fortify itself, with the expectation of the impending arrival of six more ships transporting building materials and equipment. Privileges had been awarded by the king of Britain, with printed copies of these assurances having been distributed in Curacao, even being submitted to its governor. The militaristic intent of the group was substantiated by one of the clauses of the notice, which declared that the intruders would make war against vassals of the Spanish king should efforts be undertaken to interfere with their efforts.

Berroteran proceded to elaborate on the hazards to Spain of such an initiative, pointing out that the intended destination of the Scots was within proximity of gold mines in Darien. Not only would this valued resource, which had previously been raided by the pirate Lorencillo, again be vulnerable, but there was the attendant threat of expanding illicit commerce. It would be an easy and logical next step for the Scottish force to cross to the Pacific and exchange trade goods for large sums of gold. Again referring to the history of raiding, the governor reminded Adanero that this had been accomplished by pirates previously, for the Isthmus was a mere eighteen leagues across. Moreover, the intended construction of fortifications exacerbated the threat, for it would increase the possibility of occupying Portobello, Chagres and Panama. In response to the situation's severity, Berroteran explained he was also writing the viceroy of New Spain in order that means to check the situation might be deployed from Mexico City. The president of the Audiencia of Santo Domingo, the governor of Cartagena and the president of the Audiencia of Panama would also receive the intelligence so that appropriate responses could be implemented.[7]

Given the distances, topography and means of communication available, reaction was both swift and dispersed, reflecting the perceived degree of the threat. The same circumstances assured that the response was plagued by lack of uniformity as officials grappled with often incomplete and inaccurate information. Strategies were debated, revised and sometimes obstructed as officials sought to justify their actions and decisions, or lack thereof.

Berroteran had indeed dispatched information to the Count of Moctezuma, viceroy of New Spain, who received confirmation of events from the governor of Havana. A Council of War had been convened in Mexico City where it was unanimously decided the Guardacosta fleet of General Zavala, then in port at Veracruz, would be supplemented by a collection of private vessels and deployed against the Scots. In the midst of preparations, a dispatch was received from President Canillas of Panama transmitting a new alarm received from the president of Santo Domingo: 4,000 of the enemy were anchored off the former Spanish settlement at Rancho Viejo anticipating reinforcements of six additional vessels, 6,000 men, arms, ammunition and livestock.

As anxiety concerning the Scots continued to accelerate, yet another alert complicated deployment of Zavala's fleet. Reacting to notice of French activity near Pensacola and along the Gulf Coast it was decided

by subsequent Council of War sessions in both Mexico City and Veracruz that the northern threat, despite its uncertainty, was the priority. As
months passed, however, consolidation of new intelligence from across
the region dictated yet another strategic shift. Word had arrived via Guatemala that the general of the Barlovento fleet had been summoned to
Portobello by the president of Panama to assist against the Scots, and
support from Mexico was urgently required. The vital role of the *asiento*
in information-gathering was also reinforced when its commissioner in
Jamaica, don Santiago del Castillo, reported the presence on that island
of Admiral Benbow's formidable squadron and its commander's confus-
ing assurances that the Scots had acted without the patent or authority of their king. Councils of War were again convened, downgrading
the potential threat presented by the French and affirming diversion of
resources to confront the Scots and secure the Isthmus before reported
reinforcements had time to arrive and entrench themselves with their
compatriots.[8]

While the viceroy in Mexico City pursued preparations and debated
tactics and priorities based on available information, royal officials
more directly threatened were also reacting. Panama's Canillas had
received word from a French captain within weeks of the Scots' landfall, relating the enemy's presence and their intent to establish themselves and make war. More disturbing, the informant had spoken with
indigenous Cuna who had actually been aboard the enemy ships and
been offered treaties of peace in exchange for permission to occupy
the land and construct fortifications. Everything, from women to
munitions, had been brought to create a settlement. In response, the
president of Panama convened his own Council of War. Notice was
quickly dispatched not only to the general of Portobello, the governor
of Cartagena and the local factor for the *asiento,* but also the vice-
roys in Mexico City and Lima. In recognition of international implications, Canillas also wrote to Governor Beeston of Jamaica expressing
his concern over the latest developments and their affront to Spanish
sovereignty.[9] In these and subsequent dispatches, the president also
referred to the historic vulnerability of his jurisdiction, the threat to
the Pacific coast and his decision to proceed with plans for a land operation while the fleets readied themselves. The Scots had, he reported,
been distributing printed invitations to numerous foreign and piratical interests to join their enterprise, threatening even a consolidated
Spanish opposition. It was, declared the plans submitted to Carlos II
by his president in Panama, a question of preventing total destruction
of Spain's American dominions.[10]

In Cartagena it was Governor Rios who was experiencing the most immediate repercussions of the Scottish threat. In the midst of overseeing seizures of foreign vessels furtively appearing along the coast poised to participate in contraband trade, it had at first proved challenging to evaluate the gravity of the Scottish activity. As reports began to multiply, including an anonymous warning of the intended 'English establishment' and a list of the suspect vessels, he sent a launch to gather more solid intelligence. While anticipating its return the compilation of disturbing dispatches continued from the Bishop of Santa Marta, the governor of Portobello and a passenger arriving from Havana and Curacao. Although the informants varied in the quantity of enemy, there was full agreement regarding their actual arrival and generous supplies of munitions and building materials. Upon return of the surveillance vessel, which had been thwarted by a Scottish craft on watch, the governor learned that land clearing had commenced and thirty to forty huts had been constructed. The new information was disseminated to Madrid and fellow royal officials while, in turn, Rios was informed of plans to initiate a land operation from neighbouring Panama. Turning his attention to the security of his own jurisdiction, he issued orders throughout the province requiring consolidation of reinforcements in Cartagena. The response was less than enthusiastic, typified by the report from the captain of Rio de Caucas that 'people are escaping without wishing to obey'. The governor complained of the situation to Madrid, adding that his efforts were further undermined by actions of the president of the Audiencia of Santa Fe, who had 'detained and embargoed all the appropriations' since the French raid of 1697.

Rios next had to contend with a request from Panama to dispatch the Barlovento fleet, docked in his port, to Portobello to confer over plans to expel the Scots. He doubted the wisdom of the strategy, citing contrary winds and recommending action be initiated directly from Cartagena. In this he had the unanimous support of his Council of War, including the experienced pilots he had summoned to participate. The governor also remained adamant about the necessity of concurrence and communication with the representative of the *asiento*, particularly since he had impounded two of that company's ships for use in the upcoming campaign. A dispute ensued despite Rios's self-professed best intentions and the support of his council. The admiral of the Barlovento fleet was determined to proceed to Portobello with the sequestered ships of the slave trade at his disposal. Both the governor and the *asiento* concessionaire objected, declaring the sail to be unnecessary expense without merit for the campaign.

Suddenly added to the chaos of broad and earnest debate over tactics, funding and deployment came dubious offers of external assistance. The French Captain Rache was first to arrive, offering his services against the Scots. Rios had the visiting frigate inspected, recording only subsistence, arms and water on board. Feeling reasonably confident of the captain's sincerity, he took his deposition and was provided with the erroneous information that, during the Frenchman's recent stay in Jamaica, he had witnessed that island's governor provisioning the five Scottish ships, which were transporting dismantled wooden houses and stone to construct the settlement. Considering his options amid rapidly evolving circumstances, Rios likely felt substantial relief as he arrived at the decision to send the French vessel, under the watchful guise of the Barlovento fleet, out of Boca Chica and on a fact-finding mission to Portobello, thereby ridding himself of two problematic personalities.

Respite was, however, elusive. Within a few days two vessels arrived under the 'blue squadron flag of the King of England, a surprising sight in these parts'. Admiral Benbow, whose specific interaction with Rios is discussed in Chapter 4, had entered the bay, accompanied by a ship of the slave concession and claiming his mission to be removal of the Scots. Once again the governor found himself hosting a foreign contingent professing the surprising and unsolicited motive of assuring New Caledonia's demise.

Understandably, Rios's report does not present his final release of the *asiento* ships as bowing to pressure imposed by either Benbow or merchants, but it does contain references to article 22 of the Slave Trade Concession prohibiting interference with the enterprise and the governor's claimed desire to comply as ultimate motivation for permitting the vessels to clear. Quickly returning to his efforts regarding the Scots, the governor recounts the day following the English admiral's departure, when yet another offer of French assistance reached his hands. This time the communication was from the same Admiral Du Casse who had conducted the raid on Cartagena and subjected Rios to the humiliation of having to march out of his city at the head of a 2,800-man Spanish force, effectively relinquishing his jurisdiction's fate to the raiders. In his role as governor of Petit-Goave, the Frenchman was now offering munitions, firearms and assistance. He was expecting warships, he informed the governor, 'in which he will come to confer with your majesty's president of the Audiencia of Panama, with your majesty's Governor at Portobelo, and with me, on the best method of expelling this evil people from these parts'.

Benbow had departed on 12 February 1699 and the letter from Petit-Goave had arrived on the 13th, but both events were eclipsed on the 15th with the even more dramatic occurrence of the grounding of the *Dolphin* and subsequent arrest, incarceration and interrogation of her crew. With concrete intelligence acquired from the prisoners, Rios was able to inform his fellow officials and his king of actual conditions at New Caledonia, concurrently emphasising the ambiguities and proximity of foreign interests in the entire affair and the requirement to avoid delay. He would, he assured his correspondents, 'take part with all my strength'.[11]

Isolated by distance and topography from the numerous Councils of War, debates over tactics and financial disagreements was the Count of la Monclova, viceroy of Peru. New Caledonia fell within his expansive jurisdiction, creating an administrative challenge defined by the logistical problems of coordinating a military response. Having previously served as viceroy in Mexico City and possessing a notable military career, Monclova well comprehended both the threat and impediments involved in any campaign to dislodge foreign invaders from the Isthmus. Initially questioning the validity of intelligence indicating the Scottish intrusion, reasoning that King William would not risk war with Spain and conditions in Darien were not conducive to settlement, the count continued to enthusiastically await his replacement from Spain and imminent retirement. Instead, he soon comprehended not only the accuracy of the intelligence, but that orders from Madrid would extend his tenure in Peru by three years in response to the threat created by the Scots.

From his opposite side of the continent, across the formidable obstruction of the Andes, Monclova attempted to respond to the responsibilities of his position, pleas for assistance, the changing scope of the crisis as the Scots first abandoned their colony and then returned, and the mandate from his king that he personally travel to Panama to take command. Following initial word of the Scots' presence via a December 1698 notice from President Canillas, the viceroy had responded with supplies and the annual allocation of 300,000 pesos, dispatched by warship up the Pacific coast the following month. Also provided was a contingent of 500 soldiers from Lima to augment existing military personnel in the impacted region.

Although events would eventually negate the need for either his presence or the assistance he requested from the viceroy in Mexico City, Monclova attempted to educate Madrid on the challenges created by its decisions. He wrote that mandated transportation of artillery from Lima to Cartagena, initiated after the French raid and increased in urgency with the arrival of the Scots, was plagued by the conditions of the Isthmus, making it impractical for both ground and sea transport. Land operations could be successfully undertaken only three months of the year due to intense rainfall. The immense distances involved, besides presenting a serious deterrant to effective coordination of any military response, were incomprehensible to anyone who had not actually experienced them. Illustrating his claims with the lag of communication plaguing the New Caledonia operation, he recorded that he had received notice on 9 March that the Scots had returned to Darien to reoccupy their original site. The very next day, he would eventually be informed on 21 July, General don Juan Pimienta and his vessels out of Cartagena, united with those of Admiral don Francisco Salmon out of Portobello, were present off New Caledonia assuring expulsion of the enemy. Despite the difficulties faced, the viceroy wrote to his king, Pimienta's forces had prevented nothing short of the loss of America and assured the security of the Catholic faith.[12]

SUCCESS AND AFTERMATH

Following the devastating French raid on Cartagena, the government in Madrid had recognised the need to replace the city's leadership. Don Juan Diaz Pimienta y Zaldivar, endowed with a lengthy résumé of military experience and family honour, was named to the position on 17 June 1698. He sailed from Spain in the company of Captain Diego de Peredo, 500 infantry, 110 pieces of artillery and munitions, and arms intended to improve both the security and morale of his beleaguered jurisdiction. Pimienta would assert his leadership rapidly, taking possession of the city on the afternoon of his 7 June 1699 arrival. Not only would his presence relieve disgraced Governor Rios of having to manage the continuing crisis in Darien and pressures related to the thriving contraband trade, but his soldiers, recruited principally from Andalucia and supplemented later by those who arrived with the armada sent from Cadiz to expel the Scots, would appreciably alter a population which had shrunk to 2,500 white inhabitants.[13]

In late August the new governor prepared his mandatory report for Madrid, transmitting the conditions he had found upon his arrival and including a summary of events concerning the Scots and the status of his original orders to eliminate the threat of New Caledonia. As he had immersed himself in preparing the offensive, he wrote, news reached him of seven prisoners released by the Scots who had reported abandonment of the colony. A vessel sent to verify the news had returned on

22 July with confirmation, also providing details on the structures and conditions at the site, enumerating the presence of 400 graves outside the fort and two within the interior, and noting that two ill Scots had been offered for trade by the local Cuna. Pimienta further reported he was transporting Robert Pincarton, John Malloch, James Graham and a youth named David, all Scots, to provide direct account to the Casa de la Contratación.[14]

Pimienta sent the king a duplicate of this same correspondence in early October via a Portuguese vessel headed directly to Lisbon. Included was an update of conditions, reporting continuing decimation of his troops due to illness and death and pleading for competent reinforcements. He explained that negligence perpetrated in Spain compounded the situation, for those manning the ships at departure were intent on catering for the needs of passengers with whom they had arranged for transport and eventual business collaborations in the Indies, leaving concerns for the king's ships and treasury a forgotten priority.

The governor continued with a more immediate warning. He had received notice that one of the departed ships of the Scots had been in Jamaica and surmised the remainder of the fleet to be dispersed across the region. He recommended occupation of the site of the colony, for it had been mapped by the intruders during settlement and the potential for them to reappear with reinforcements was high. Pimienta underscored his opinion with a reference to the ruinous financial and military costs of the recent ground offensive led by the president of Panama against the Scots, so effectively halted by the incessant seasonal rainfall and impassable terrain characteristic of the Isthmus.

Of most immediate importance, however, were the governor's concluding remarks. He had received notice via a sloop from Panama only the day before of two ships of Scotsmen once again present at their original encampment. Pimienta was preparing his own expedition to confront the situation, but did not waste the opportunity to inform his king of the implications of diverting valuable resources away from Cartagena. He would take necessary troops with him, having the day before ordered an equivalent number to be deployed into the city as he departed. Sceptical as to their effectiveness, he added, 'I do not exaggerate to your majesty how difficult it is to do this for besides the trouble it costs to drag these troops to anything that looks like fighting your majesty lacks everything here.' Addressing the international response he had quickly identified as exploiting the emergency, Pimienta added his assessment of the recent offer from Admiral and Governor Du Casse of Petit-Goave:

> Your majesty will observe that the governors, and particularly this Frenchman with all his offers and all his compliments, are only seeking a way, be it under the pretext of driving away Scotsmen from Darien (though hard) or of cleaning these seas, to get into our ports loaded to the brim with merchandise.[15]

Pimienta's identification of the opportunity seized by the French to ingratiate themselves with the Spanish and his concerns over unchecked illegal commerce, both exacerbated by his necessity to deal with the Scottish threat, provide evidence for two of the major immediate impacts of the attempt to establish New Caledonia. Not only would merchants, legal and otherwise, be free of the governor's interference while he commanded the situation in the Bay of Caledonia, but the same man who had participated in devastating Cartagena two years earlier was actively pursuing redemption through offers of military assistance. Substantiating Pimienta's cautionary words, but unknown to him, was the concurrent activity in Spain of the Archbishop of Milan, Papal Nuncio to the king, who was formally presenting offers of French assistance to assure expulsion of the Scots.[16]

Regardless of the consequences of his absence, reemergence of the Scots demanded a definitive response and Governor Pimienta initiated his expedition against New Caledonia on 12 February 1700, departing Cartagena in the squadron of Diego de Peredo, with whom he had transitted the Atlantic the previous year. A vital addition to the contingent, signifying the critical status of the campaign, was military engineer Juan de Herrera y Sotomayor, recently arrived from Havana and entrusted with overseeing construction of trenches and bastions.[17] As the men sailed towards confrontation with the Company of Scotland, a letter from their king dated 11 January 1700 was making its way west across the Atlantic, informing Pimienta of the existence of the Scottish fleet he was about to face and ordering him to do everything possible to eliminate the threat.[18]

The tribulations and eventual success of the coordinated effort of forces from Panama, Portobello and Cartagena, well documented in Pimienta's journal and reports, culminated in the erratically negotiated capitulation of the Scots at the end of March 1700.[19] The following day a message was sent to President Canillas in Panama, conceding future governance of the site to his discretion and offering him the opportunity to forward word to Spain. In the same dispatch was a request that all assistance possible be provided to don Antonio de Paredes, who had been ordered to proceed to Lima as rapidly as possible to inform the viceroy of the campaign's positive resolution.[20]

Pimienta returned in triumph to Cartagena on 8 May, filing his full report to the king on 1 July. With the submission he included two maps produced by his military engineer, documenting both the vicinity and specific site of New Caledonia, as well as fortifications involved in the recent campaign.[21] As anticipated, there was to be no respite from his myriad of gubernatorial duties, two activities demanding immediate attention and resources. With the Scottish threat resolved, the services of Herrera could now be applied in Cartagena, where repair and strengthening of the city's defences became a priority.[22] Pimienta also resumed frustrated attempts to control the continuing, pervasive contraband trade of his jurisdiction, submitting a report in early October testifying to the fraudulent market in textiles and slaves that flourished under the guidance of the *asiento*'s factors.[23]

There would also be one more unanticipated negotiation with his prior Scottish foes. Two days following the governor's own return, the *Hope* arrived on one of Cartagena's nearby off-shore islands with twelve men, seven of them Scots. The pilot, Alan Waugh, spoke some Spanish and entered the city to announce their arrival and submit a proposal. The small vessel had been taking on so much water and the crew was so decimated by illness that they were unable to continue their voyage. An Irish resident of Cartagena was summoned to assist with translation and it was soon fully understood that the men had agreed among themselves to attempt to sell their vessel and its contents to the Spanish and trade their personal possessions to fund their way home. Although the *Hope* was deemed unworthy for royal service, declarations were taken, a full inventory completed, a price negotiated and the men allowed to depart.[24]

Pimienta would not be the sole governor faced with a desperate group of survivors. Shipwrecked off Cuba, fourteen veterans of New Caledonia would find themselves echoing Captain Pincarton's route across the Atlantic via a Spanish warship. Arriving in Cadiz, their reception would, however, markedly contrast with their five predecessors. An order dispatched from the secretary of the Council of the Indies in Madrid to the Casa de la Contratación in Seville demanded their immediate liberation due to the capitulation. On 18 July 1701 the fortunate men would find themselves before Company of Scotland directors being relieved of a series of debts incurred on their homeward journey. Among contributions to be repaid was a loan from the governor of Havana.[25]

Over the four months following the capitulation, Cartagena welcomed the 2,000-man squadron of Pedro Fernández de Navarette y Ayala. The armada had departed from Cadiz on 19 June 1700 and anchored off Cartagena on 18 August, having been financed and deployed specifically in response to the Scottish threat. Preceded by additional engineers, the arrival of the new force and its accompanying ample rations, arms and ammunition provided a substantial supplement of personnel and resources. Despite having lost 180 men during the Atlantic crossing and immediately placing sixty into Cartagena's two hospitals, Navarette's remaining contingent of healthy crew members offered a valuable sense of security to an apprehensive region.[26]

While disputes resumed between the returned governor of Cartagena and *asiento* representatives, and while Navarette's fleet had been crossing the Atlantic expecting to engage the Company of Scotland, don Antonio de Paredes reached Lima to report to the viceroy on 21 July 1700, having completed his journey from New Caledonia across the Isthmus and down the coast of Peru in slightly over three months. His arrival in the city with fortunate notice of the expulsion of the Scots was, however, not unanticipated. Pimienta's emissary had been preceded by a communication through the prosecuting attorney for the viceregal court of Quito, who had been in Guayaquil and duly forwarded several private notices from Panama recounting the positive outcome at Darien. Thus, even before official word was received, Lima celebrated. The same day that the viceroy received initial notice he gathered the Royal Tribunal, Finance Board and City Council and led the way to the cathedral 'to give Our Lord thanks for such a happy outcome . . . the *Te Deum laudamus* was sung, and there was a solemn high mass with exposition of the Sacred Host.' Soon to follow were additional expressions of gratitude

> That night the city celebrated with fireworks and illuminations, the Viceroy Palace, the balconies of the archbishop's house, the galleries of the Town Hall, and Main Square being all decorated with long candles of white wax. His Excellency ordered that solemn high mass be sung the following day at the Presidio of Callao, and this was done with many artillery salvoes. Said fortress celebrated for three days with bullfights in a ring with parapets. . .
>
> And in order that the due and just happiness resulting from such good news might not be marred by the unpleasant regret for the severe punishment and sad death of three unfortunates who already were in the death house ready to be hung next day, His Excellency, who until then had been inexorable to the insistent pleas of those who appealed to his clemency for their pardon, in commemoration and honor of the happy event saved their lives, commuting the sentence of death to perpetual exile in the Presidio of Valdivia, that they might serve the King in the fortress.

While the pardoned trio of prisoners adjusted to their astonishing change of fortune gifted by expulsion of the Scots, another confirmation arrived from Quito on the 16th, followed by the entry of the first eyewitness, Paredes, five days later. The viceroy was briefed on the details of the campaign, likely transfixed by details of events and strategies employed given his own service in France, Flanders, Sicily, Portugal and Africa, his associated imprisonments, and the loss of his right arm, in place of which he had been fitted with a metal prosthesis.[27]

For the benefit of the citizenry an account of events was printed in a *Gazeta extraordinaria* for public distribution. Not surprisingly, the document emphasised Pimienta's professional orchestration of operations, but it further acknowledged the vital supportive roles of the military engineers and critical intelligence provided by an ample number of deserters, the French and allied natives. Pimienta's denial of an initial, unacceptable offer of peace was described, along with his explanation to the Scots that they were 'a company of merchants; that if they were troops of their king he would, and not otherwise, as it would be a disgrace to the troops of his own king'. Paredes was credited with having served as a hostage during final negotiations, hosted by the enemy on one of their ships for twenty-two hours. Other details, some of which are related in Chapter 8, described troop movements, specific placement of cannon, mortars and bombs, dimensions of batteries and size of enemy shells. There was a recounting of negotiations leading up to the final capitulation as well as the stipulations of the agreement itself. Events undertaken to evaluate and relinquish infrastructure at New Caledonia to Spanish control and deal with those Cuna who had allied themselves with the Scots were included. Also mentioned was the role of a 'Scotch boy', servant to Pimienta, who confirmed his loyalty by reporting 'he had heard one of the newcomers say that reinforcements of 2,200 men and 300 women were to come'. In closing, the account included Pimienta's later communication that the Scotch had finally sailed from the site on 26 April and a notice had been sent to Spain on the 29th. A contingent of 200 Spanish troops remained behind to secure the location. The final words of the *Gazeta*, communicating the triumph and power of Spain to the population of Lima at the behest of the viceroy, reiterated the underlying premise 'May the Lord be thanked for all'.[28]

FAITH AND FINANCE

In addition to the elimination of the economic and territorial threat that the establishment of New Caledonia had presented, the viceroy was expressing gratitude for preservation of the Catholic faith. In a 9 May

1699 *consulta* to Carlos II, the Council of the Indies had expressed severe regret over confirmation of the Scottish foothold in Darien. Citing the consequences of allowing foreign intrusion to go unchecked, the Council signified its most dire concern that 'the Catholic religion will perish, which is what will most deeply grieve your majesty's Catholic heart'.[29]

The absolute necessity to protect Catholicism from the heresy of the Scots is reflected in the words of the *Gazeta* and the religious nature of events conducted in response to the capitulation, yet the Church did not restrict its activities against such a fundamental affront to conducting masses or enforcing royal edicts to evangelise resistant native populations. As previously noted, the Bishop of Santa Marta submitted instrumental intelligence to the governor of Cartagena regarding initial arrival of the Scots. Although incorrect in its reporting of the presence in St Thomas of 3,000 men and 500 women, all Scots fully supported by their king, the correspondence did confirm their entry into the region and their intent to establish themselves near Golden Island.[30] The new Bishop of Panama, Lima native Juan de Argüelles, had immediately ascertained that evangelisation of troublesome indigenous groups within his bishopric was being seriously hampered by unrest relating to the establishment of New Caledonia. Having only arrived on the Isthmus in 1699 he nevertheless took it upon himself to submit a detailed account to the king following the colony's elimination.[31]

Nor was the expansive scope of the Church's role in protecting the faith limited by provision of intelligence or analysis of events. A lasting and significantly more concrete affirmation of the degree of concern was witnessed by financial responsibilities assigned to churches and associated facilities across Spanish America. Although generally exempted from forms of taxation required of secular sources, there was no equivalent prohibition against imposition of a *donativo*, utilised with frequency during the reign of Carlos II as a funding mechanism to satisfy military needs during periods of armed conflict.[32] Once necessary papal permission was granted to the king, ecclesiastical institutions would find themselves funding improvements to defensive fortifications across Spain's West Indian dominions. Pope Innocent XII had, in 1693, set a precedent by creating a subsidy to be paid from incomes of churches, convents and hospitals in the Spanish Indies for a period of three years. The fund's declared purpose was the repression of piracy and, although initially unimplemented, its form and function were revitalised in response to the papacy's recognition of the threat presented by the Company of Scotland. Not only did the Church actively intervene with a warning to Carlos II 'although the Scotch have abandoned the country of Darien, your majesty should now be more than ever alert', but in July 1699 the Pope issued a revision and reconfirmation of the earlier dispensation of one million ducados. The new brief was explicit in its targeted enemy and was followed by a set of instructions from the king, signifying the resources were to be used in preparing for war against the heretic Scots attempting to populate Darien and others who might attempt to occupy or commit hostilities against Spain's American dominions. Accompanying the royal orders in the thirty-four packets prepared for the designated recipients were copies of the brief itself, translated from the original Latin and printed for distribution.[33]

The necessary mandates to implement collection of the subsidy, to be comprised of 10 per cent of annual income until the eventual sum of one million ducados was reached, were prepared in Madrid in duplicate and triplicate for the recipient prelates. In addition to the documents' submission to archbishops and bishops for further dispersal, they were also distributed to officials of the Inquisition in the Americas. The geographical extent of the order was vast, ranging from Puebla and Michoacan in New Spain to Guatemala, Nicaragua and Honduras, Santo Domingo, Puerto Rico, Cuba, Venezuela and Lima. Florida was also to be included, although the isolated regions of the Philippines and Marianas were specifically exempted. The resulting revenue-producing campaign would last over two decades and its records, including a summary dated 1721, would state clearly and repeatedly that it had been motivated by the attempt of the Scots to establish New Caledonia.[34]

Although duty was acknowledged, the financial imposition was not necessarily enthusiastically embraced across the intricate network of ecclesiastical institutions. In a letter to the king, the Archbishop of Lima assured his sovereign of compliance but also described the intense hardships already caused by diminishing sources of revenue. The extreme poverty of the region, he explained, had been exacerbated by a series of earthquakes over the previous decade, destroying homes and reducing the fertility of the soil, simultaneously reducing the Church's income by over a third while increasing demands for assistance.[35] That the continuing challenges cited by the archbishop impacted actual collection of the *donativo* can be assumed from resubmissions of the order issued in November 1713 to all the prelates of Peru and their viceroy.[36] Regardless of problems inherent in the administration and success of the programme, its existence and repetitive reminder of the Company of Scotland invasion served as a continuing warning to both the population and its Church of the incessant, sinister danger of foreign heretics.

NOTES

1. MHS-Hart, *Gazeta*-English, p. 1. Preparation and distribution of the document testifies to the importance of events to which it relates. The first appearance of such a printed public notice had occurred in 1594 to disperse news of the capture of English privateer Richard Hawkins. Although gazettes usually extended up to four pages, the unique edition quoted here runs to double that length. Haring, *The Spanish Empire*, pp. 230–1.
2. Galvin, *Patterns of Pillage*, pp. 64–5.
3. Arciniegas, *Caribbean*, pp. 240–2 and Lemaitre, *Historia General, tomo II*, p. 238.
4. McNeill, *Mosquito Empires*, pp. 145–7. McNeill stresses that the 1690s witnessed particularly bad outbreaks due to increased arrivals of vulnerable populations as well as meteorological conditions conducive to survival of larvae of *Aedes aegypti*, the yellow fever-transmitting mosquito.
5. Haring, *Trade and Navigation*, pp. 249–50.
6. The *piraguas* were well suited for deployment in coastal areas as they were flat bottomed, having a draft of only a foot and a half. They could accommodate a crew of 120 and were typically armed with a single long gun located in the bow and four additional pieces in the stern. Ibid., pp. 256–7.
7. MHS-Hart, Darien Item 1, translation of letter from Francisco de Berroteran to Conde de Adanero, Caracas, 15 November 1698. Berroteran's reference to Cornelis Boudewijn de Graff, 'Lorencillo', signifies the degree of alarm being communicated. The Dutch pirate, who had served in the Spanish navy prior to becoming a buccaneer, eventually entered the service of the French king, so terrorising the region that special prayers were invoked to protect communities from his attacks. Haring, *The Buccaneers*, p. 246, ft. 2.
8. Hart, *The Disaster*, App. XXI, pp. 299–305.
9. AGI, Panamá 181, ff. 167r–73v.
10. Hart, *The Disaster*, App. XVI, pp. 261–82.
11. MHS-Hart, Darien Item 8, English translation of Rios' submittal to Carlos II dated 24 February 1699 covering events from the previous December, and Crouse, *The French Struggle*, p. 232. It is intriguing to speculate on the degree to which Rios's actions in response to the Scots were conducted under the guise of potential redemption for his 1697 humiliation.
12. Moreyra y Paz-Soldán and Céspedes del Castillo, *Virreinato peruano, tomo III*, pp. xxii–xxx, 58–9, 63–4, 69 and AGI, Panamá 181, ff. 631–48v.
13. Castillo Mathieu, *Los Gobernadores*, pp. 79–80.
14. AGI, Santa Fé 79, testimony dated August 1699.
15. Hart, *The Disaster*, App. XXVII, pp. 319–21.
16. AGS, Estado 3091, *consulta* from Council of State to Carlos II, October 1699.
17. Castillo Mathieu, *Los Gobernadores*, p. 80.
18. AGI, Panamá 113, *Ramo 3*.

19. An English translation of the journal is in Hart, *The Disaster*, App. XXXI, pp. 353–93. A copy of the original Spanish version is in AGI, Panamá 164.
20. Hart, *The Disaster*, App. XXXII, pp. 394–5. Don Juan Pimienta to the Conde de Canillas, 12 April 1700.
21. AGI, Santa Fé 435, Don Juan Pimienta to Carlos II, 1 July 1700.
22. Castillo Mathieu, *Los Gobernadores*, p. 81.
23. AGI, Santa Fé 435, testimony dated 5 October 1700.
24. AGI, Panamá 181, ff. 691r–735v, from a collection of documents submitted by Pimienta on 27 October 1700.
25. RBS Archives, D/1/2 and NA, SP94/75, *Copia del Despacho de Dn Manuel de Aperiguy, 14 de Marzo de 1701.*
26. Moreyra y Paz-Soldán and Céspedes del Castillo, *Virreinato peruano, tomo III*, p. xxvii and AGI, Panamá 182, report of Navarette's accountant, f. 230r.
27. MHS-Hart, *Gazeta*-English, pp. 2–4 and Moreyra y Paz-Soldán and Céspedes del Castillo, *Virreinato peruano, tomo III*, p. vii.
28. MHS-Hart, *Gazeta*-English, pp. 6–14.
29. MHS-Hart, Darien Item 13.
30. AGI, Panamá 215, ff. 5v–6r.
31. Rojas y Arrieta, *History of the Bishops*, pp. 87–90.
32. Storrs, *The Resilience*, pp. 129–34.
33. MHS-Hart, Darien Item 70, Storrs, 'Disaster', pp. 22–3, and AGI, Panamá 162, ff. 277–99r.
34. AGI, Panamá 166, ff. 805r–929v.
35. AGI, Lima 520, Archbishop of Lima to Felipe V, 20 November 1701.
36. AGI, Panamá 166, f. 908r.

7

The View from Disparate America

Beyond Spanish America existed an array of competing colonial interests, watching the Company of Scotland with a mixture of curiosity, anxiety, irritation and open hostility. Earlier chapters have introduced the range of consequences the Darien initiative provoked among varied interests and jurisdictions, from impressments of sailors on Jamaica to the interruption of the Portuguese slave trade to political frustrations imposed upon the royal governor of New York. The impacts were, however, even more varied in character and intensity, indicative of the political and economic environment of the larger, highly competitive Caribbean and Atlantic Worlds. Perhaps the greatest challenge, given the rash intent of the Company of Scotland to impose itself permanently on the lands of the Spanish king, was to maintain a semblance of disinterested neutrality.

FACING THE DANES

The Caribbean of 1698 reflected two centuries of a fluid mosaic of European interests in the southern portion of the Atlantic, evolving along with a savvy, experienced cast of participants ever alert to new competition. Denmark had for over a decade maintained her own operation based on St Thomas and it was to that island's free port that two ships of the Company of Scotland sailed to secure a pilot for the final crossing to Darien. The remainder of the fleet sailed to nearby Crab Island (now Vieques, part of the United States territory of Puerto Rico), Commodore Pennycook logging his completion of instructions as the site was secured for the Company and a camp established onshore.[1]

The initial welcome for the contingent arriving in St Thomas was cordial, with Governor Lorentz extending hospitality to Captain Pincarton and William Paterson, as their companion Colin Campbell enthusiastically recorded his wonder at the novel vegetation and fruits he saw as he explored the port.[2] Upon the governor's receipt of word that other of the Scots' fleet had landed on Crab Island, however, events quickly evolved in a less amiable direction. Submitting a sharply worded written response to Pincarton's introduction, Lorentz stressed that the king of Denmark and Norway had claimed the territory since 1682 and any effort undertaken by the Scots to take possession would be protested against in a strong manner. To reinforce the warning, Captain Claus Hansen was dispatched to the island the same day with instructions to secure the territory and defend it with whatever action was required.

In his eventual report, Hansen records anchoring at the designated location referred to as Settlement and sighting two vessels offshore. As instructed, the Danish flag was planted on a rise and left under guard while the pair of foreign ships was observed sailing out of sight. That afternoon one vessel reappeared and shot several signals, causing their larger fleet to consolidate. The strangers then raised their own flag and sailed to the Danes, sending across a rowing boat to determine the identity of those ashore and the nature of their business. In turn, they were instructed to approach the Danish command established on the beach, a directive that appeared to make the visitors hesitate and return to their own ship. The following morning the requested land meeting was conducted, Hansen demanding the reason for the strangers' presence on Crab Island and the Scots replying that they required water and asking where it could be found. Being told that fresh supplies were only available on the island's west end, the visitors again returned to their vessels. Later in the day the Scots returned to shore, this time accompanied by armed personnel. Hansen reapproached the group and again enquired why they were present on his king's land. Captain Robert Jolly replied that Crab Island did not appear to be worth any trouble or expense, but assumed that its former occupation by the English gave him as much right to it as anyone. The Scots proceeded to ask Hansen if he had a commission, to which he responded in the affirmative, adding that he was not going to show them anything. Again the Scots returned to their ships and continued the search for water while maintaining their distance from the Danes.

The following afternoon the two ships (repeatedly referred to by the Danes as 'English') that had been at St Thomas arrived and joined their countrymen, an event soon followed by intelligence reaching Hansen that three or four tents had been erected while watering was being undertaken. The next day the Danish captain and three soldiers walked overland to question the purpose of the camp and again assert the king of

Denmark and Norway's sovereignty. The Scots replied that they would have to discuss the matter with their commodore, who was on board his ship. Asserting their authority, the Danes dispatched three men by canoe to make the same protest directly to the designated Scot, who responded that they held no claim on Crab Island and were acting appropriately upon arrival in unoccupied territory by maintaining an armed guard as they secured water. He reiterated that they would be able to take the land if they wanted it, but it was not worth taking. Furthermore, they intended to sail that evening or the following morning, pointedly refusing to discuss their destination. Upon witnessing the promised departure of the entire 'English' fleet prior to daylight, Hansen ordered his own forces to return to St Thomas.[3]

Scottish accounts of the days at Crab Island fail to acknowledge actual friction with the Danes, even reporting the host's express wish that the visitors remain in order to provide a buffer against Spanish settlements in adjacent Puerto Rico. One comment included in a journal maintained by an anonymous Scot, however, supplies additional motivation for Governor Lorentz's active assertions of his king's territorial claims. Guaranteed to alarm any colonial administrator was the approach and proposal by twenty-five St Thomas families to Captain Pincarton, offering to accompany the Scots to Darien should transportation be available to accommodate them.[4]

TRADING PURSUITS

As Crab Island's strained diplomacy evolved and Captain Pincarton successfully obtained a pilot to guide the fleet towards the mainland, William Paterson had been utilising his time on St Thomas to renew his acquaintance of many years with Captain Richard Moon of Jamaica, initiating what would become a series of tentative trading efforts. Convinced to divert from his journey between New York and Curacao, Moon followed the Scots back to the remainder of the fleet anchored at Crab Island, where negotiations commenced in the hope of acquiring much-needed provisions. When the attempt failed, Paterson warned his fellow colonists of the negative consequences, not only of the lack of new and high quality supplies, but of the negative and long-lasting reputation that would be established regarding their own trade goods and expertise. As his advice went unheeded and Moon prepared to sail, Paterson reapproached his old friend and proposed that he prepare a sloop with provisions and dispatch it directly to the fledgling colony, where he would be likely to experience a more favourable reception.

Despite sullying specifics contained in any subsequent report, curiosity and potential profit soon established a procession of mercantile traffic entering Caledonia Bay. Shortly before Christmas a sloop dispatched by Moon and his associates under the command of Edward Sands arrived. The second round of negotiations had a positive outcome, with Scottish goods in payment for desperately needed supplies to be transferred to Captain Moon personally upon his arrival in approximately a month. Sands's subsequent homeward passage to Jamaica not only strengthened ties and communication between the nascent colony and the island, but also transported the first emissaries dispatched to report to directors in Edinburgh, accompanied by the soon-to-be infamous Walter Herries.

Moon reappeared as promised, bringing with him another hard lesson in Caribbean economics. Aboard was the ship's owner Peter Wilmot, demanding return of the goods awaiting payment, complaining that prices charged by the Scots were no better than he could negotiate in Jamaica and warning the would-be trading entrepôt that he would not sell further provisions at such prices. Following Moon's departure came the return of Captain Sands, accompanied by a second vessel under one Pilkington, both successfully arranging the sale of their cargo.

Lacking a single craft designed for the coastal environment, a deficiency ignored when brought to the attention of Edinburgh directors a full two years prior to the departure by London-based merchant Robert Douglas, the Jamaican vessels' suitability for local conditions was quickly recognised and secured. While Sands was contracted to hunt turtle to augment the diminishing food supply, Pilkington was dispatched with a load of goods to trade along the Spanish coast. The trading assignment, acknowledged by William Paterson in his subsequent written report to his Council of Directors, substantiates the intent of the Company to indulge in the illicit commerce that would become a vital concern to the judges of the Casa de la Contratación.[5]

During the second week of February 1699, shortly after the departure of Captain Pincarton and the *Dolphin* on their doomed expedition, two additional Jamaican sloops arrived in close succession. Although their principle motivation, illustrating the speed with which a Caribbean opportunity could be relayed and exploited, was salvaging gold and silver from the recently sunken *Maurepas*, they also carried provisions and were willing to consider a sale, but only in exchange for money, a commodity in insufficient supply in the colony. Regardless of the treasure seekers' growing awareness of the precarious circumstances of the colony they adhered to their stipulations for doing business and retained their cargo.[6]

Captain Pilkington returned to New Caledonia in early March, claiming little success in his contraband trade mission due to an inappropriate cargo. Of more immediate concern, he also brought news of capture of the *Dolphin* and her crew. Both Pilkington and Sands suddenly found themselves recipients of a novel diplomatic assignment, the transport of a representative from New Caledonia to Cartagena to demand the *Dolphin*, her stores and her personnel. Should that mission be unsuccessful, the Jamaicans were issued with another contract granting them permission to commit reprisals. Both vessels and the colony's ambassador returned to New Caledonia by the end of the month, communicating complete failure of the diplomatic effort and carrying the governor of Cartagena's abrupt letter of refusal.

The *Articles of Agreement* with Pilkington (See Appendix 2) comprised a clear and provocative extension of contacts with Jamaica and its merchant community. Not only did the contract arrange for hire of the ship, but it also constituted nothing short of a letter of marque, allowing for shares of any prizes taken and compensation for wounded and disabled men. The document is also notable in that it includes one of the few references to involvement in the slave trade. The Fifth Article, considering compensation for disability incurred during the voyage, assures that 'in such case, the same man shall have and receive six hundred pieces of eight, or six able slaves, if so much be made in the said voyage'.[7]

Although Paterson's later report to Company directors indicated a poor financial return from the reprisals, declaring the proceeds limited to a single abandoned sloop acquired during two weeks of effort, Walter Herries once again provides a sharply contrasting opinion intimating aggressive illegal activity. The surgeon included in one of his pamphlets that Pilkington and Sands 'sometimes shared 2 or 300 pieces of eight a man (tho' little came into your colony's treasury)' and related that the two captains ranged along the coast 'snapping up every Spanish thing that came in their way'.[8]

Regardless of the relative success or failure of their efforts, while pursuing reprisals the two hired captains were themselves recipients of threats originating from Jamaica based on their involvement with the Scots. Upon their return to New Caledonia they informed the colony of the disturbing communication and sailed for home, Pilkington apparently undeterred and promising to send another sloop with provisions and eventually to return himself, accompanied by his family and effects.[9]

JAMAICAN FAITH AND FINANCE

Pilkington and Sands were not the only enterprising Jamaican merchants to be warned of pursuing commercial partnerships with the Company of Scotland. Jewish and English merchants had sought to coexist since the British acquisition of the island in 1655, the former continuing to benefit from a long history of trade in the region, family connections with Christian converts across Spanish America and proficiency in speaking Spanish. Although permitted to openly practise their religion, the Jews of Jamaica were restricted from holding public office and voting, and were subject to special taxation, estimated at up to three times the normal level in 1700.[10]

Inevitably, the opportunity presented by the arrival of the Scots in the region had been quickly evaluated and plans formulated to capitalise on the advantages of a new trading link, a step by the Jewish mercantile community that quickly provoked reaction from competing English companies. As recorded in the *Journals of the Assembly of Jamaica* on 14 March 1699, an inflammatory paper attributed to Jacob Mears and John Sadler was read before the body, resulting in an order to take the authors into custody due to the 'great grievance and prejudice to the island, and contempt of his majestys government' the content was perceived to present. Messengers were dispatched to Port Royal to seize the books and papers of the accused, their boats to be held in port and Mears to be confined to close custody without pen, ink or paper.

The suspect document, entitled *A Scheme for the Improvement and Good Management of a Trade for the Scots Colony at Caledonia in America,* comprised a strategic business plan for profitable trade with the Company of Scotland. It had been signed by Mears and Sadler in Port Royal on 23 January 1699 and listed seven pertinent points, each indicating familiarity with current realities of general commerce and the slave trade across the Atlantic and within the Caribbean:

1. Jamaica had the most to offer the colony, including the supply of provisions and Africans.
2. Jamaica was the most advantageous site for communicating with Europe.
3. The Company of Scotland should assign a factor to reside in Jamaica, securing from the king assurances that the appointed individual would not be susceptible to interference by the governor.

4. A sum of cash should be provided to the factor so that advantage could be taken of low prices for provisions, liquors and Africans.
5. The Spanish trade would be served by sending large parcels of goods to Caledonia, which should realise substantial profit within a year.
6. Because the Spanish would not conduct trade with the Scots, or anyone who sailed under their flag, sloops should be purchased in Jamaica and outfitted with English colours, under English command and include some English crew. The said ships should go to Caledonia, load their respective goods and proceed on trading missions giving every indication of being Jamaican-owned vessels.
7. The designated factor should be well acquainted with affairs of both Europe and America, and particularly the Spanish trade, in order to provide the best advice to both the colony and Company directors in Scotland.

The investigating committee reported back to the Assembly on 21 March, presenting their discovery of an incriminating letter dated December 1698 that appeared to be a solicitation to become a factor for the Company of Scotland from one Joseph Cohen D'Asevedo. Other evidence included additional letters written in an unrecognisable script that the investigators could not comprehend. Furthermore, there was correspondence pertaining to a debt Mears was attempting to recover for a client from a man purported to be a member of the Assembly, a circumstance the investigators concluded required some form of response.

Sadler and Mears quickly petitioned to be heard. Appearing before the Assembly's Committee of Grievances on 29 March they explained they had discussed supplying the Scots with provisions with Mr Cunningham, who had promised substantial gains. They had also consulted with Sir James del Castillo, the local factor for the *asiento*, after which they had drawn up the controversial proposal. The involvement of Castillo caused particular alarm, the factor finding himself called before the committee the following week. He was informed that aspects of the subject document not only exhibited negative attitudes toward the king, but constituted direct threats to Jamaican commerce. Told he was considered to be supporting the initiatives of the Jewish merchants, Sir James replied that he recalled seeing the paper, but had no hand in creating it. Sadler and Mears were then recalled and informed they were guilty of no less than subverting the king's authority and the government of the island. They were fined and consigned to good behaviour for twelve months.[11]

An explanation of the conflict's context, indicative of the extent of concern it provoked, was provided by Secretary of State Vernon in a report to the king dated June 1699. Initially the secretary related several other items of troubling news from Jamaica, including active promotion of New Caledonia by a Scottish resident of the island. Vernon then addressed the growing dispute between Jewish and English merchants over access to potential profits from trade with Darien Scots. The Assembly of Jamaica had determined there was preferential treatment given to the Jews, he wrote, adding his criticism of Governor Beeston for not having provided notice of the conflict. Notably, the secretary of state named his source as none other than Walter Herries.[12]

Traces of the debate would also find their way into the highest level of Spanish correspondence and acknowledge concern over religious threats beyond the influence of Protestant heretics. Ambassador to London Canales, actively receiving intelligence from Herries, reported his concerns to his own king in late August by noting that current conditions had begun 'to assume the aspect of Conquest, and especially the element of the Jews, which element is strong in capital and altogether unchecked by Law, Divine or human.'[13]

FORCED ADAPTATION AND ACCOMMODATION

Competition for and speculation about New Caledonia trade was soon muted by the issuing of proclamations forbidding commerce or assistance to the colony and the final capitulation to Pimienta's forces. Governor Beeston, in spite of Secretary of State Vernon's insinuations of a lack of zeal in thwarting the designs of the Company of Scotland, was first to issue a ban in the king's name, on 8 April 1699. Shortly afterwards came equivalent orders from Barbados, Virginia, New York, Rhode Island, Massachusetts Bay, East New Jersey, Connecticut, South Carolina, New Hampshire, New Providence and Maryland.[14] In addition to their targeted impact on New Caledonia, the proclamations provided a deterrent against any consideration of trade with the Scots while inadvertently mapping the geographical extent of interest in the venture. A significant percentage of the far-flung locations would receive numbers of survivors, adding an unforeseen, unsolicited and sometimes unwelcome contingent of distressed newcomers to various colonial communities.

Due to its location and commercial activity, Jamaica found itself inextricably tied to the fortunes of New Caledonia. Besides its piqued economic interests, the island also served as a communications entrepôt between Edinburgh and those coming and going from Darien. Capitalising on the existence of an established community of Scots, the principal conduit for much of the contact was one Dr Blair, credited with directly corresponding with Company directors in Edinburgh and keeping them updated regarding the arrival of relief ships and acquisition of pilots for the final crossing to the Isthmus.[15] Although Blair resided in Kingston, where he had routine exposure to events of the port and seat of royal government, a Dr Stewart living near the eastern anchorage of Port Morant often provided the first point of contact. As designated in her sailing orders, the relief ship *Margaret of Dundee* made her initial Jamaican call at that port, her command seeking out Stewart and a Captain Robertson, both designated links in the chain of communciation.[16]

In the aftermath of successive abandonments of New Caledonia, many survivors also either transitted through or settled in Jamaica. Following the capitulation, Reverend Francis Borland would recuperate for a month in the home of planter Charles Graves. Equipped with a marketable occupation, he preached and baptised on the island, eventually finding his way to Port Royal. As he prepared to sail to New England to join his brother he was gifted with provisions from a lengthy list of residents, including the previously mentioned Dr Blair. Following months of convalescence at his sibling's home in Boston, the reverend would prove an exception among all Darien participants, returning permanently to Scotland and reuniting with his children in August 1701.[17]

Documented in early histories of the island, the substantial needs of Jamaica created permanent opportunities for a significant number of other survivors. In his unpublished chronicle, Dr Henry Barham describes the arrival of many Scots from Darien, citing several who experienced economic success through marriage to wealthy widows. He also recounts the near tragedy that accompanied the *St Andrew*'s entry into port. As the ship was saluted, the magazine on shore burst into flame, heroically extinguished by a sailor who stripped off his shirt, saturated it with water, and eliminated what could have been a catastrophe. His quick action failed to be duly recognised, however, as his major later claimed credit for the response and was rewarded with a knighthood.[18] Charles Leslie, in his 1740 *A New History of Jamaica, from the Earliest Accounts, to the Taking of Porto Bello by Vice-Admiral Vernon*, provides a wider perspective of the arrival of survivors. He writes of the high mortality on board the two ships that reached Jamaica, but also records the eventual successes of several of the group. Among those who rose to prominent positions within affairs of the colony were Colonels Dowdall and Guthrie, the former initially finding employment as an overseer, the first step to eventual acquisition of his own estate.[19]

In a twenty-first-century treatment of Jamaica's past, Douglas Hamilton also addresses the increase of Scots following Darien, specifically identifying the community of Argyll in the western part of the island as dating from the period. Notable among its settlers was Colonel John Campbell, who eventually served in both the Assembly of Jamaica and its council and would entice additional immigration through family and community ties in Scotland.[20]

The majority of survivors faced far less lucrative prospects. What appears to be one such group, finding themselves alive but without sustenance or material goods, solicited, and at length obtained, permission to settle as planters between Bluefields and Luana Point.[21] The net result was integration into a marginally populated colonial island of a seasoned group of survivors who had expected to settle elsewhere, but now effectively adapted to their latest unforeseen circumstances. Governor Beeston, who had originally expressed concern over losing population to the Scots, affirmed the influx of population to the island, commenting that it was better to have the new arrivals support the king's territories than to settle among the French or Dutch.[22]

What neither Beeston nor the survivors that made Jamaica home could have imagined was the voluntary arrival over a decade later of an individual central to the Darien expeditions and undoubtedly an acquaintance of many who had established new lives in the Caribbean. In 1711 Roderick McKenzie, former secretary of the Company of Scotland and later honoured by Queen Anne with admission to her Company of Archers, arrived to serve Governor and Captain General Archibald Hamilton as his private secretary. McKenzie would hold the position until 1716, exhibiting his experience dealing with conflict as he quickly became enmeshed in heated political debate precipitated by his acceptance of the additional position of clerk of the Council of Jamaica.[23]

Although the Company of Scotland's legacy bore a heavy imprint on its history, Jamaica was by no means the sole locality in the Caribbean to be impacted. In March of 1700, as Pimienta's fleet anchored off New Caledonia, a controversy sprang to the forefront of problems confronting Barbados. A certain George Duncan, Governor Grey reported to the Council of Trade and Plantations, had spoken out against the king in the offices of the island's clerk. Depositions were taken and prosecution undertaken. The defendant had been declared drunk, but not before expressing his unwelcome opinion that Scots were equal to English, they were not King William's subjects, and changes would be coming. Also causing alarm was a subversive book supporting the Scottish right to Darien that had infiltrated the island and caused several additional offensive remarks to be duly relayed to Grey. The governor confidently reported the example he had made of Duncan would suffice to keep the Scots in order.[24] From Nevis came a more dire but ultimately false alarm, warning that the notorious pirate Captain Kidd, who had been in Madagascar and would be eventually arrested in Boston, transported to London and executed, was heading to Darien to join forces with his Scottish countrymen.[25]

Accumulated resentment and suspicion would not readily disappear as the Scots strove to integrate themselves into new communities. In 1707 Governor Park of the Leeward Islands, writing to London during the War of the Spanish Succession concerning the vulnerability of his small domain, added a postscript offering his solution to multiple problems:

> If the Queen will not spare English troopes, send us Ten Thousand Scotch, this Warm Climate will Meliorate them, and make them of a more Sociable Religion, the Queen need be at no great Expence, only furnish them with arms and Transports, and Some Oatmeal, we will join them with what men can be spared here. If We take Martinique the Queen gains a fine Island, the Scotch shall have the Land, and we will have the Plunder. The Queen ventures little, and may gain the Sugar Trade , This will be a better Project than their beloved Darien . . . I promise they shall never trouble the Queen's affairs more, If they do not take Martinique I will get them Disposed of; And I think that will be some Service.[26]

Further to the north events in Darien had been followed with high interest, not solely of a commercial nature. Judge Samuel Sewall of Boston had been particularly intrigued by potential religious influence the Company of Scotland might impose. Writing in his diary that the intentions of the Scots were much discussed in his city, Sewall offered his private assessment that Spanish America was the Antichrist and the Company of Scotland the Sixth Angel. Reflecting maintenance of correspondence between his city and the Isthmus, he wrote to the surviving ministers in New Caledonia, providing support and expressing concern over the potential for Pimienta to overcome them before they were fully settled. The judge also recorded receipt of a letter of appreciation from William Paterson for two books that had been sent to the colony. Further indicating the web of interrelationships that linked New Caledonia with other portions of the Americas was Sewall's friendship with local merchant John Borland, brother to Reverend Borland discussed above, and future business associate of Samuel Vetch, whose story is recounted later in this chapter.[27]

Another clergyman, Archibald Stobo, did forge a new life in the Americas against a backdrop of great tragedy. He had accompanied Borland on the second expedition, parting from his fellow surviving minister following the capitulation as he sailed from New Caledonia aboard the *Rising Sun*. The ship eventually reached South Carolina, anchoring off a bar outside Charleston harbour, where Stobo and a delegation of fourteen others, including his wife and a Lieutenant Graham, went into the city to meet a delegation from the Congregational Church. Remaining on board, Captain Gibson and ninety-six passengers and crew found themselves helpless against an approaching hurricane. Having lost the *Rising Sun*'s masts in a storm off Florida and vulnerable to the open sea, the anchors could not hold the ship, finally giving way and causing vessel and passengers to be flung relentlessly against sandbars. All aboard perished, their bodies washing ashore on the nearby island appropriately named Coffin Land (later Folly Beach), wreckage and additional corpses also being deposited on James Island. The following day Stobo and Graham, along with others from the fortunate contingent who had gone ashore, spent the day burying corpses in the sand while scavengers probed the debris.[28] A year later, surveyor John Lawson and his party would find themselves hospitably received at the Dix's Island residence of a Scot, their meal consisting of oatmeal salvaged from the *Rising Sun* and their attention being diverted by the array of other goods its remains had provided their host.[29] As for Stobo, he would soon be assigned his own congregation in Charleston, leaving after four years to practise among Presbyterian-leaning Protestant Dissenters in more rural areas and establishing his reputation as a tireless minister over thirty-seven years of service.[30]

More positive yet complicated circumstances surrounded the arrival of survivors in the Jerseys, where simmering hostilities had surfaced, exacerbated by events on the Isthmus. Governor Basse documented his frustration following the passage of the Jamaica Act by the Assembly of East Jersey. The legislation was, he explained, aimed at privateers and pirates, but was vehemently opposed by Scottish residents enabled by the king's consideration of one of their countrymen for a local governmental appointment and early reports of success from New Caledonia. The principal traders of not only East and West Jersey but also Pennsylvania were Scots, Basse stated, and there were active assertions that King William would not dare to oppose activities at Darien. The governor further offered his advice that the only effective means of resolving the situation was to assure exclusion of any Scot from colonial administrative positions.[31]

Basse addressed his concerns to the extent possible by issuing the requisite proclamation prohibiting commerce with New Caledonia, but he could not prevent the influx of survivors who chose to establish themselves near the existing Scottish community of Perth-Amboy and create the new settlement of Scots Plains.[32] Among them was Colonel John Anderson, who had successfully commanded the *Unicorn* to safety following the first abandonment of New Caledonia. Anderson's role in his new home would run counter to Basse's recommendations, for the Scot would establish himself as a trader and planter and, despite efforts to block his nomination, serve on His Majesty's Council for the Province of New Jersey, becoming president of the body just prior to his death in 1736.[33]

THE CASE OF SAMUEL VETCH

Also reaching New York and New England, but following an entirely different course encompassing both sides of the Atlantic, was Samuel Vetch. Having been educated at Utrecht and rising to the rank of captain during service against the French in the Netherlands he would become a citizen of the empire, personifying the often entangled motivations that had propelled his native country towards Darien. Exhibiting the pragmatic realities of colonial survival, he would initially struggle into New York with the Drummonds following the first expedition and assist in the successful manipulation of the port's politics and resources to outfit and commandeer a sloop for return to New Caledonia. Vetch, however, would opt against accompanying Drummond back to the Isthmus. Claiming the need to oversee Company of Scotland assets left in New York, he would choose the far more attractive pursuit of marriage into the family of prominent local Scot Robert Livingston and participation in trading ventures which adroitly manoeuvred between legality and opportunity. Building on the established network of Scottish trading interests, he became an associate of the previously introduced John Borland of Boston and began decades of individual ambition and unfulfilled speculation. Following an unsuccessful request for commission as captain of one of the Crown's companies stationed in New York, a 1705 prisoner exchange requiring a voyage to Canada presented convenient cover for the more commercial motives of the Borland–Vetch collaboration. Having raised suspicions, the vessel and captain were seized upon their return, Vetch pleading from prison that stormy weather had forced him into Acadian ports and compelled him to trade in order to assure welfare of his ship and crew.

Capitalising on both his Darien and Canadian experience, Vetch diverted his energy to the formulation of a plan to defeat France through a northern offensive. He proposed Scots as practical colonists for Canada, explaining the region was far more appropriate for those from a cold country than the proven fatal life of the West Indies. Personally presenting a detailed scheme to the Board of Trade in 1708 he emphasised the interconnectedness of the colonies and the vulnerability of British holdings in North America to French invasion. Supported by a cast reminiscent of Darien: William Paterson, Seafield, Carstares and the Duke of Hamilton, his proposal was approved and forwarded to the Privy Council and Queen Anne. The scheme conveniently not only strove to expel the French from portions of their Canadian territory, but also provided a mechanism to ameliorate lingering dreams of a Scottish colony and residual opposition to the Treaty of Union. In February 1709 long-sought orders were signed and sealed for the campaign, assigning Vetch a colonel's commission and responsibility for overseeing preparations in the colonies. Although he would serve under a British field officer he was to be rewarded with the governorship of Canada following the territory's acquisition.

The new colonel returned to the colonies and proceeded with provisioning, implementing the orders of his queen across the disparate northern colonies. Harkening back to Darien experience, factions of the diverse indigenous population and former prisoners of the French were used to obtain intelligence, news soon emerging that the adversary was well aware of the impending campaign. Prepared and impatiently awaiting arrival of ancillary forces from England, the colonial troops instead received deflating news that the expedition had been tabled and the anticipated fleet diverted to Spanish waters.

Recovering again from the disappointment Vetch strove to take advantage of successive opportunities and debate. As he promoted himself for several denied colonial governorships, he also attempted to press action against New Spain, activity for which his Darien experience would be of the highest value. A viable project finally arrived from London with orders for a smaller expedition to the northern port of Annapolis Royal, where Vetch at last achieved an appointment as governor. After successfully overseeing a conquered foreign population and his own troops through a harsh winter of death, insufficient stores, desertion and constant fear of attack, Vetch found himself recalled to New England in the summer of 1711 to command forces designated to attack Quebec. Although implemented, success also eluded that campaign, with colonial and English forces blaming each other for its failure.

Reapplying his efforts to the survival and promotion of the outpost at Annapolis Royal, Vetch attempted in vain to determine what conditions being negotiated in Utrecht to end the War of the Spanish Succession would mean for his struggling colony. Coping with the need to sustain his forces, he finally received word that he would continue as adjutant general to the new governor of Newfoundland and Nova Scotia, eventually receiving the highest position himself while in London in 1715. In England his expertise was further solicited through appointment to a commission investigating boundaries between France and Great Britain in the Americas, a position providing audiences before the Board of Trade and an accompanying platform to advocate for his own future, the future of Nova Scotia and the colonial world in general. His proposals, including putting himself forward as candidate for governor of Massachusetts, remained unfulfilled and he would never return to the colonial world. Suffering his ultimate reversal of fortune, he would die while imprisoned for debts in London in 1732.[34] Perhaps more than any other individual, Vetch had taken his practical experience, including the tragic, divisive months in Darien, and attempted to apply it to future attempts at colonisation, repeatedly facing tenuous conditions and the challenges of survival frustrated by unfulfilled promises of political support and practical sustenance.

Far from the huts of New Caledonia, the arrival of the Company of Scotland on the Isthmus produced a litany of consequences across the Americas, forcing communities throughout both continents to come to terms with a novel set of circumstances and fear of uncertain and threatening change. From Danes protecting the uninhabited Crab Island to an international coterie of intrigued merchants to expedition participants fighting for recognition and survival in locations they never expected to settle, the entry of the Scots into the Caribbean added to an already unstable political and economic environment. As unintended bands of survivors dispersed across the map of British America from Jamaica to New England, often echoing prior paths taken by deserters, they would alter the face of Atlantic colonies, assisting in forging new communities, adding to discord in others, and serving as an indication of more change to come.

NOTES

1. Insh, *Papers*, pp. 78–9.
2. NLS, MS846, *Colin Campbell's Journal – Journey of the Unicorn*.

3. Host, *Efterretninger om Oen Sanct Thomas*, pp. 40–52. English translation by Dr Melissa Lucas, 2016.
4. Burton, *The Darien Papers*, p. 61, and Maidment, *Analecta Scotica*, p. 359.
5. Barbour, *A History of William Paterson*, pp. 93–4, 98–101, 105.
6. Ibid., p. 106. The French *Maurepas* had sunk on Christmas Day while attempting to leave the bay, suffering the loss of twenty-four crew. Among the survivors was the lieutenant who would accompany the *Dolphin* to Cartagena and play an integral part in that crew's identification and imprisonment. Insh, *The Company*, pp. 138–9.
7. Barbour, *A History of William Paterson*, pp. 106–8, 112–13.
8. Ibid., p.113 and Herries, *An Enquiry*, p. 37.
9. Barbour, *A History of William Paterson*, p. 114.
10. Arbell, *The Portuguese Jews*, pp. 13, 41, 44.
11. NLJ, MS J28L434, *Journals of the Assembly of Jamaica*, Volume I, pp. 190–8.
12. BL, ADD MS40774, f. 50v.
13. MHS-Hart, Darien Item 37, translation of letter from the Marquis of Canales to Carlos II, 31 August 1699.
14. Hart, *The Disaster*, pp. 153–4.
15. NLS, Adv. MS 83.7.5, f. 152r.
16. Burton, *The Darien Papers*, p. 307.
17. University of Edinburgh Library, Centre for Research Collections, MS Laing 262, *Memorial or Diary of Mr Francis Borland, 1661–1722*, pp. 26–31.
18. BL, ADD MS12422, Dr Henry Barham, M.D., *The Civil History of Jamaica to the Year 1722*, p. 222.
19. Leslie, *A New History*, pp. 264–5.
20. Hamilton, *Scotland, the Caribbean*, pp. 4, 55–6.
21. Bridges, *The Annals of Jamaica*, p. 328.
22. UGSp, MS 1686, Governor William Beeston to the Council of Trade and Plantations, 14 April 1699.
23. Bodleian Library, MSS Rawlinson, A290, f. 62, and A312, ff. 8, 29, 90–9.
24. Headlam, *CSP, Colonial, 1699*, Items 245 and 245ii, pp. 133–4.
25. Ibid., Item 501, p. 276.
26. MHS-Hart, MS N-189.
27. Thomas, *The Diary, Vol. 1*, entries for 20 December 1698 and 8 May 1699, Pears, 'The design of Darien', p. 81, and Sewall, *Letter-book, Vol. 1*, pp 82–3.
28. Ludlum, *Early American Hurricanes*, p. 42, Hewatt, *An Historical Account, Vol. 1*, p. 142, Fraser, *Lowcountry Hurricanes*, p. 9 and McCrady, *The History of South Carolina*, p. 311.
29. Lawson, *A New Voyage to Carolina*, p. 7.
30. Clarke, *Our Southern Zion*, p. 43.
31. Headlam, *CSP, Colonial, 1699*, Item 512, p. 281, letter from Mr Basse, governor of Jerseys to Secretary Popple, 9 June 1699.

32. M'Robert and Bridenbaugh, 'Tour through part', p. 169.
33. Lockhart, 'The Scottish origin of Colonel John Anderson', pp. 1–3.
34. Waller, *Samuel Vetch*, pp. 11–13, 34–43, 56, 70, 79–86, 102–19, 124–56, 168–206, 238–84. See Lyons, *The 1711 Expedition to Quebec*, for specific discussion of that campaign.

8

Darien Consequences

T HE LOCATION CHOSEN FOR New Caledonia was far from an isolated territory devoid of its own history and society. Not only was the site currently surrounded by populations of native Cuna, well versed in international negotiation following two centuries of European contact, but there were also pronounced indicators of current foreign presence, exemplified by the French resident, accompanied by two Martinique Creoles, who provided the Scots with both a welcome and an informal review of Darien politics.[1] This chapter will examine the intricate local sociopolitical fabric into which the Company of Scotland attempted to weave itself and, conversely, the short- and long-term consequences the colony, regardless of its ephemeral establishment, imposed upon the region. Unlike the remainder of the Americas, which either coped with the arrival of groups of expedition survivors or celebrated their departure, the province of Darien and its people would experience an intensified and disquieting focus of attention. Although eventually empty of would-be Scottish colonists, the area would nonetheless be severely impacted by their aborted effort, convulsing through both attempts to inaugurate the settlement and reciprocal military efforts to assure its demise and prevent its re-establishment. The lengthy and volatile record of interaction between Cuna and Spaniard would be exacerbated by the former's alliances with the Scots, resulting in new campaigns to bring the notoriously independent native populations under colonial control. The Company of Scotland's flagrant attempt to establish a permanent settlement provided an eloquent reminder that Darien possessed not only uniquely strategic assets and valuable resources, but that these same benefits were highly vulnerable to domestic threat and foreign incursion, both of which demanded a strong, prolonged response to assure any semblance of Spanish dominance.

A CROWDED AND TURBULENT STAGE

By the time of the Scots' arrival, local Cuna had established their own history of simultaneously defending their sovereignty and accommodating the presence of foreigners. Although Rodrigo Bastides first sailed along Darien in 1501 and Columbus, hardly creating goodwill with native groups, forayed upon its coast during his fourth voyage a year later, it was the establishment of Santa Maria la Antigua del Darien in 1511 that initiated protracted interaction between Spanish and indigenous groups. To their advantage the Cuna then inhabited lands on the periphery of this initial interface with Spain. From their vantage point they would have had the opportunity to witness and assess initial favourable relations with Governor Vasco Núñez de Balboa, his beheading by fellow Spaniard and successor Pedrarias de Avila, and the decimation through disease and slavery of the contemporary resident indigenous group, the Cuevas. By 1519, when the Spanish removed themselves and their livestock to anticipated improved conditions in Panama, lessons had been learned. The Cuna expanded into the newly vacated region, firmly anti-Spanish and predisposed to alliances, assistance and commerce with other foreign interests, particularly those seeking a share of the wealth of the Americas at the expense of Spain. The disaffection created by Pedrarias would be acknowledged centuries later when military engineer Antonio Arevalo, reporting in 1761 on the jurisdiction he had been ordered to bring under control, would reference the durability of the region's violent history.[2]

Despite abandonment of their initial settlement, Spanish officials fully comprehended the necessity of asserting authority over the Isthmus and struggled to contain the dual hazards of foreign penetration and domestic strife. The actuality was that colonial policies had failed to check either vulnerability. Efforts to evangelise and resettle the native population into Spanish-style nuclear villages were met with tenacious and violent opposition. Two attempts by the Capuchin order, departing from Cadiz in 1647 and 1681, to establish Cuna missions resulted in complete failure.[3] Restrictions intended to control Cuna access to weapons and tools served only to perpetuate continued welcome of Dutch, British and French smugglers offering the desired goods. A coordinated effort between jurisdictions, indicative of later action against the Scots, resulted in the appointment from Panama and Cartagena of Julian Carrisoli, a Spaniard reared by Cuna, as Protector of the Indians. It had brought some measure of relief when, in 1645, a Dutch force landed on the northern coast of Darien and promised accommodation of Cuna customs in return for support of a settlement. Carrisoli used his diplomatic and language skills, reinforced by ties of kinship, to persuade vacillating Cuna to refuse the proposition. Despite the success, and the deep impression it made on Spanish officials, there was to be no reign of uniform or persistent peace in the region. A plea to Madrid for military assistance from Panama in 1651 indicated only the latest insurrection, attributing it to the natural character of the indigenous population and discounting any malevolent treatment by Spaniards.[4]

The continuing lure of Darien's gold mines, coupled with treasure shipped from Peru for transport across the Isthmus and on to Spain, provided unrelenting enticement for foreign intrusions, a point reinforced by a series of piratical raids conducted between 1680 and 1695. Among those succumbing to the aggregate of adventure and potential fortune was Lionel Wafer, a surgeon whose experience living with the Cuna for several months while recuperating from wounds would gain him fame and financial reward. Wafer's subsequent return to London and successful efforts to publish his story came to the attention of the Company of Scotland and would provide significant impetus for the designation of Darien as the chosen destination. Wafer would ultimately be brought to Scotland to consult with the 'Secret Committee' regarding assets of the Isthmus and be escorted out of Edinburgh by fellow surgeon Walter Herries.[5]

Whatever decisions Wafer's short duration in Darien may have facilitated, he would have been challenged to fully relay the kaleidoscope of entangled and shifting alliances, chaotic at best, that greeted the Company of Scotland fleet into what would become Caledonia Bay. Although Luis Carrisoli, now serving in his father's role, had measures of military success with his Cuna defensive forces, other groups of Cuna had simultaneously established vital roles for themselves as guides and informants for the cast of plundering and trading foreigners. The sociopolitical landscape was profoundly fragmented and subject to rapid and unanticipated change, conditions relayed to Company councillors within days of their arrival and hinting at the fact they had entered a world as complex as any they had left behind. Captain Andreas was one of the first Cuna to approach the Scots, enquiring if they were friends of the Spanish, explaining he understood they intended to cross to the South Sea, and relating his friendships with English privateers. Four days later arrived a group of visitors including the previously mentioned Frenchman and two individuals from Martinique, one of whom spoke Cuna fluently. They clarified to the Scots that the story of a supreme leader over the Cuna was untrue and proceded to describe the intricate network of diverse contemporary leaders, their territories and variety of political affiliations. Captain Diego, with an estimated 3,000 men under his control, was regarded as the most powerful and had spent the last year at odds with the Spanish over gold mines within his jurisdiction. Most recently, the strife had resulted in the murders of twenty

Spaniards and three priests. Captain Paussigo's lands lay between those of Diego and Andreas, the latter allied with his brother and residing closest to the Scottish settlement. The two siblings had traditionally maintained a more amicable relationship with the Spanish, even allowing some of them to reside in the area and keep officials in Panama abreast of events. All had changed within the previous two months, however, when Captain Ambrosio, quasi-leader of yet another adjacent territory, had convinced them to join him in the killing of ten Spaniards on nearby Golden Island.[6]

What the Scots' informant could not have known was the transatlantic reverberations of the recent crimes, nor the region's impending interface with the aftermath. The president of Panama, just prior to receiving word of the Scots' appearance in Caledonia Bay, had dispatched word to Madrid regarding the latest Cuna atrocity, including his higher tally of victims as three Franciscan priests and thirty-two Spaniards. Walter Herries would later provide additional details, relating that following the murders and associated robbery of the chapel's furniture, Diego's son brought vestments and a chalice to New Caledonia and presented them to Captain Fraser. Ambrosio, also involved in the killings, had expressed his opinion that he would receive no pardon.[7]

The various captains also possessed a range of personal résumés reflecting impressive experience and acquisition of skills that allowed them to promote their interests both within their own territories and on foreign soil, circumstances that would deeply influence their individual actions during the periods of Scottish residence. Ambrosio's son-in-law Pedro was a fluent Spanish speaker, having learned the language in Panama while detained there as a slave. His language skills also included French, which he had acquired while living in Petit-Goave. French support also characterised Captain Corbete, who had assisted a group of French privateers and been offered compensation from Governor Du Casse. Sailing to meet with the governor, Corbete had been captured by the English and taken to Jamaica, where he and two companions had been sold into slavery. Du Casse, learning of the incident, had successfully demanded release of the three, allowing Corbete not only to travel twice to the French stronghold at Petit-Goave, but also to Cartagena. Neighbouring Corbete's lands was Captain Nicola, who had been brought up among the Spanish and was not only a fluent speaker, but also able to read and write. He had remained a Spanish ally until only twelve months earlier, when he had relinquished a treasured French firearm, acquired from a buccaneer, to a Spaniard for repair. The weapon had captured the attention of and been retained by the governor of Portobello, resulting in Nicola's transition to those firmly opposed to the Spanish.[8]

The Scots were also quickly made aware not only of differences, but also of discord, among Cuna communities. Ambrosio warned that Andreas was not to be trusted and was functioning as a spy. Questioned about the accusation, the latter captain related a critical account that was to be echoed following final departure of the Scots. Andreas explained that sixteen or seventeen years previously his people had assisted the French and English in raids on both sides of the Isthmus, receiving in return promises for continued protection from Spanish reprisals. Two years later, once the raids had reaped sufficient treasure, the foreigners departed and the Cuna were subjected to Spanish retribution, forcing them to seek sanctuary in the mountains for several years. Beyond verbal accusations levelled between the Cuna leaders, the underlying hostilities soon exhibited more concrete manifestations. Despite attempts by the Scots to negotiate between the two men, an alcohol-fuelled physical altercation erupted between them on board one of the Scottish vessels and Andreas was discovered dead the following morning, victim of a suspicious fall through an open hatch.[9]

The situation was further complicated by other, non-indigenous constituencies. The presence of Frenchmen had been, of course, quickly made obvious to the Scots. These ex-buccaneers had integrated themselves into Isthmian society, rearing half-Cuna families and considering themselves citizens of Darien, not of the French king. They welcomed the Scots as another intruding group who would not only provide trading opportunities, but would also deflect unwanted Spanish attention. A non-resident French contingent was also active and willing to provide its own unique narrative of regional sociopolitics. Captain Thomas of the *Maurepas*, which would sink attempting to sail out of Caledonia Bay on Christmas Day 1698, related to Commodore Pennycook that about eight months prior there had been a slave revolt in Portobello. The original 700 rebels had rapidly increased to 1,500, aided by arms and ammunition from English, French and Dutch traders. The force had been too powerful for the governor, who offered a guarantee of freedom in return for peace.[10]

Although the specific Portobello insurrection cannot be verified, the account is indicative of a series of local slave uprisings. Acquisition of slave labour had created the inevitable attendant problem of slave escapees, or maroons (*cimarrones*), which could involve up to 300 of every 1,000 individuals. Their sheer numbers, coupled with a jungle environment providing unique conditions of shelter and security, resulted in the creation by 1570 of at least three maroon settlements or *palenques* on the Isthmus. The largest of these, Ronconcholon, was said to include 1,700 fighting men and sustained not only persistent tension across the area but also an ample supply of conspirators for intruders. As early as 1572 Francis Drake had discovered the benefits of allying with such communities, which provided invaluable survival and guiding skills, including intelligence on movements of the ultimate incentive of Spanish treasure shipments. Returning to England, Drake had praised the overwhelming importance of such alliances, assuring their use by successive expeditions.[11]

In return, desperate to retain the vital source of labour, some modicum of security and prevent potential wholesale revolt, Spain attempted evangelisation, general amnesty and military action, resorting to mutually beneficial capitulations only in extreme circumstances. The threat of rebellion, and the economic strain of military deployments attempting to remedy it, resulted in imposition of a *cimarron* tax on local slave owners in 1639. Previously established in Mexico City, Cartagena and Havana, the funds were to be collected from slave owners and applied to offset military expenses. However successful revenue collection may have been, the problem continued. In 1697 ninety-four maroons were reported to be residing in the vicinity of Panama, subsisting off small farm plots which allowed them to mobilise quickly and avoid capture.[12]

While the recent purported capitulation in Portobello related by Captain Thomas may have created an apparent pause in slave insurrections, the latest developments presented both a novel intruder and a potential opportunity for the Spanish. Acknowledging the reality of possible assistance to the Scots by remaining fugitives and echoing concerns transmitted by Mexico's viceroy, in May 1699 the Council of War of the Indies recommended to the king that the inducement of amnesty be offered to communities of outlaw slaves in return for assistance in eradicating New Caledonia.[13]

At best the dynamic conditions of the Isthmus verged on unchecked disorder devoid of effective Spanish control. In addition to problems related to established residents, there was the vague mission of the newly arrived French, currently resting in the bay alongside the Scots and allegedly hunting pirates. There was also the ill-defined expedition of Captain Richard Long. Claiming to be searching for old wrecks, the Englishman had been cruising along the coast for a month prior to the Company of Scotland's arrival. His furtive presence made even the Scots suspicious, resulting in adoption of a policy to indulge the captain's propensity for alcohol as a means to discover his true motivations. Revealing no firm intelligence, Long did maintain a small English presence on the Isthmus by leaving three men and one woman behind with Cuna Captain Diego. One of the quartet made his way to New Caledonia in December 1698, reporting that he and his comrades, joined by local natives, had killed seven Spaniards. He requested powder and shot, neither of which could be spared, and added that Long had been emphatic in explaining to indigenous groups just how bad the Scots were.[14]

As if any Spanish official needed a reminder of the incessant, potentially violent equation of local unrest and foreign intrusion, there were now five heavily armed ships of Scots in the heart of Darien. Not only were they expressing their intent to establish themselves by constructing fortifications, but they were actively forging alliances with the Cuna and speaking of substantial reinforcements from Scotland.

COSTLY REHEARSAL

As the clearing and construction of New Caledonia commenced, there was no lack of intelligence warning the Scots of impending Spanish reaction. French Captain Thomas provided notice that the president of Panama had alerted Portobello and Cartagena officials of the Company's arrival and increasing Spanish anxiety up and down the coast was evident. Thomas maintained that the Mississippi River was assumed to be the Scots' final destination, but three vessels of the Barlovento fleet remained at anchor in Cartagena's port. Furthermore, Mexico City had also been alerted and its viceroy was preparing his own campaign. Captain Long also passed on the alarm regarding the Barlovento fleet, notifying the newcomers that it was currently provisioning to attack them in a few days, prompting the Scots to accelerate completion of their battery and position their ships in a battleline across their bay's mouth. From Cuna Captain Andreas came word of actual mobilisation of a ground force marching from Panama to Portobello to augment the naval contingent consolidating from the latter port and Cartagena.[15]

The providers of intelligence, however, in no way restricted themselves to communicating solely with the intruders. The value of information as a commodity was fully comprehended and exploited by a selection of native captains who not only possessed the highest degree of proximity and access to events at New Caledonia, but also knowledge of how most efficiently and effectively to transmit the information and to whom the substance of the message would be of greatest importance. The president of Panama, while highly critical of Cuna truthfulness, soon found himself formulating strategies based largely on the intelligence they provided. Canillas had originally dispatched Spanish Captain Betancur to assess the threat of the French presence and arrest Cuna leaders Ambrosio and Pedro for the recent murders, including further orders to burn their villages as punishment. In return came the even more disturbing report that five Scottish warships were in the vicinity. Much of the information had been acquired during an interview with Corbete, who readily conceded he had actually been aboard one of the Company of Scotland's vessels, adding that eighteen Cuna captains had declared themselves allied with the new arrivals.[16]

Corbete's remarks encompassing recent alliances forged with the Scots were accurate, for a written treaty was formulated between the Council of Caledonia and Chief Diego and signed on 24 February 1699. The document, declaring the parties to be perpetual allies obligated to defend each other's population and territories, also included a critical stipulation providing for inclusion of additional Cuna groups. Among the names of potential future signators were Ambrosio and Pedro, the specific pair of leaders the president of Panama was seeking to have arrested.[17] New Caledonia had not taken long to firmly enmesh itself in the convoluted political world of Darien.

The alert created by the arrival of the Scots initially resulted in the creation of companies of Spanish, Creole and black volunteers to reinforce regulars guarding Panama, Portobello and Chagres.[18] Meanwhile, President Canillas initiated a land operation from Panama, followed by a report to the king seeking to justify its wasteful expense and abject failure. Claiming that delays necessary to careen the fleet of General de Pez in Portobello would create an opportunity for the Scots to entrench themselves, Canillas intimated that the naval commander had proposed the alternative of a land operation, with which he had agreed. The resulting fifty-two-day campaign, which faced the environmental challenges of Darien that thwarted Scot and Spaniard alike, extended through March and April 1699 and was intended to be completed prior to the onset of the rainy season. Although Canillas was careful to concede that the land expedition had the potential to fail in eliminating the Scottish settlement, he justified its implementation by declaring the importance of exhibiting a show of force that would both alarm New Caledonia and provide a powerful lesson to those Cuna who had committed the recent murders and habitually chose to ignore Spanish authority.

Resources deployed for the mission were impressive. Ten large barks were used to ferry troops on the six-day sail to El Escuchadero on the Pacific side of Darien. From there an assembly of canoes had been convened to transport men and supplies to the outpost of Tubacanti, a plan that had to be altered when the inadequate capacity of the vessels was realised. Forced to change tactics, Canillas would instead find himself led by native guides through dense jungle to the outpost, where he joined four companies of militia under Carrisoli to create a combined force of 1,500 men. Conditions worsened as the troops, without any option of water transport, were forced to carry their personal ten-day supplies of rations in addition to required arms and ammunition.

Darien's topography severely impaired progress as the men forded rivers confined by steep cliffs, often marching within the actual watercourse. Falls were common, saturating food and ammunition. Eventually traversing a steep range, the men reached a marshy area two leagues from New Caledonia. From their campsite the Spanish could hear regular intervals of artillery fire, taken as an indication of the Scots' knowledge of their presence. Rest and preparation for a final offensive failed to materialise as heavy rains began to inundate the camp and continued for three days, restricting any movement and destroying rapidly diminishing food supplies. The dire conditions were underscored with the arrival of 100 black porters, subjected to the same incessant rainfall and flooding, whose anticipated supplementary supplies of bread and cheese had also become saturated. Inability to proceed was evident, forcing a decision to retreat.

The aborted land campaign was accompanied by the abandonment of a concurrent strategic effort assigned to foreigners. In return for 10,000 pesos to be delivered upon completion of the task, a contingent of Frenchmen, with native support, had been positioned to burn or cut cables mooring Scottish vessels once Spanish troops were reported within sight of New Caledonia. The combined French and Cuna company had, however, been subjected to the same problems of weather and inadequate rations. Upon notification of their condition, and the critical factor of their perception by the Scots, they were also recalled.[19] As if challenges of climate and topography were not sufficient to destroy the mission, a message had also reached General de Pez that mandated urgent return to his fleet: English warships (unknown to de Pez, those of Admiral Benbow) had arrived in Portobello where the vulnerable, minimally manned vessels were undergoing maintenance.[20]

The failed initial assault on New Caledonia did, however, facilitate the first incident of armed confrontation between Scot and Spaniard. In his account of the colony's history, Reverend Francis Borland describes 'one small skirmish' with a forward patrol approaching the colony 'either to spy . . . or to see if they could apprehend any . . . stragglers in the woods, or to entice the Indians to forsake our men'. Informed of the Spanish presence by native allies, the Scots deployed 150 men under Captain Montgomery. Along with their company were two previously apprehended Spanish prisoners who successfully shouted a warning as the New Caledonia force moved through thick woods. Firing began, killing two Scots and wounding fourteen, as the Spanish patrol, vastly outnumbered, retired.[21]

The failed outcome of the Panamanian land operation, irrespective of initial abandonment of New Caledonia by the Scots less than two months later, would cost Canillas dearly. Pending an investigation, he would find himself relieved of his presidency. The suspension would, however, be as short-lived as the disappearance of the Company of Scotland, for reinstatement would occur by the end of the year following a letter from the king citing the value of the president's military experience.[22]

Significant changes in the administration of Darien were not limited to the unpopular president in Panama. Initiated by Canillas prior to his suspension, a new governor of the province of Darien had presented himself, his appointment threatening to supplant Luis Carrisoli and the decades of supremacy his family had held over the conduct of local affairs. Arriving from Cadiz with the daunting mandate to populate his jurisdiction, promote gold mining activities, pacify the natives and impede the activity of pirates, Miguel de Cordones would find himself not only with an established and resentful local authority, but also immersed in the immediate crisis of a new wave of Scots arriving in Darien.[23]

RESTORING AUTHORITY OVER THE KING'S LAND

While the second expedition struggled to establish itself in an abandoned, overgrown New Caledonia, one commodity consistently in ample supply was intelligence about forces assembling against them. A visiting Jamaican brigantine, attempting to market its cargo of dry goods and forty slaves near Portobello, had been chased by a Spanish warship and recognised it to be part of the fleet consolidating against the Scots. It was also said that bakers in Portobello were fully employed in preparing bread for the amassing forces.[24] As February 1700 progressed, such communications began to be a daily occurrence, culminating in a specific alarm from Cuna allies of a force approaching by land. Deciding to seize the initiative, on the 13th the newly arrived Captain Campbell of Fonab led a company of 200 Scots, joined by sixty natives under Captains Pedro, Augustine and Brandy, out of New Caledonia. Two days later, while approaching Tubacanti, they engaged in heavily forested terrain with a mixed contingent of 300 mullatoes, Creoles, blacks and natives under the new Governor Cordones, killing nine or ten and taking three prisoners. Casualties within the allied New Caledonia force numbered eight dead and eighteen wounded. Among those requiring the attention of Scottish surgeons was Captain Campbell, as well as Captain Pedro, the latter among several Cuna commended for their service. The skirmish, regarded by the Scots as an impressive victory, was reported so to Edinburgh, prompting celebrations for what was actually a minor prelude to a remarkably contrasting reality.[25]

Relief and elation were soon overshadowed by full comprehension of the composition, size and strategies of the emerging Spanish operation under command of Cartagena's Governor Pimienta. As introduced in Chapter 4, Reverend Borland documented visits by an English sloop claiming to be Jamaican and a group of nine Frenchmen purporting to trade in tortoises, both eventually exposed as spying for the Spanish. Borland, a witness to these events, relates that as anxiety surrounding ultimate arrival of Spanish forces increased, a flurry of activity was undertaken to repair and enhance batteries surrounding Fort Saint Andrew. Simultaneously, two sloops and the *Rising Sun*'s longboat were dispatched to determine the identity of vessels detected off the coast. In turn chased by their unidentified prey, the sloops made it back safely, but the longboat was abandoned on the beach as her crew fled, resulting in the loss of a key resource.

The anticipated debut of the full offensive force was finally detected on 23 and 25 February, consisting of 'eleven sail of Spanish vessels great and small'. As Borland recorded:

> We daily expected their coming into our harbour to attack our Fort and ships . . . all hands, sea-men and Land-men, were put to work, to fortify the place as well as they could: They also made several Fire-ships of their smaller vessels, putting themselves in as good a posture of defence as they could. But the Spaniards did not come in with their ships, for they knew this harbour well enough, which is easy for great ships to come into, but difficult and dangerous to get out again; the wind this season of the year, generally blowing right into it. So they went another way to work, less dangerous to themselves, and more disadvantageous to us, which was, To hem us in both by sea and land.

While the naval blockade secured the mouth of the bay, Pimienta landed men near Careto, merging his own forces with those arrived overland 'from Panama and Santa Maria, accompanied with numbers of Indians, Negroes and Molattoes, who were expert in knowing the woods, and cutting passages through the thorny thickets of the woods in their way'.[26]

Fully exploiting the restrictions of New Caledonia's wind-locked harbour, the governor strategically directed the landing of men on either side of the bay's mouth. As he pushed the Scots toward capitulation, Pimienta would remind his adversaries of their predicament, writing to them of his regret should he be required to order his own naval fleet into the port, for then he would have to rush their defences and would find himself stranded, conditions which would prevent any opportunity of giving quarter. The governor would return to the same issue as negotiations faltered, reminding the Scots of their vulnerability by lamenting that his own vessels would face difficulty in leaving the anchorage for up to two months should he be forced to enter.[27]

Accompanying Pimienta was Cartagena's chief military engineer Juan de Herrera y Sotomayor, who provided a graphic representation of the governor's evolving strategy (Figure 8.1 and cover). As illustrated on Herrera's map, a stranglehold was established and gradually tightened around New Caledonia (A) as the Spanish coordinated land and sea forces. Denoted as (D) are the initial points where troops were landed at Rancho Viejo and Careto, on either side of the Scots, succeeded by the improved site of Caleta (F). Following engagement with the Scots at their forward point (E) on 11 March, the progress of confining the colonists is demarcated by the advancing locations of the third (G), fourth (H), fifth (I) and, finally, sixth (L) Spanish encampments, the last of which was established with artillery on 7 April.

Instrumental to both Herrera's work and Pimienta's orders was the continual stream of sound, timely intelligence. With the arrival of allied Spanish forces the diverse, fluid Cuna factions had to expediently evaluate anticipated outcomes of the impending armed conflict. Not only were actual military confrontations taking place within their home territory, but they had to consider their own and their families' futures within the context of two volatile centuries of contact with both Spanish governance and foreign intruders. The opportunity to ingratiate themselves to Pimienta's command would at least provide some measure of future security over the less attractive alternative of continued allegiance to a faltering and unstable group of Scots who only months previously had abandoned their fledgling colony and promises of defensive support against the Spanish.

Reaching the Isle of Pines and waiting to assemble with vessels dispatched from Portobello, Pimienta had sent a launch from his flagship to secure information. It returned with an unidentified native, followed by the parade of informants discussed in Chapter 2, who had deserted the Scottish encampment and provided critical details regarding New Caledonia fortifications, manpower, supplies and munitions. The initial landing at Careto also featured indispensable native intelligence, as the 200 men, three captains, two engineers and three Frenchmen were guided by the omnipresent Corbete as they reconnoitered the mountainous terrain. The value of detailed local intelligence was acknowledged in Pimienta's campaign journal on 13 March 1700 as he recorded disembarkation and placement of artillery initially frustrated by steep slopes and multiple drainages. The remedy had been provided once engineers acquired information from Cuna of an inlet closer to Caledonia meeting Spanish requirements. Indigenous participation from other parts of Darien was also evident with the arrival of Luis Carrisoli and a force of 120 allied

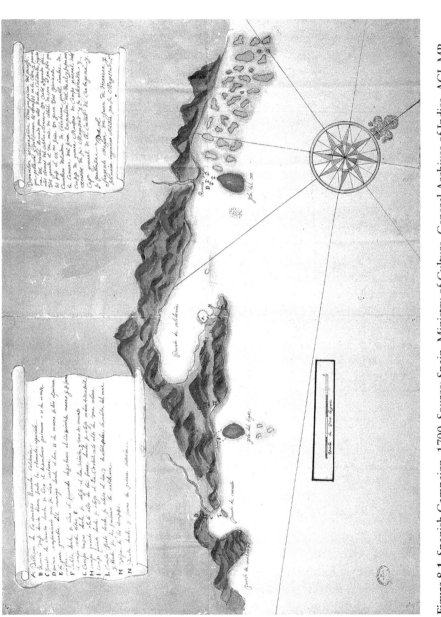

Figure 8.1 Spanish Campaign, 1700. Source: Spain. Ministry of Culture. General Archives of Indies, AGI, MP Panamá 120_R.

natives from their base near the Cana gold mines. The Pacific groups, constituting their own incursion into Cuna territory, were assigned to protect rear positions as the Spaniards advanced, Pimienta later complaining that they did little more than consume rations.[28]

As the Spanish, reinforced by diverse regional and foreign participants, and the Scots, successively reduced to operating from within their fortifications and isolated from their water supply, played out their conflict, the changing political conditions and growing discomfort facing the Cuna did not go unrecognised by either principal party. With the Spanish stranglehold intensifying around New Caledonia and an estimated 2,000 men engaged in the immediate area, Borland noted the impact of the loss of support previously provided by 'our Indian friends', who now had to 'shift for themselves, for fear of the Spaniards'. He also commented on a pragmatic fact of Darien existence, that some had approached and given intelligence to the Spaniards, offering his assessment 'for they commonly join with the strongest side, and little trust is to be put in most of them'.[29] The Spanish perspective was roughly equivalent, Pimienta directing natives be cordially welcomed, but maintained under a watchful eye

> the Indians who may come aboard these ships they will detain, or, if they desire to join me, they will send to my port. They will treat these Indians well and in such manner that they shall not resent their detention, seeking pretexts to keep them aboard; especially if they come aboard with their bands they will send them to me with the first vessel going to Carreto, assuring these Indians always of our friendship.[30]

ATTEMPTING TO RESTORE CONTROL

As negotiations lurched towards capitulation and ultimate abandonment of New Caledonia, the Scots made an attempt to assure the welfare of their Cuna allies. Article 7 of a draft of the agreement stipulated that natives who had aligned themselves with the Scots since their initial arrival would suffer no retribution. Asserting his king's authority, Pimienta adamantly vetoed the proposal and directed particular anger at Scottish Reverend Shiels, who had presented the specific petition. 'The Indians were the king of Spain's subjects,' the governor stated, 'and he knew best how to treat his own subjects, and if the Indians would keep out of his way, he would not search after them.' The proposal and subsequent refusal of amnesty was also included in the account related in the *Gazeta extraordinaria*, accompanied by the explanation that Pimienta had not regarded the condition as advantageous to his king.[31]

A deliberate and public assertion of control over the native population continued as the Scots prepared to embark and the Spanish force began to occupy the site of the colony. Pimienta, having finally entered the harbour and anchored at its fortified dock, dispatched men to inspect the enemy's ships and relay to land all Cuna found aboard. Eleven individuals were discovered and brought before the governor, who ordered them to be handcuffed, transferred to the Spanish base camp and maintained under guard. That night a general alarm went up as three shots were heard. As troops seized their weapons, notice spread that two of the detainees had thrown themselves into the sea, causing their guards to fire after them. Orders also directed a Spanish officer to take twenty-five men to find and arrest Captain Brandy, identified by the Scots as the individual who had sold them land. Yet another incident occurred when Pimienta noticed a canoe tied to one of the Scottish ships as it was being prepared to depart. The subsequent investigation revealed that a group of Cuna had been delivering supplies of food. Once the perpetrators were in custody they, too, were transferred to the main camp.[32]

There is marked silence in contemporary documents regarding eventual action taken against the prisoners, with the exception of that provided by Walter Herries. As noted in Chapter 3, the surgeon and spy, who would have had to obtain the information from returning contacts, reported a number of the indigenous allies were 'impaild alive' by the Spaniards for the service they provided the Scots at Tubacanti. Taking into account the murders committed prior to arrival of the Scots, combined with obvious continuing alliances forged with intruders, it is not inconsistent that Pimienta elected to impose on both foreign and native populations an explicit demonstration of Spanish authority over rebellious subjects. Such outcomes for the indigenous population were not atypical. A 1779 report, relating reasons for the closure of a Darien mining operation, noted that five natives, recognised as rebels and enemies of the Crown, had been executed.[33]

While addressing the issue of Cuna betrayals, the Spanish simultaneously turned their attention to the fortifications, artillery and ammunition they had acquired. Stipulations of the capitulation did allow the Scots personal arms, baggage and weaponry necessary for the defence of their ships on the journey home. There was also a reciprocal exchange of prisoners and agreement that no vessel affiliated with the Company of Scotland arriving within two months would be attacked, providing it made no hostile gesture. The governor, following the late afternoon signing of the capitulation, ordered a force of 200 men to immediately occupy Fort Saint Andrew, now renamed Saint Charles in recognition of the Spanish king. 'Accompanied by officers and some curious persons',

Pimienta personally surveyed the facility and considered it to be of adequate strength. In addition to the structure itself, there were twenty-eight or thirty pieces of artillery, up to seventy dwellings of thatch, a headquarters and storehouses. Having taken formal possession, the governor retired to his headquarters and its assorted population of injured and allied personnel, assigning command of Fort Saint Charles to *Maestro de campo* Melchor Ladron de Guevara.[34]

Once again, the technical skills of the military engineers were mobilised to document what, with inadvertent assistance of Scottish lives and labour, was now a well-fortified Spanish military outpost in the volatile region of Darien. Documentation of Fort Saint Charles's infrastructure, along with its relative position to the Spanish headquarters, was completed (Figure 8.2), illustrating fortifications of the Scots (A), their warehouses (B), batteries (C), the principal encampment of Spanish forces (D), sequence of Spanish offensive positions and fortifications (E to I), the embarkation point for Spanish artillery (L), routes utilised to implement the campaign (M), the Scottish flag (N) and the housing area within the fort (O).

Active participation of engineers was essential not only to implementation and documentation of military success securing New Caledonia, but would also have far-ranging impacts regarding institutional understanding of regional geography. Engineering units within the Spanish military had evolved significantly during the final decades of the seventeenth century and would spread across Spain's American dominions, nowhere better exemplified than by the activities of brothers José and Juan de Herrera y Sotomayor. The latter, whose efforts supported the Darien campaign, would eventually be appointed as the king's leading military engineer in the Americas and continue his work strengthening Cartagena's defences. His and his colleagues' projects would be further credited in an anonymous 1739 Spanish manuscript on Darien addressing expulsion of the Scots and priority given to the area's security following the ultimate demise of New Caledonia. Citing personal conversations with veterans of the 1700 campaign, the author would stress the value of the knowledge gained and catalogued of the Cuna homeland.[35]

While the Spaniards imposed their authority over the former Fort Saint Andrew, the engineers completed surveys and mapping, and the Cuna sought whatever security they could determine, an assertion of the Catholic faith was also conducted. As the Scots struggled out of their wind-locked bay, finally succeeding 'with the help of the Spaniards, who were glad to be rid of us, as we were of them', Pimienta did not fail to acknowledge religion or king, designating one of the now vacant warehouses as a church and hearing the first mass as the site was dedicated in the name of Saint Charles.[36]

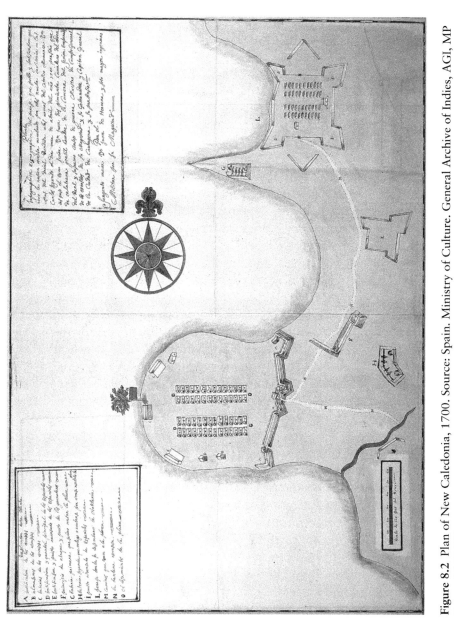

Figure 8.2 Plan of New Caledonia, 1700. Source: Spain. Ministry of Culture. General Archive of Indies, AGI, MP Panamá 119 BIS.

NO RESTORATION OF PEACE

A flurry of activity followed cessation of military action on Darien soil, although peace continued to elude the region on several fronts. The president of Panama, restored to his post, had remained in Portobello with reinforcements, receiving regular correspondence from Pimienta regarding developments. Canillas duly included these updates in his report to Carlos II, along with references to his own sacrifices and timely initiatives and complaints he had received regarding the governor of Cartagena's administration of the campaign. Characteristically, the president had not been reluctant to offer counsel to Pimienta, advising the man enmeshed in orchestrating military action about the hardships and frustrations of running an operation so divorced from those in Europe.[37] Pimienta's reaction to the unsolicited commentary, particularly following Canillas's dismal land campaign against the Scots, can only be imagined.

For his questionable efforts the president of Panama would be amply rewarded. His capital city would respond in a manner similar to Lima, providing a mix of military, civil and church expressions of celebration while bestowing equal credit to its own Canillas along with Pimienta. Of higher value to its recipient was appointment as interim viceroy of Peru, a prize that would go unclaimed due to Canillas's death in Panama prior to his departure for Lima. The diversion of credit did not go unnoticed, for the 1739 manuscript quoted previously also recorded opinions in Cartagena regarding the viceregal appointment. An informant related that the position had been awarded regardless of the fact that Pimienta actually executed the campaign and Canillas never even left Panama nor made any valuable contribution, instead relinquishing effort and eventual success to troops from Cartagena and associated naval forces.[38]

For his part Pimienta appears to have opted out of debate with the president of his neighbouring jurisdiction from whose lands he had just effectively expelled the enemy. Focusing on bringing the successful operation to conclusion, he issued orders for an officer and 200 men to remain in New Caledonia and returned to the formidable challenges of his own government in Cartagena.[39] In his notification of success to Canillas the governor tactfully acknowledged that New Caledonia was in Panamanian territory but did not glorify his own role in the mission. Instead, he reported that he was leaving the fort in secure condition and that two men had expressed their wish to be placed in charge of the garrison, one Canillas's appointee to the governorship of Darien and the other *Maestro de campo* Melchor de Guevara. The decision as to which man was to receive the permanent appointment Pimienta deferred to

Panama's president, stating he should have the opportunity to choose the individual most agreeable to him for the assignment.[40]

Intended permanent occupation of the newly acquired outpost by Spanish forces would not last. Admiral Navarette, fulfilling orders to assess the state of regional defences should his resources not be required against the Scots, visited the site and, in his report written from Cadiz in April 1701, noted the majority of the guard had either deserted or died. He had reinforced the fort with 100 men and appropriate provisions, along with a chaplain sent by Governor Pimienta. These supplementary resources failed to eliminate the challenges of the assignment and an attack by twenty-two pirates in the summer of 1701, along with the opportune arrival of a brigantine providing a source of evacuation, facilitated yet another abandonment. Citing lack of supplies, prevailing illness among the men, and the chronic inability to protect themselves either from the recent or any future assault, a junta held in 'Plaza Caledonia' unanimously decided to evacuate, a decision Canillas would use against Pimienta by complaining that it had been implemented without notice to or permission from Panama. Despite King Carlos's recent declaration of Santa Theresa as patron saint and protector of Darien and the designation of 15 October for an annual local fiesta to commemorate successful expulsion of the Scots, the challenges facing sustained occupation of New Caledonia continued to impede any permanent European presence.[41]

The Cuna lacked, of course, either a viable alternative or the desire to vacate what was their homeland, yet their situation was no less problematic. Although their territory had involuntarily hosted an influx of domestic and foreign forces and the actual combat, there were no assessments or documentation of losses asked of them and their opinion was not solicited by either colonial administrators or Madrid. Nevertheless, two intriguing sources addressing their reaction can be elicited from later documents. The first is contained in annotations accompanying the 'Anonymous Spanish manuscript from 1739 on the province Darien'. Editor Henry Wassén explains that although the episode of interaction with the Scots was not included in the oral chronicle of Cuna history dictated to ethnographer Erland Nordensklold, the latter's Cuna collaborator, Ruben Perez, did recount the Scots had suffered from illnesses released by a powerful Cuna religious authority, forcing them to abandon the region. Commentary addressing a more explicitly historic context is found in another oral history documented by the governor of Portobello in 1741 during a visit to his city by a group of Cuna, one of whom was able to converse in Spanish. The visitor related that disparity and autonomy among various groups of Cuna had been reflected in interaction with foreigners, the French and English often being readily accepted for the tools and textiles they traded. The people identifying themselves as Scots, however, had solicited a licence to establish themselves in the area. The novelty of that request had created a substantial level of discord, as some factions supported the Spanish effort to expel the newcomers and others did not. Perhaps more importantly, promises of continued defence against the Spanish included in the forged alliance proved false, for the Scots abandoned their site within a mere sixteen months, leaving the Cuna once again fully responsible for their own security.[42]

DARIEN EPILOGUE

While ramifications of the failed Scottish expeditions across the remainder of the Americas were manifested through dispersal of its survivors, lasting impacts in Darien centred on a reinvigorated Spanish commitment to secure the region from the continuing lures of Isthmian resources and geography. As the acquired infrastructure of New Caledonia, successively rebuilt and fortified by the Spanish, would serve as a concrete reminder of vulnerability to foreign intrusion, relentless domestic strife would continue to seed the potential for menacing indigenous alliances with foreigners. The audacious attempt by the Scots to establish themselves within the dominions of the Spanish king could and would not be forgotten as attempts to pacify the region continued through the decades of the eighteenth century.

The territory's alluring attributes would rapidly reassert themselves, enabled by open conflict in Spanish American waters during the War of the Spanish Succession of 1701–14. In September 1702, a mere two and a half years following final departure of the Scots, Darien was subjected to an assault on its gold mines in Cana by a force of 700 English and 300 rebel natives. This and a number of subsequent raids, afflicting primarily the southern side of the Isthmus, were followed two decades later by a major regional native uprising led by mestizo Luis Garcia. The years 1725 and 1726 witnessed abandonment not only of the aforementioned mines, but also livestock, sugar and timber operations along the Pacific slope. The severity of the insurrection became so acute that the safety of Spaniards in the area would be compromised for the next half century and long-established French and French–Cuna families would be murdered.[43]

Despite permanent establishment in 1739 of the new viceroyalty of New Granada, based in Bogotá to provide more effective administration of the region, internal turmoil continued to suppress Spanish economic development and the world of illicit commerce continued to thrive. The

newly appointed president of Panama, don Dionisio de Alsedo y Herrera, would be specifically reminded in his 1742 orders of the former
Scottish incursion, and how Cartagena, Portobello and Panama had
been left inadequately defended during the ensuing campaign. As the
new president made his way up the coast from Cartagena towards his
post, surveying his jurisdiction and attempting to ascertain how some
measure of control might be attained, he gathered first-hand knowledge
of the challenges he faced. In his report he documented interviews with
Cuna who verified current English activity, including specific information that a Major Cunningham had recently been in the area trading
substantial quantities of arms and ammunition. After exploring the ruins
of New Caledonia and considering all he had witnessed, he commented
that the indigenous population had been living in complete liberty, ben-
efiting from foreign traders but devoid of any equivalent positive interaction with Spaniards.[44]

A dramatic illustration of rewards derived from interrelationships
with foreigners was later described in Jacob Walburger's 1748 *Relación
sobre la Provincia del Darién*. The Jesuit recorded the case of two sons of
a Cuna captain residing in the region referred to as Caledonia who had
gone to Jamaica and been taught to read and write the English language.
The brothers returned a year and a half later, impressively dressed, bearing gifts and soliciting additional Cuna men to return with them to the
island. From that point, according to Walburger, it had been forbidden
to criticise the English.[45] Substantiating the continuity of the range of
exchanges are references in Jamaican government correspondence to
interactions with Cuna emissaries during the first half of the eighteenth
century. In 1706 the island's governor Thomas Handasyd wrote of four
indigenous men who had arrived and requested arms and munitions following purported murders by the French. Handasyd received unanimous
approval from his Council of War to provide each visitor with thirty-five
arms and supplies of powder, ball and flints, following which the group
was dispatched home on the identical sloop which had brought them. In
1741 interaction is again indicated by an expenditure in the accounts of
Governor Trelawny for gifts to native leaders from Darien.[46]

Sustained failure to either establish domestic peace or effectively sty-
mie illegal commerce mustered support for a far-reaching plan in the final
two decades of the eighteenth century that would once again emphasise
the strategic importance of New Caledonia. The gravity of the situation
and its accompanying challenge of persistent native trade with English,
Dutch and French pirates and merchants went so far as to provoke a
royal order in 1783 for outright elimination of the Cuna population.
Two years later, in an attempt to install a permanent Spanish presence,

governor of Panama Andres de Ariza initiated construction of a road towards Caledonia Bay, supported by the fort of El Principe approximately half way across the Isthmus. Heading to the military outpost from Caledonia three years later, a Spanish engineer would report sightings of groups of Cuna rebels.[47] Verification of their activity underscored the urgency of the colonial administration's full intentions, for more than military subjugation of the territory was intended. Elaborate plans had been formulated to establish five communities, one of which was to be Caledonia, to be inhabited by a spectrum of civilian and military personnel. The network of new settlements would be deliberately located not only to secure coastal anchorages, but also to impress authority on the interior, thus creating a living statement of possession while simultaneously providing networks of communication and a semblance of civilisation. In addition to military support, each site was to include the various professions necessary to make a viable community. Among the minimum fifty families at each enclave would be ten or twelve carpenters, a bricklayer, two blacksmiths, a surgeon and a chaplain. Likely reflecting the understandable hesitancy of any local Spaniard to participate in the enterprise, colonists were to be imported from outside the area (in this case, the newly independent United States, specifically Philadelphia) and would eventually comprise an international group consisting of 113 English, Irish and German individuals, along with fifteen French who had previously been in Caledonia. Unlike the unfortunate Scots before them, however, these expectant settlers would never reach their destination. Arriving and maintained in Cartagena at the Crown's expense, they would eventually find themselves reboarded on a Spanish vessel and sent back to Philadelphia, never glimpsing what was to have been their new home. Citing enduring concerns over allowing immigration of foreigners into such a strategic region, the recently assigned viceroy of New Granada had abruptly cancelled the project.[48]

Perhaps the best witness to the unmitigated and enduring insecurity of Darien is correspondence from the governor of Jamaica to the viceroy dated November 1785. Responding to concerns expressed over activities of English merchants, the island's Governor Clark ironically echoed virtually the identical claims his predecessor Sir William Beeston had made during the occupation of the Scots almost a century before:

The persons calling themselves British subjects, who have dispersed themselves into Caledonia Darien . . . have had no encouragement from this government. On the contrary, every effort in my power shall be exerted to recall such as are there.[49]

NOTES

1. Insh, *The Company*, p. 129.
2. Spain's tumultuous early years in Darien are recounted in Howarth, *Panama*, Chapters 1–2 and Romoli, *Balboa of Darién*. For Arevalo's report see Cuervo and Vergara y Velasco, *Colección de documentos inéditos, tomo II*, p. 256.
3. Castillero Calvo, *Conquista*, p. 227.
4. Gallup-Diaz, *The Door*, pp. 43–53.
5. Insh, *The Company*, pp. 109–14.
6. Burton, *The Darien Papers*, pp. 63–7.
7. AGI, Panamá 105, *consulta* from Council of War to Carlos II, 14 July 1699 and Herries, *A Short Vindication*, p. 35.
8. Burton, *The Darien Papers*, pp. 67–9 and Langebaek, 'Cuna long distance journeys', pp. 371–80. Langebaek elaborates on the importance of foreign experiences and acquisition of exotic goods and knowledge as instrumental to attainment of prestige and position within Cuna communities.
9. Herries, *A Defence*, pp. 58–60.
10. Gallup-Diaz, *The Door*, pp. 108–9 and Insh, *Papers*, pp. 92–3.
11. Howarth, *Panama*, pp. 59, 67–80
12. Rodriguez, *Cimarron Revolts*, pp. 4–7, 152–3.
13. AGS, Estado 4183, *consulta* dated 12 May 1699.
14. Insh, *Papers*, pp 88–9, 93–4. As late as 1707 Long was still promoting treasure to be realised from the Isthmus, soliciting funds from the Duke of Hamilton for a private expedition. NRS, GD406/1/5437.
15. Insh, *Papers*, pp. 92–4.
16. Gallup-Diaz, *The Door*, pp. 127–9.
17. Burton, *The Darien Papers*, pp. 87–8.
18. Carles, *220 años*, p. 169.
19. Hart, *The Disaster*, App. XVI, pp. 261–82.
20. Torres Ramírez, *La Armada*, pp. 164–5.
21. Borland, *The History*, p. 21.
22. AGI, Panamá 113, Carlos II to the Count of la Monclova, 14 August 1699 and Alba, *Cronología de los gobernantes*, pp. 104–5.
23. Gallup-Diaz, *The Door*, p. 141, AGI, Panamá 113, assignment of title of governor of the Province of Darien to Don Miguel Cordones, 9 January 1699, and AGI, Panamá 167, Cordones to Carlos II, 20 February 1699.
24. Burton, *The Darien Papers*, p. 244.
25. Ibid., p. 251 and Hart, *The Disaster*, p. 138.
26. Borland, *The History*, pp. 59–60.
27. Hart, *The Disaster*, App. XXXI, pp. 374, 380.
28. MHS-Hart, *Gazeta*-English, p. 4 and Hart, *The Disaster*, App. XXXI, pp. 371, 385.
29. Borland, *The History*, pp. 70–1.
30. Hart, *The Disaster*, App. XXXI, p. 371.

31. Ibid., App. XII, p. 249 and MHS-Hart, *Gazeta*-English, p. 10.

32. MHS-Hart, *Gazeta*-English, p. 13 and Hart, *The Disaster*, App. XXXI, p. 391.

33. Herries, *An Enquiry*, p. 40 and Martínez Cutillas, *Colonial Panama*, pp. 582–4.

34. MHS-Hart, *Gazeta*-English, pp. 10–12 and Hart, *The Disaster*, App. XXXI, p. 390.

35. Buisseret, 'Spanish military engineers', p. 52, Marco Dorta, *Cartagena de Indias*, p. 211 and Wassén, 'Anonymous Spanish manuscript', p. 111.

36. Borland, *The History*, p. 74 and Hart, *The Disaster*, App. XXXI, p. 391.

37. Hart, *The Disaster*, App. XXXIII, pp. 396–426.

38. Severino de Santa Teresa, *Historia documentada*, p. 251, Alba, *Cronología de los gobernantes*, p. 105 and Wassén, 'Anonymous Spanish manuscript', p. 111.

39. MHS-Hart, *Gazeta*-English, p. 14.

40. Hart, *The Disaster*, App. XXXII, p. 394. The situation was not resolved by Canillas, for a letter from the king dated 20 October 1700 acknowledged the dispute and advanced the decision on to the viceroy in Peru. AGI, Panamá 113, *Ramo* 3.

41. AGI, Panamá 181, report of Alm. Gen. Don Pedro Navarette, Cadiz, 6 April 1701, AGI, Panamá 177, ff. 1039r–43v, Canillas to the King, August 1701 and Severino de Santa Teresa, *Historia documentada*, pp. 252–3.

42. Wassén,'Anonymous Spanish manuscript', p. 126 and AGI, Panamá 307, ff. 1197r–209v.

43. Castillero Calvo, *Conquista*, p. 228 and Joyce, *A New Voyage*, App. III, pp. 169–70.

44. AGI, Panamá 255, orders to the president elect of Panama, don Dionisio de Alsedo y Herrera, Cadiz, July 10 1742 and AGI, Panamá 255, *Diario de Don Dionisio de Alsedo y Herrera, Governador y Comandante General del Reyno de Tierra Firme y Presidente de la Real Audiencia de Panamá*.

45. AGI, Panamá 307, ff. 1168r–84v. A record of parallel lessons is provided in a manuscript describing a language exchange during the Scottish presence at New Caledonia. Gentleman, *The History of Caledonia*, pp. 43–4, 51.

46. NA, CO137/45, f. 351v. and CO137/48, f. 157.

47. Weber, *Bárbaros*, pp. 175 and 334, ft. 232 and Joyce, *A New Voyage*, App. III, pp. 169–70.

48. AGI Panamá 307, ff. 1040r–7r, 1153r–65v, AGS, Secretaria del Despacho de Guerra 7054, 46 and Vásquez Pino, 'Políticas Borbónicas', pp. 89–103.

49. AGI, Panamá 307, f. 1607r.

Appendix I

Caledonia: The Declaration of the Council Constituted by the Indian and African Company of Scotland, for the Government and Direction of their Colonies and Settlements in the Indies

The said Company pursuant to the Powers and Immunities granted unto them by His Majesty of Great Britain, our Sovereign Lord, with Advice and Consent of His Parliament of Scotland, having granted and conceded unto us and our Successors in the Government for all times hereafter, full Power to equip, set out, freight, and navigate our own or hired Ships, in warlike or other manner, from any Ports or Places in amity, or not in hostility with His Majesty; to any Lands, Islands, Countries, or Places in Asia, Africa, or America; and there to plant Colonies, build Cities, Towns or Forts, in or upon the places not inhabited; or in or upon any other place, by consent of the Natives or Inhabitants thereof, and not possest by any European Soveraign, Potentate, Prince, or State; and to provide and furnish the aforesaid Places, Cities, Towns, or Forts, with Magazines, Ordinance, Arms, Weapons, Ammunition and Stores of War; and by force of Arms to defend the same Trade, Navigation, Colonies, Cities, Towns, Forts, Plantations, and other Effects whatsoever; and likewise to make Reprizals, and to seek and take reparation of damage done by Sea or by Land; and to make and conclude Treaties of Peace and Commerce with Soveraign Princes, Estates, Rulers, Governours or Proprietors of the aforesaid Lands, Islands, Countries, or places in Asia, Africa or America.

And reserving to themselves five per Cent, or one twentieth part of the Lands, Mines, Minerals, Stones of value, precious Woods, and Fishings, have further conceded and granted unto us, the free and absolute Right and Property in and to all Such Lands, Islands, Colonies, Towns,

Forts and Plantations, as we shall come to, establish, or possess in manner aforesaid; as also to all manner of Treasures, Wealth, Riches, Profits, Mines, Minerals and Fishings, with the whole Product and Benefit thereof, as well under as above the Ground, as well in Rivers and Seas as in the Lands thereunto belonging; or for or by reason of the same in any sort, together with the right of Government and Admiralty thereof; as likewise that all manner of Persons who shall settle to inhabit, or be born in any such Plantations, Colonies, Cities, Towns, Factories, or Places, shall be, and be reputed as Natives of the Kingdom of Scotland. And generally the said Company have communicated unto us a Right to all the Powers, Properties and Privileges granted unto them by Act of Parliament, or otherwise howsoever, with Power to grant and delegate the same, and to permit and allow such sort of Trade, Commerce and Navigation unto the Plantations, Colonies, Cities, and Places of our Possession, as we shall think fit and convenient.

And the chief Captains and Supream Leaders of the People of Darien, in compliance with former Agreements, having now in most kind and obliging manner received us into their Friendship and Country with promise and contract to assist and join in defense thereof, against such as shall be their or our Enemies in any time to come: Which, besides its being one of the most healthful, rich, and fruitful Countries upon Earth, hath the advantage of being a narrow ISTHMUS, seated in the heighth of the World, between two vast Oceans, which renders it more convenient than any other for being the common Store-house of the insearchable and immense Treasures of the spacious South Seas, the door of Commerce to China and Japan, and, the Emporium and Staple for the Trade of both Indies.

And now by virtue of the before-mentioned Powers to us given, We do here settle, and in the name of GOD establish Our Selves: and in Honour and for the Memory of that most Ancient, and Renowned Name of our Mother Kingdom, We do, and will from hence-forward call this Country by the Name of Caledonia; and our selves, Successors; and Associates, by the name of Caledonians.

And suitable to the Weight and greatness of the Trust reposed, and the valuable Opportunity now in our hands, being firmly resolved to communicate and dispose thereof in the most just and equal manner for increasing the Dominions and Subjects of the King Our Soveraign Lord, the Honour and Wealth of our Country, as well as the benefit and advantage of those who now are, or may hereafter be concerned with us: We do hereby declare, That all manner of People soever, shall from hence-forward be equally free and alike capable of the said Properties,

Privileges, Protections, Immunities, and Rights of Government granted unto us; and the Merchants and Merchants Ships of all Nations, may freely come to and trade with us, without being liable in their Persons, Goods or Effects, to any manner of Capture, Confiscation, Seizure, Forfeiture, Attachment, Arrest, Restraint or Prohibition, for or by reason of any Embargo, breach of the Peace, Letters of Mark, or Reprizals, Declaration of War with any foreign Prince, Potentate or State, or upon any other account or pretence whatsoever.

And we do hereby not only grant and concede, and declare a general and equal freedom of Government and Trade to those of all Nations, who shall hereafter be of, or concerned with us; but also a full and free Liberty of Conscience in matter of Religion, so as the same be not understood to allow, connive at or indulge the balspheming of God's holy Name, or any of his Divine Attributes; or of the unhallowing or prophaning the Sabbath Day.

And finally, as the best and surest means to render any Government successful, durable, and happy, it shall (by the help of Almighty God) be ever our constant and chiefest care that all our further Constitutions, Laws, and Ordinances, be consonant and agreeable to the Holy Scripture, right Reason, and the Examples of the wisest and justest Nations, that from the Truth and Rightcon . . . thereof we may reasonably hope for and expect the Blessings of Prosperity and Increase.

By Order of the Council,
Hugh Ross, Secretary
New Edinburgh
Decemo. 18, 1698.

Source: Anonymous, *An Enquiry into the Causes of the Miscarriage of the Scots Colony at Darien or an Answer to a Libel Entituled* 'A Defence of the Scots Abdicating Darien'. *Submitted to the Consideration of the Good People of England*. Glasgow, 1700, pp. 67–9.

Appendix II

Articles of Agreement betwixt the Council of Caledonia and Captain Ephraim Pilkingtoun

WITNESSETH AS FOLLOWES.

First, The said Ephraim Pilkingtoun shall have and receive for the hyre of his Shalloop twelve full shares.

2d, The said Ephraim Pilkingtoun shall have and receive for himselfe two shares and a halfe.

3d, The Doctor shall have one hundred pieces of eight for his chest of Medicins, and one share in comon.

4th, The said Council reserves to themselves one tenth part of all the loading of any prize taken at sea – the wounded and disabled men being first provided for, and the like share of all booty taken upon land.

5. If any man be disabled in the service of the voyage, in so much that he be put from geting a future lyvlyhood, in such case the same man shall have and receive six hundred peeces of eight, or six able slaves, if so much be made in the said voyage.

6. All the remaining part of the profit of the voyage to be equaly divided amongst the men belonging to the vessels, share and part alike.

7. That the said Ephraim Pilkingtoun have his choice of first, second, or third prize taken in the voyage in the lieu of his, not exceeding three in number.

In virtue wherof, both parties have herto set their hands at Fort St Andrew the Elevinth day of March One thousand six hundred nynty nyn

Robert Jolly, J Ephr Pilkington

Source: John H. Burton (ed), *The Darien Papers: Being A Selection of Original Letters and Official Documents Relating to the Establishment of a Colony at Darien by the Company of Scotland Trading to Africa and the Indies. 1695–1700.* Edinburgh: Bannatyne Club, 1849, p. 101.

Bibliography

MANUSCRIPT SOURCES

England
Bodleian Library (Oxford)
MSS Rawlinson, A290 and A312

British Library (London)
ADD MS12403 Long, E., *Political History of Jamaica to 1717*
ADD MS12422 Barnham, Dr Henry, *The Civil History of Jamaica to the Year 1722*
ADD MS28903 Papers of J. Ellis, Vol. VIII, March–August 1699
ADD MS28904 Papers of J. Ellis, Vol. IX, September 1699–April 1700
ADD MS28905 Papers of J. Ellis, Vol. X, May–September 1700
ADD MS37992 W. Blathwayt Letter Book, 1698–1701
ADD MS40774 Vernon Papers, Vol. IV
ADD MS46542 Lexington Papers – letters and documents concerning the Council of Trade and Plantations of which he was a member, 1699–1702
Sloane MS 50 Voyages and Travels: journal of a voyage from S. Domingo to the wreck of a Spanish vessel off Porto Plato, and thence to England: 1686–1687

Kent History and Library Centre (Maidstone)
U1590 Stanhope of Chevening Manuscripts

National Archives (Kew)
ADM1 Admiralty Correspondence and Papers (Vols 1435, 1462, 1463, 2003, 2004, 2033, 5261)
ADM2 Admiralty, Out-Letters (Vol. 25)

ADM3 Admiralty, Minutes (Vol. 15)

ADM6 Admiralty Service Records (Vol. 5)

ADM7 Collection of Memos and Remarks on a Voyage to the West Indies (Vol. 833)

ADM33 Admiralty, Navy Board, Ships' Pay Books (Vols 204, 206, 207)

ADM36 Admiralty, Royal Navy Ships' Musters (Vol. 3378)

ADM51 Admiralty, Captains' Logs (Vols 341, 389, 571, 3892)

ADM52 Admiralty, Masters' Logs (Vols 34, 39)

ADM106 Admiralty, Navy Board Records (Vols 525, 533)

CO137 Colonial Office and Predecessors: Jamaica (Vols 4, 5, 44, 45, 48)

CO142 Colonial Office: Misc. Jamaica, Shipping Returns, 1680–1705 (Vol. 13)

CO324 Commissions, Instructions, Board of Trade Correspondence (Vol. 5)

SP32 Secretaries of State: State Papers Domestic, William and Mary (Vols 11, 12)

SP89 Secretaries of State: State Papers Foreign, Portugal (Vols 17, 18)

SP94 Secretaries of State: State Papers Foreign, Spain (Vols 74, 75, 212, 229)

SP103 Secretaries of State: State Papers Foreign, Treaty Papers (Vol. 66–1)

SP104 Secretary of State's Letter Book 1695–1701 (Vol. 198)

SP113 State Papers: Gazettes and Pamphlets: Treaties (Vol. 6)

T4 Treasury: Reference Book of Applications (Vol. 7)

T70 Company of Royal Adventurers of England (Vols 61, 119)

National Maritime Museum/Caird Library (Greenwich)
Lieutenants' Logs (ADM/L/F/28, ADM/L/G/47, ADM/L/M/21)
Phillipps Collection (PLA/23)

Jamaica
National Library of Jamaica (Kingston)
J28L434 Journals of the Assembly of Jamaica (Vol. 1)
MS60 Legislative Council Minutes (Vol. 12)
MS1049 Notes on the Illicit Trade Carried on by Sloops from Jamaica with the Spanish in the Gulf of Mexico

Scotland
Collection of Blair Castle (Perthshire)
NRAS 234, Box 45, Bundle 1

National Records of Scotland (Edinburgh)
GD1/649/2 Diary of George Home of Kimmerghame

GD26/13/119 Petition to the King by the Council-General of the Company of Scotland
GD406/1 Hamilton Papers
GD446 Papers of the Douglas Family of Strathendry, Fife
PA7/17 Parliamentary Papers
PC12/1700 Records of the Privy Council

National Library of Scotland (Edinburgh)
Adv. MS 83.2.5–83.9.3 Darien Papers
MS70
MS846 Journey of the *Unicorn*
MS1914 Darien Company
Ch.A.238–42 Company of Scotland Letter Book
RY.II.b.8 *The Edinburgh Gazette*

Royal Bank of Scotland Archives (Edinburgh)
Manuscripts of the Company of Scotland

University of Edinburgh Library, Centre for Research Collections
MS Laing 262, *Memorial or Diary of Mr Francis Borland*, 1661–1722

University of Glasgow Library, Special Collections
Spencer Collection, MS General 1681, 1685, 1686, 1687

Spain
Archivo General de Indias (Seville)
Casa de la Contratación, Legajos 4887, 4987, 5726A
Audiencia de Lima, Legajos 91, 407, 520
Audiencia de Mexico, Legajo 61
Audiencia de Panamá, Legajos 105, 109, 110, 113, 159, 160, 161, 163, 164, 165, 166, 167, 175, 177, 181, 182, 215, 243, 255, 306, 307
Audiencia de Santa Fé, Legajos 48, 79, 435
Audiencia de Santo Domingo, Legajo 375
Contaduría, Legajo 1780A
Escribania de Cámara, Legajos 477A, 622A–C, 1048B, 1108B, 1179A, 1192
Indiferente General, Legajos 316, 2015
Mapas y Planos, Panamá, Legajos 119, 119BIS, 120, 149, 255

Archivo General de Simancas
Estado, Legajos 3091, 3944, 3970, 3971, 3996, 4183

Secretaria del Despacho de Guerra, Legajos 7054, 7242

Archivo Historico Nacional (Madrid)
Estado, Legajos 195, 702, 1778

United States
Huntington Library (San Marino, California)
Huntington Manuscripts, West Indies: MS32282, MS32283
Papers of John Egerton, 3rd Earl of Bridgewater, 1594–1700: MS9714
Papers of William Blathwayt, 1657–1770: MSBL6, MSBL7, MSBL8, MSBL9, MSBL10

Massachusetts Historical Society (Boston)
Francis Russell Hart Collection

PRINTED MANUSCRIPT COLLECTIONS AND INDICES

Bateson, Edward (ed.), *Calendar of State Papers, Domestic Series, of the Reign of William III, 1699–1700, Preserved in the Public Record Office* (London: His Majesty's Stationery Office, 1937).

Bateson, Edward (ed.), *Calendar of State Papers, Domestic Series, William III, April 1700–March 1702, Preserved in the Public Record Office* (London: His Majesty's Stationery Office, 1937).

Burton, John H. (ed.), *The Darien Papers: Being a Selection of Original Letters and Official Documents Relating to the Establishment of a Colony at Darien by the Company of Scotland Trading to Africa and the Indies, 1695–1700* (Edinburgh: Bannatyne, 1849).

Camacho Sánchez, Miguel, Alberto Zabaleta Lombana and Pedro C. Covo Torres, *Bibliografía general de Cartagena de Indias: desde el siglo XV hasta 2007, tomo III* (Cartagena de Indias: Ediciones Pluma de Mompox, 2007).

Collections of the Connecticut Historical Society, Volume XXIV (Hartford, CT: Connecticut Historical Society, 1932).

Cuervo, Antonio (ed.), *Colección de documentos inéditos sobre la geografía y la historia de Colombia, Sección 1–Geografía y viajes, tomo I, Costa Atlántica* (Bogotá: Imprenta de Vapor Zalamera Hermanos, 1891).

Cuervo, Antonio and Francisco Javier Vergara y Velasco (eds), *Colección de documentos inéditos sobre la geografía y la historia de Colombia, Sección 1–Geografía y viajes, tomo II, Costa Pacifica, provincias litorales y campañas de los conquistadores* (Bogotá: Casa Editorial de J. J. Perez, 1892).

González Palencia, Ángel, *Extracto del catálogo de los documentos del Consejo de Indias conservados en la Sección de Consejos del Archivo Histórico Nacional*, (Madrid: Tip. de la 'Revista de Archivos, Bibliotecas y Museos', 1920).

Goslinga, Marian, *A Bibliography of the Caribbean* (Lanham, MD: Scarecrow Press, 1996).

Grant, James (ed.), *Seafield Correspondence from 1685 to 1708* (Edinburgh: Scottish History Society, 1912).

Grimblot, Paul (ed.), *Letters of William III and Louis XIV and of Their Ministers, Illustrative of the Domestic and Foreign Politics of England from the Peace of Ryswick to The Accession of Philip V of Spain, 1697 to 1700* (London: n. pub., 1848).

Headlam, Cecil (ed.), *Calendar of State Papers, Colonial Series, America and West Indies, 1699. Also Addenda,1621–1698. Preserved in the Public Record Office* (London: His Majesty's Stationery Office, 1908).

Headlam, Cecil (ed.), *Calendar of State Papers, Colonial Series. America and West Indies, 1700. Preserved in the Public Record Office* (London: His Majesty's Stationery Office, 1910).

Ingram, K. E., *Manuscript Sources for the History of the West Indies: with Special Reference to Jamaica in the National Library of Jamaica and Supplementary Sources in the West Indies, North America, and United Kingdom and Elsewhere* (Barbados: University of West Indies Press, 2000).

Insh, George P. (ed.), *Papers Relating to the Ships and Voyages of the Company of Scotland Trading to Africa and the Indies 1696–1707* (Edinburgh: Scottish History Society, 1924).

James, G. P. R. (ed.), *Letters Illustrative of the Reign of William III from 1696 to 1708 Addressed to the Duke of Shrewsbury, by James Vernon, Esq., Secretary of State* (London: H. Colburn, 1841)

Maidment, James (ed.), *Analecta Scotica: Collections Illustrative of the Civil, Ecclesiastical, and Literary History of Scotland. Chiefly from Original Mss. First Series–Second Series* (Edinburgh: T. G. Stevenson, 1834–37).

McCormick, Joseph (ed.), *State-papers and Letters, Addressed to William Carstares, Confidential Secretary to K. William During the Whole of his Reign: Relating to Public Affairs in Great-Britain, To which is Prefixed the Life of Mr Carstares* (Edinburgh: printed for W. Strahan and T. Cadell, London and John Balfour, Edinburgh, 1774).

Moreyra y Paz-Soldán, Manuel and Guillermo Céspedes del Castillo (eds), *Virreinato peruano documentos para su historia, Colección de cartas de virreyes, Conde de la Monclova, tomo II (1695–1698)* (Lima: Instituto Histórico del Perú, 1955).

Moreyra y Paz-Soldán, Manuel and Guillermo Céspedes del Castillo (eds), *Virreinato peruano documentos para su Historia, Colección de cartas de virreyes, Conde de la Monclova, tomo III (1699–1705)* (Lima: Instituto Histórico del Perú, 1955).

Nelson, William and A. V. D. Honeyman (eds), *New Jersey Archives, 1st Series, Extracts from American Newspapers, Relating to New Jersey, 1704–1775, Volume I, 1704–1739* (Trenton, NJ: n. pub., 1894).

Ortega Ricaurte, Enrique, *Misiones colombianas en los archivos europeos* (Mexico, D. F.: Instituto Panamericano de Geografía e Historia, 1951).

Paz, Julián and Ricardo Magdaleno Redondo, *Archivo General de Simancas, Catalogo XVII, Secretaría de Estado, Documentos relativos a Inglaterra (1254–1834)* (Madrid: National Government Publication, 1947).

Plaza Bores, Angel de la and Ascención de la Plaza Santiago, *Archivo General de Simancas, guia del investigador* (Madrid: Ministerio de Cultura, 1980).

Sánchez Belda, Luis, *Guia del Archivo Historico Nacional* (Madrid: Dirección General de Archivos y Bibliotecas, 1958).

Scott, John, *A Bibliography of Printed Documents and Books Relating to the Darien Company* (Edinburgh: n. pub., 1904).

Scott, W. R., *Scottish Economic Literature to 1800, a List of Authorities Prepared for the Committee* (Glasgow: William Hodge, 1911).

Sewall, Samuel, *Letter-book, Volume 1* (Boston, MA, Massachusetts Historical Society, 1886).

Stanhope, Alexander, *Spain under Charles the Second, Or, Extracts from the Correspondence of the Hon. Alexander Stanhope, British Minister at Madrid, 1690–1699. From the Originals at Chevening* (London: John Murray, 1840).

Thomas, Daniel and Lynn Case (eds), *Guide to the Diplomatic Archives of Western Europe* (Philadelphia: University of Pennsylvania Press, 1959).

Thomas, M. (ed.), *The Diary of Samuel Sewall, Volume I: 1674–1708* (New York: Farrar, Straus and Giroux, 1973).

Walne, Peter (ed.), *A Guide to Manuscript Sources for the History of Latin America and the Caribbean in the British Isles* (London: Oxford University Press 1973).

Whitehead, William A., Frederick Ricord and William Nelson (eds), *New Jersey Archives, First Series, Volume II, Documents Relating to the Colonial History of New Jersey (1631–1776)* (Newark, NJ: printed at the Daily journal establishment, 1881).

CONTEMPORARY PUBLISHED PAMPHLETS AND CORRESPONDENCE

Allen, Robert, *An Essay on the Nature and Methods of Carrying on a Trade to the South Sea, by Robert Allen, Who Resided Some Years in the Kingdom of Peru* (London: John Baker, 1712).

Allen, Robert, *Essay on the Nature and Methods of Carrying on a Trade to the South Sea, a New Trade Laid Open from the Islands of Tobago, Granados, . . . to the Spanish Main, in the Kingdom of Peru, and from Cape Florida to the Havana and La Vera Cruz, in the Kingdom of Mexico, By a Gentleman Who Resided Many Years in Both Kingdoms* (London: Mrs Hinxman and D. Wilson, 1763).

Allen, Robert, *The Great Importance of the Havannah, Set Forth in an Essay on the Nature and Methods of Carrying on a Trade to the South Sea, and the Spanish West Indies. By Robert Allen, Esq.; Who Resided Some Years in the Kingdom of Peru* (London: J. Hinxman and D. Wilson, 1762).

Anonymous, *An Enquiry into the Causes of the Miscarriage of the Scots Colony at Darien or an Answer to a Libel Entituled* 'A Defence of the Scots Abdicating Darien'. *Submitted to the Consideration of the Good People of England* (Glasgow: n. pub., 1700).

Anonymous (with English trans. by G. Rivera), *Gazeta extraordinaria del feliz successo: que las Armas Españolas invieron en el desaleja-miento del Escoces que se avia fortificado en el Playon, Costa de Portovelo, Provincia del Darien en el Reyno de Tierra firme, á 11 de Abril de este presente año 1700* (Lima: Imprenta de Ioseph de Contreras, 1700).

Borland, Francis, *The History of Darien 1700* (Glasgow: John Bryce, 1779).

Byres, James, *Letter to a Friend at Edinburgh from Roterdam* (Edinburgh?: n. pub., 1702).

Gentleman Lately Arrived, *The History of Caledonia: or, The Scots Colony in Darien in the West Indies: With an Account of the Manners of the Inhabitants, and the Riches of the Countrey* (London: John Nutt, 1699).

Herries (Harris), Walter and James Hodges, *A Defence of the Scots Abdicating Darien: Including an Answer to the Defence of the Scot's*

Settlement There/authore Brittano sed Dunensi (Edinburgh?: John Nutt, 1700).

Herries (Harris), Walter, *A New Darien Artifice Laid Open; in a Notable Instance of Captain Maclean's Name Being Used (in the Flying Post, February 11 and 13 1700/01) to Vouch for the Caledonian Company, after that Gentleman Hath Been Persecuted by Them These Thirteen Months Past for Vouching Against Them* (London: n. pub., 1701).

Herries (Harris), Walter, *A Short Vindication of Phil. Scot's Defence of the Scots Abdicating Darien Being in Answer to the Challenge of the Author of the Defence of that Settlement, to Prove the Spanish Title to Darien, by Inheritance, Marriage, Donation, Purchase, Reversion, Surrender or Conquest: with a Prefatory Reply to the False and Scurrilous Aspersions, of the New Author of, the Just and Modest Vindication, &c., and Some Animadversions on the Material Part of It, Relating to the Title of Darien* (London: n. pub., 1700).

Herries (Harris), Walter, *An Enquiry into the Caledonian Project, with a Defence of England's Procedure (in point of Equity) in Relation Thereunto, in a Friendly Letter from London, to a Member of the Scots African and Indian Company in Edinburgh, to Guard againft Paffion* (London: John Nutt, 1701).

Philo-Caledon, George Ridpath, Andrew Fletcher and Archibald Foyer, *A Defence of the Scots Settlement at Darien: with an Answer to the Spanish Memorial Against It. And Arguments to Prove that it is the Interest of England to Join with the Scots, and Protect It. To Which is Added, a Description of the Country and a Particular Account of the Scots Colony* (Edinburgh: n. pub., 1699).

Ridpath, George, *An Enquiry into the Causes of the Miscarriage of the Scots Colony at Darien, or, An Answer to a Libel Entitled A Defence of the Scots Abdicating Darien Submitted to the Consideration of the Good People of England* (Glasgow: n. pub., 1700).

Ridpath, George, *Scotland's Grievances Relating to Darien etc., Humbly Offered to the Consideration of the Parliament* (Edinburgh?: n. pub., 1700).

BOOKS

Alba C., Manuel María, *Cronología de los gobernantes de Panamá 1510–1967* (Panama: n. pub., 1967).

Alsedo y Herrera, Dionisio de and Justo Zaragoza, *Piraterías Y agresiones de los Ingleses Y de otros pueblos de Europa en la América Española desde el siglo XVI al XVIII* (Madrid: Hernándes, 1883).

Anderson, C. L. G., *Old Panama and Castilla del Oro, a Narrative History of the Discovery, Conquest, and Settlement by the Spaniards of Panama, Darien, Veragua, Santo Domingo, Santa Marta, Cartagena, Nicaragua, and Peru: Including the Four Voyages of Columbus to America* (Boston, MA: The Page Company, 1911).

Araúz, Celestino Andrés, *Panamá y sus relaciones internacionales, Vols 1 y 2* (Panama: Editorial Universitaria, 1994).

Araúz, Celestino Andrés, Argelia Tello Burgos and Alfredo Figueroa Navarro, *Manual de historia de Panamá, tomo I* (Bethania, Panama: Litho Editorial Chen, 2006).

Arbell, Mordechal, *The Portuguese Jews of Jamaica* (Kingston, Jamaica: Canoe Press, 2000).

Arciniegas, Germán, *Caribbean: Sea of the New World*, trans. by H. de Onis (New York: A. A. Knopf, 1946).

Armitage, David and Michael Braddick (eds), *The British Atlantic World 1500–1800, 2nd ed.* (Basingstoke: Palgrave Macmillan, 2009).

Bailyn, Bernard, *The New England Merchants in the Seventeenth Century* (Cambridge, MA: Harvard University Press, 1955).

Baker, Emerson and John Reid, *The New England Knight, Sir William Phips, 1651–1695* (Toronto: University of Toronto Press, 1998).

Bakewell, Peter, *A History of Latin America, Empires and Sequels 1450–1930* (Cambridge, MA: Blackwell Publishers, 1997).

Barbour, James, *A History of William Paterson and the Darien Company: with Illustrations and Appendices* (Edinburgh: W. Blackwood and Sons, 1907).

Baxter, Stephen, *William III* (London: Longmans, 1966).

Bécker, Jerónimo and José María Rivas Groot, *El Nuevo Reino de Granada en el siglo XVIII* (Madrid: Imp. del Asilo de húerfanos del S.C. de Jésus, 1921).

Benjamin, Thomas, *The Atlantic World-Europeans, Africans, Indians and Their Shared History, 1400–1900* (Cambridge: Cambridge University Press, 2009).

Bourne, Ruth, *Queen Anne's Navy in the West Indies* (New Haven: Yale University Press, 1939).

Bridenbaugh, Carl and Roberta Bridenbaugh, *No Peace Beyond The Line: the English in the Caribbean 1624–1690* (New York: Oxford University Press, 1972).

Bridges, George, *The Annals of Jamaica* (London: J. Murray, 1828).

Brooks, George, *Eurafricans in Western Africa: Commerce, Social Status, Gender and Religious Observance from the Sixteenth to the Eighteenth Century* (Athens, OH: Ohio University Press, 2003).

Browne, Patrick, *The Civil and Natural History of Jamaica* (London: B. White and Son, 1789).

Buisseret, David, *The Mapmaker's Quest; Depicting New Worlds in Renaissance Europe* (Oxford: Oxford University Press, 2003).

Burnet, Gilbert, *History of His Own Time, Volume II, from the Revolution to the Conclusion of the Treaty of Peace at Utrecht in the Reign of Queen Anne* (London: Thomas Ward, 1734).

Burns, Alan, *History of the British West Indies, 2nd ed.* (London: G. Allen and Unwin, 1965).

Campbell, John, *Lives of the Admirals, and Other Eminent British Seamen: Containing Their Personal Histories, and a Detail of All Their Public Services; Including a New and Accurate Naval History from the Earliest Account of Time; and Clearly Proving by a Continued Series of Facts, our Uninterrupted Claim to, and Enjoyment of Our Seas; Interspersed with Many Curious Passages Relating to Our Discoveries, Plantations, and Commerce; Supported by Proper Authorities* (London: Osborne, 1761).

Carles, Rubén D., *220 años del período colonial en Panamá* (Panama: Imprenta Nacional, 1959).

Castillero Calvo, Alfredo, *Conquista, evangelización y resistencia, triunfo o fracaso de la política indigenista?* (Panama: Instituto Nacional de Cultura, 1995).

Castillero Calvo, Alfredo, *Historia general de Panamá: Volumen 1, Tomo 1- Las sociedades originarias, el orden colonial* (Panama: Comité Nacional del Centenario de la República, 2004).

Castillero Reyes, Ernesto and J. Conte Porras, *Historia de la comunicación interoceánica y de su influencia en la formación y en el desarrollo de la entidad nacional panameña* (Panama: Producciones Erlizca, 1999).

Castillo Mathieu, Nicolás, *Los Gobernadores de Cartagena de Indias, 1504–1810* (Bogotá: Academia Colombiana de Historia, 1998).

Clarke, Erskine, *Our Southern Zion, a History of Calvinism in the South Carolina Low Country, 1690–1990* (Tuscaloosa: University of Alabama Press, 1996).

Crouse, Nellis, *The French Struggle for the West Indies, 1665–1713* (New York: Octagon Books, 1966).

Crowhurst, Patrick, *The Defence of British Trade, 1689–1815* (Folkestone: Dawson, 1977).

Cullen, Edward, *Isthmus of Darien Ship Canal, with a Full History of the Scotch Colony of Darien, Several Maps, Views of the Country, and Original Documents* (London: E. Wilson, 1853).

Cundall, Frank, *The Darien Venture* (New York: The Hispanic Society of America, 1926).

Davenport, Frances (ed.), *European Treaties Bearing on the History of the United States and its Dependencies, Volume II 1650–1697* (Washington, DC: Carnegie Institution of Washington, 1929).

Davenport, Frances (ed.), *European Treaties Bearing on the History of the United States and its Dependencies, Volume III 1698–1715* (Washington, DC: Carnegie Institution of Washington, 1934).

Delevante, Marilyn and Anthony Alberga, *The Island of One People – an Account of the History of the Jews of Jamaica* (Kingston, Jamaica: Ian Randle, 2008).

Devine, T. M., *The Scottish Nation* (New York: Viking, 1999).

Earle, Peter, *Sailors: English Merchant Seamen 1650–1725* (London: Methuen, 1998).

Elliott, John, *Imperial Spain 1469–1716* (New York: St Martin's Press, 1964).

Elliott, John, *Spain and Its World 1500–1700, Selected Essays* (New Haven: Yale University Press, 1989).

Elliott, John, *Empires of the Atlantic World: Britain and Spain in America, 1492–1830* (New Haven: Yale University Press, 2006).

Ferguson, William, *Scotland's Relations with England: Survey to 1707* (Edinburgh: Saltire Society, 1994).

Fernández Nadal, Carmen María, *La política exterior de la monarquía de Carlos II-el Consejo de Estado y la Embajada en Londres, 1665–1700* (Gijon: Ateneo Jovellanos, 2009).

Fisher, John, *The Economic Aspects of Spanish Imperialism in America, 1492–1810* (Liverpool: Liverpool University Press, 1997).

Fisher, Lillian, *Viceregal Administration in the Spanish-American Colonies* (Berkeley, CA: University of California Press, 1926).

Forrester, Andrew, *The Man Who Saw the Future* (New York: Texere, 2004).

Foster, George, *Doctors' Commons: Its Courts and Registries* (London: Reeves, 1871).

Francis, A. D., *The Methuens and Portugal 1691–1708* (Cambridge: Cambridge University Press, 1966).

Fraser, Walter, *Lowcountry Hurricanes: Three Centuries of Storms at Sea and Ashore* (Athens, GA: University of Georgia Press, 2006).

Fry, Michael, *The Scottish Empire* (Edinburgh: Birlinn, 2001).

Fry, Michael, *The Union: England, Scotland and the Treaty of 1707* (Edinburgh: Birlinn, 2006).

Gallup-Diaz, Ignacio, *The Door of the Seas and the Key to the Universe: Indian Politics and Imperial Rivalry in the Darién, 1640–1750* (New York: Columbia University Press, 2004).

Galvin, Peter, *Patterns of Pillage: a Geography of Caribbean-based Piracy in Spanish America, 1536–1718* (New York: Lang, 1999).

García Casares, Joaquín, *Historia del Darién: cuevas, cunas, españoles, afros, presencia y actualidad de los chocoes* (Panama: Editorial Universitaria Carlos Manuel Gasteazoro, 2008).

Góngora, Mario, *Studies in the History of Spanish America* (Cambridge: Cambridge University Press, 1975).

Graham, Eric, *Seawolves: Pirates and the Scots* (Edinburgh: Birlinn, 2005).

Grahn, Lance, *The Political Economy of Smuggling; Regional Informal Economies in Early Bourbon New Granada* (Boulder, CO: Westview Press, 1997).

Grosjean, Alexia and Steve Murdoch (eds), *Scottish Communities Abroad in the Early Modern Period* (Leiden: Brill, 2005).

Hamilton, Douglas, *Scotland, the Caribbean and the Atlantic World, 1750–1820* (Manchester: Manchester University Press, 2005).

Hamshere, Cyril, *The British in the Caribbean* (London: Weidenfeld and Nicolson, 1972).

Haring, Clarence, *The Buccaneers in the West Indies in the XVII Century* (New York: E. P. Dutton, 1910).

Haring, Clarence, *Trade and Navigation between Spain and the Indies in the Time of the Hapsburgs* (Cambridge, MA: Harvard University Press, 1918).

Haring, Clarence, *The Spanish Empire in America* (New York: Harcourt, Brace and World, 1947).

Hart, Francis, *Admirals of the Caribbean* (Cambridge, MA: The Riverside Press, 1922).

Hart, Francis, *The Disaster of Darien, the Story of the Scots Settlement and the Causes of its Failure 1699–1701* (Cambridge, MA: The Riverside Press, 1929).

Hattendorf, John, *England in the War of the Spanish Succession: a Study of the English View and Conduct of Grand Strategy, 1702–1712* (New York: Garland, 1987).

Herzog, Tamar, *Defining Nations – Immigrants and Citizens in Early Modern Spain and Spanish America* (New Haven: Yale University Press, 2003).

Hewatt, Alexander, *An Historical Account of the Rise and Progress of the Colonies of South Carolina and Georgia, Vol. 1* (London: A. Donaldson, 1779).

Holton, Robert, *Globalization and the Nation-state* (New York: St Martin's Press, 1998).

Host, Georg, *Efterretninger om Oen Sanct Thomas og dens Governeurer, optegnede der paa Landet fra 1769 indtil 1776* (Copenhagen: N. Moller og son, 1791).

Houston, James, *Memoirs of the Life and Travels of James Houston, M.D. from the Year 1690 to this Present Year 1747 . . . Collected and Written by His Own Hand* (London: Jacob Bickerstaff, 1747).

Howarth, David, *Panama, Four Hundred Years of Dreams and Cruelty* (London: McGraw-Hill, 1966).

Howe, James, *Chiefs, Scribes, and Ethnographers, Kuna Culture from Inside and Out* (Austin: University of Texas Press, 2009).

Insh, George, *The Company of Scotland Trading to Africa and the Indies* (London: Charles Scribner's Sons, 1932).

Insh, George, *Historian's Odyssey: the Romance of the Quest for the Records of the Darien Company* (Edinburgh: Moray Press, 1938).

Jacobsen, Gertrude, *William Blathwayt: a Late Seventeenth-century English Administrator* (New Haven: Yale University Press, 1932).

Joyce, L. E. Elliott (ed.), *A New Voyage and Description of the Isthmus of America by Lionel Wafer, Surgeon on Buccaneering Expeditions in Darien, the West Indies, and the Pacific from 1680 to 1688* (Oxford: Hakluyt Society, 1934).

Kamen, Henry, *The War of Succession in Spain 1700–15* (Bloomington: Indiana University Press, 1969).

Kamen, Henry, *Spain in the Later Seventeenth Century 1665–1700* (London: Longman, 1980).

Kamen, Henry, *Spain 1469–1714, a Society of Conflict, 2nd ed.* (London: Longman, 1991).

Kamen, Henry, *Spain's Road to Empire: The Making of a World Power 1492-1763* (London: Penguin, 2003).

Klooster, Wim, *Illicit Riches – Dutch Trade in the Caribbean, 1648–1795* (Leiden: KITLV Press, 1998).

Koot, Christian, *Empire at the Periphery, British Colonists, Anglo-Dutch Trade, and the Development of the British Atlantic, 1621–1713* (New York: New York University Press, 2011).

Lane, Kris, *Pillaging the Empire; Piracy in the Americas 1500–1700* (Armonk, NY: M. E. Sharpe, 1998).

Langdon-Davies, John, *Carlos: the King Who Would Not Die* (Englewood Cliffs, NJ: Prentice-Hall, 1962).

Lawson, John, *A New Voyage to Carolina; Containing the Exact Description and Natural History of that Country: Together with the Present State Thereof. And a Journal of a Thousand Miles, Travel'd Thro' Several Nations of Indians. Gving a Particular Account of their Customs, Maners, &c.* (London: n. pub., 1709).

Lemaitre, Eduardo, *Historia General de Cartagena, tomo II, La colonia* (Bogotá: Banco de la República, 1983).

Lenman, Bruce (ed.), *Military Engineers and the Development of the Early–Modern European State* (Dundee: Dundee University Press, 2013).

Leslie, Charles, *A New History of Jamaica, from the Earliest Accounts, to the Taking of Porto Bello by Vice-Admiral Vernon* (London: J. Hodges, 1740).

Long, Edward, *The History of Jamaica: or General Survey of the Ancient and Modern State of that Island: with Reflections on Its Situation, Settlements, Inhabitants, Climate, Products, Commerce, Laws, and Government* (London: T. Lowndes, 1774).

Ludlum, David, *Early American Hurricanes 1492–1870* (Boston, MA: American Meteorological Society, 1963).

Lynch, John, *Spain under the Hapsburgs, Volume Two: Spain and America, 1598–1700* (New York: Oxford University Press, 1969).

Lynch, John, *New Worlds, a Religious History of Latin America* (New Haven, CT: Yale University Press, 2012).

Lyons, Adam, *The 1711 Expedition to Quebec: Politics and the Limitations of British Global Strategy* (London: Bloomsbury, 2013).

MacKay, Ruth, *Lazy, Improvident People* (Ithaca, NY: Cornell University Press, 2006).

Marchena Fernández, Juan, *La Institución militar en Cartagena de Indias en el siglo XVIII* (Seville: Escuela de Estudios Hispano-Americanos, 1982).

Marco Dorta, Enrique, *Cartagena de Indias: puerto y plaza fuerte* (Cartagena, Colombia: Alfonso Amadó, 1960).

Marsh, Richard, *White Indians of Darien* (New York: G. P. Putnam's Sons, 1934).

Martínez Cutillas, Pedro, *Colonial Panama, History and Images* (Madrid: Ediciones San Marcos, 2006).

Martínez Reyes, Gabriel, *Finanzas de las 44 diócesis de Indias 1515–1816* (Bogotá: Ediciones Tercer Mundo, 1980).

Martínez Shaw, Carlos, *La emigración a América (1492–1824)* (Colombres, Asturias: Archivo de Indianos, 1994).

Mathieson, William, *Scotland and the Union, a History of Scotland from 1695 to 1741* (Glasgow: J. Maclehose, 1905).

Matson, Cathy, *Merchants & Empire, Trading in Colonial New York* (Baltimore, MD: Johns Hopkins University Press, 1998).

McCrady, Edward, *The History of South Carolina under the Proprietary Government, 1670–1719* (New York: Macmillan, 1901).

McCullough, David, *The Path between the Seas* (New York: Simon and Schuster, 1977).

McLachlan, Jean, *Trade and Peace with Old Spain, 1667–1750: a Study of the Influence of Commerce on Anglo-Spanish Diplomacy in the First Half of the Eighteenth Century* (Cambridge, MA: The University Press, 1974).

McNeill, J. R., *Mosquito Empires: Ecology and War in the Greater Caribbean, 1620–1914* (Cambridge: Cambridge University Press, 2010).

M'Crie, Thomas (ed.), *Memoirs of Mr William Veitch and George Brysson, Written by Themselves: with Other Narratives Illustrative of the History of Scotland, from the Restoration to the Revolution* (Edinburgh: William Blackwood, 1835).

Means, Philip, *The Spanish Main, Focus of Envy 1492–1700* (New York: C. Scribner's Sons, 1935).

Mijers, Esther and David Onnekink (eds), *Redefining William III: the Impact of the King-Stadholder in International Context* (Aldershot: Ashgate, 2007).

Mirow, Matthew, *Latin American Law, a History of Private Law and Institutions in Spanish America* (Austin: University of Texas Press, 1962).

Moses, Bernard, *The Establishment of Spanish Rule in America* (New York: G. P. Putnam's Sons, 1907).

Nordensklold, Erland, *An Historical and Ethnological Survey of the Cuna Indians/by Erland Nordensklold, in Collaboration with the Cuna Indian, Ruben Pérez Kantule: Arranged and Edited from the Posthumous Ms. and Notes, and Original Indian Documents at the Gothenburg Ethnographical Museum by Henry Wassén* (New York: AMS Press, 1979).

Oldmixon, John, *Memoirs of North-Britain; Taken from Authentick Writings, as Well Manuscript as Printed.: In Which it is Prov'd, that the Scots Nation have Always Been Zealous in the Defence of the*

Protestant Religion and Liberty. Containing, I. An Account of the Cruelties Exercis'd by the Tories, against the Protestants, in King Charles's and King James's Reigns. II. Of the Trials and Murder of the Earl of Argyle, and Robert Bailie of Jerviswood Esq; III. Of the Revolution, and Dundee's Rebellion. IV. Of Glenco's Death, and the Darien Colony; with a Vindication of King William's Honour and Justice Therein. V. Of the Designs of the Jacobites in Opposing the Union, and of Their Invasion-plot after It. VI. The Agreement between the English and Scots Tories, since the Change of the Old Ministry, in Their Attempts against the Protestant Succession. (London: J. Baker, 1715).

Olsen, Margaret, *Slavery and Salvation in Colonial Cartagena de Indias* (Gainesville: University Press of Florida, 2004).

Omar, Jaén Suárez, *La población del Istmo de Panamá desde el siglo XVI al XX, estudio sobre la población y los modos de organización de las economías, las sociedades y los espacios geograficos* (Panama: Impresa de la Nación, 1978).

Oviedo, Gonzalo Fernández, *Writing from the Edge of the World: the Memoirs of Darién, 1514–1527,* trans. by G. F. Dille (Tuscaloosa: University of Alabama Press, 2006).

Palacios Preciado, Jorge, *La Trata de Negros por Cartagena de Indias 1650–1750* (Tunja, Colombia: Universidad Pedagógica y Tecnológica de Colombia, 1973).

Pares, Richard, *War and Trade in the West Indies 1739–1763* (Oxford: Clarendon Press, 1936).

Pares, Richard, *Yankees and Creoles. The Trade between North America and the West Indies before the American Revolution.* (Cambridge, MA: Harvard University Press, 1956).

Parnell, Arthur, *The War of the Succession in Spain during the Reign of Queen Anne 1702–1711 Based on Original Manuscripts and Contemporary Records* (London: G. Bell, 1905).

Parry. J. H., *The Spanish Seaborne Empire* (London: Hutchinson, 1966).

Pereira de Padilla, Joaquina and Ricardo Segura (eds), *Aproximación a la obra de Reina Torres de Arauz* (Panama: Instituto Nacional de Cultura, 1983).

Prebble, John, *Darien; the Scottish Dream of Empire* (Edinburgh: Birlinn, 2000).

Preston, Diana and Michael Preston, *A Pirate of Exquisite Mind-Explorer, Naturalist, and Buccaneer: the Life of William Dampier* (New York: Berkley Books, 2004).

Price, Richard (ed.), *Maroon Societies, Rebel Slave Communities in the Americas* (Baltimore, MD: Johns Hopkins University Press, 1979).

Rahn-Philips, Carla, *The Treasure of the San José; Death at Sea in the War of the Spanish Succession* (Baltimore, MD: Johns Hopkins University Press, 2007).

Riley, P. W. J., *King William and the Scottish Politicians* (Edinburgh: J. Donald, 1979).

Ritchie, Robert C., *Captain Kidd and the War against the Pirates* (Cambridge, MA: Harvard University Press, 1986).

Roberts, Orlando, *Narrative of Voyages and Excursions of the East Coast and in the Interior of Central America* (Edinburgh: Constable and Company, 1827).

Rojas y Arrieta, Guillermo, *History of the Bishops of Panama* (Panama: Imprenta de la Academia, 1929).

Romoli, Kathleen, *Balboa of Darién: Discoverer of the Pacific* (New York: Doubleday, 1953).

Rose, Craig, *England in the 1690s: Revolution, Religion and War* (Oxford: Blackwell Publishers, 1999).

Schafer, Ernesto, *El Consejo real y supremo de las Indias: su historia, organización y labor administrativa hasta la terminación de la Casa de Austria, Tomo 1: Historia y organización del Consejo y de la Casa de la Contratación de las Indias* (Seville: Centro de Estudios de Historia de América, 1935).

Schafer, Ernesto, *El Consejo real y supremo de las Indias: Su historia, organización y labor administrativa hasta la terminación de la Casa de Austria, Tomo II: La labor del Consejo de Indias en la administratción colonial* (Seville: Escuela de Estudios Hispano-Americanos, 1947).

Serrera Contreras, Ramón María, *La América de los Habsburgo (1517–1700)* (Seville: Universidad de Sevilla, 2011).

Severino de Santa Teresa, Father, *Historia documentada de la iglesia en Urabá y el Darién, desde el descubrimiento hasta nuestros días, volumen IV, segunda parte, 1550–1810* (Bogotá: Editorial Kelly, 1956).

Smout, T. C., *Scottish Trade on the Eve of Union 1660–1707* (Edinburgh: Oliver and Boyd, 1963).

Sojo Zambrano, José Raimundo, *El comercio en la historia de Colombia* (Bogotá: Cámara de Comercio de Bogotá, 1970).

Squibb, G. D., *Doctors' Commons, a History of the College of Advocates and Doctors of Law* (Oxford: Clarendon Press, 1977).

Stein, Stanley and Barbara Stein, *Silver, Trade and War – Spain and America in the Making of Early Modern Europe* (Baltimore, MD: Johns Hopkins University Press, 2000).

Storrs, Christopher, *The Resilience of the Spanish Monarchy 1665–1700* (Oxford: Oxford University Press, 2006).

Thompson, I. A. A. and Bartolomé Yun Casalilla (eds), *The Castilian Crisis of the Seventeenth Century: New Perspectives on the Economic and Social History of Seventeenth-century Spain* (Cambridge: Cambridge University Press, 1994).

Thompson, William, *The Emergence of the Global Political Economy* (London: Routledge, 2000).

Torres Ramírez, Bibiano, *La Armada de Barlovento* (Seville: Escuela de Estudios Hispano-Americanos, 1981).

Veitia Linage, Joseph de, *The Spanish Rule of Trade to the West-Indies: Containing an Account of the Casa de Contratacion. Written in Spanish by D. Joseph de Veitia Linage. Made English by Capt. John Stevens* (London: S. Crouch, 1702).

Walker, Geoffrey, *Spanish Politics and Imperial Trade, 1700–1789* (Bloomington: Indiana University Press, 1979).

Waller, George, *Samuel Vetch: Colonial Enterpriser* (Chapel Hill: University of North Carolina Press, 1960).

Ward, Christopher, *Imperial Panama – Commerce and Conflict in Isthmian America, 1550–1800* (Albuquerque: University of New Mexico Press, 1993).

Watt, Douglas, *The Price of Scotland: Darien, Union and the Wealth of Nations* (Edinburgh: Luath Press, 2007).

Weber, David, *Bárbaros: Spaniards and Their Savages in the Age of Enlightenment* (New Haven, CT: Yale University Press, 2005).

Weddle, Robert, *The French Thorn, Rival Explorers in the Spanish Sea, 1682–1762* (College Station, TX: Texas A&M Press, 1991).

Whatley, Christopher, *The Scots and the Union* (Edinburgh: Edinburgh University Press, 2007).

Willis, Sam, *The Admiral Benbow, the Life and Times of a Naval Legend* (London: Quercus, 2010).

JOURNAL AND BOOK ARTICLES, REPORTS, THESES

Agostini, Thomas, 'Deserted His Majesty's service: military runaways, the British–American press, and the problem of desertion during the Seven Years' War', *Journal of Social History*, Vol. 40:4 (Summer 2007), pp. 957–85.

Alexander, Arthur, 'Desertion and its punishment in revolutionary Virginia', *William and Mary Quarterly*, 3rd Series, Vol. 3:3 (July 1946), pp. 383–97.

Alsop, J. D., 'A Darien epilogue: Robert Allen in Spanish America', *The Americas*, Vol. 43 (1986), pp. 197–201.

Armitage, D., 'Making the Empire British: Scotland in the Atlantic World 1542–1707', *Past and Present*, Vol. 155 (May 1997), pp. 34–63.

Arroyo Vozmediano, Julio Luis, *El gran juego-Inglaterra y la sucesión española*, unpublished PhD thesis (Universidad Nacional de Educación a Distancia-España, 2013).

Barbour, Violet, 'Dutch and English merchant shipping in the seventeenth century', *The Economic History Review*, Vol. 2:2 (January 1930), pp. 261–90.

Bassett, W. G., 'English naval policy in the Caribbean, 1698–1703', *Bulletin of the Institute of Historical Research*, Vol. XI (1933–34), pp. 122–5.

Bassett, W. G., *The Caribbean in International Politics 1670–1707*, unpublished PhD thesis (University of London 1934).

Bingham, Hiram, 'Virginia letters on the Scots Darien colony, 1699', *American Historical Review*, Vol. X:4 (July 1905), pp. 812–15.

Bingham, Hiram, 'The early history of the Scots Darien Company', *Scottish Historical Review*, Vol. 3:10 (January 1906), pp. 210–17, 316–26, 437–48.

Botella-Ordinas, Eva, 'Debating empires, inventing empires: British territorial claims against the Spaniards in America, 1670–1714', *Journal for Early Modern Cultural Studies*, Vol. 10:1 (Spring 2010), pp. 142–68.

Brown, Vera Lee, 'Contraband trade: a factor in the decline of Spain's empire in America', *The Hispanic American Historical Review*, Vol. 8:2 (May 1928), pp. 178–89.

Buisseret, David, 'Spanish military engineers in the New World before 1750', in Dennis Reinhartz (ed.), *Mapping and Empire: Soldier-Engineers on the Southwestern Frontier* (Austin: University of Texas Press, 2005), pp. 44–56.

Burnard, Trevor, 'European migration to Jamaica, 1655–1780', *The William and Mary Quarterly*, 3rd Series, Vol. 53:4 (October 1996), pp. 769–96.

'Campaña de don Juan Pimienta, Gobernador de Cartagena, contra los escoceses del Darién, Diario de operaciónes. Año 1700', *Boletin de Historia y Antiguedades*, Vol. XIX: 224–5 (Bogotá, October–November 1932), pp. 646–64 (No. 224); pp. 730–44 (No. 225).

Cappon, Lester, 'The Blathwayt Papers of Colonial Williamsburg, Inc.', *The William and Mary Quarterly*, 3rd Series, Vol. 4:3 (July 1947), pp. 317–31.

Céspedes del Castillo, Guillermo, 'La defensa militar del istmo de Panamá a fines del siglo XVII y comienzos del XVIII', *Anuario de Estudios Americanistas, Tomo IX* (Seville: Escuela de Estudios Hispanoamericanos, 1952), pp. 235–75.

Christelow, Allan, 'Contraband trade between Jamaica and the Spanish Main', *Hispanic American Historical Review*, Vol. 22 (1942), pp. 309–43.

Cromwell, Jesse, 'Life on the margins: (ex) buccaneers and Spanish subjects on the Campeche Logwood periphery, 1660–1716', *Itinerario*, Vol. 33:3 (November 2009), pp. 43–71.

Cruxent, José María, 'Informe sobre un reconocimiento arqueológico en el Darién, Panamá', *Publicaciones de la revista Lotería, No. 9* (Panama: La Academia, 1959).

Fortune, Armando, 'Los negros cimarrones en Tierra Firme y su lucha por la libertad', *Lotería*, Vol. 171 (February 1970), pp. 17–43; Vol. 172 (March 1970), pp. 32–53; Vol. 173 (April 1970), pp. 16–40; Vol. 174 (May 1970), pp. 46–65.

Fradera, Josep, 'The Caribbean between empires: colonists, pirates, and slaves', in Stephan Palmié and Francisco Scarano (eds), *The Caribbean, a History of the Region and its Peoples* (Chicago: University of Chicago Press, 2011), pp. 165–77.

Gallup-Diaz, Ignacio, '"Haven't we come to kill the Spaniards?" The Tule Upheaval in eastern Panama, 1727–1728', *Colonial Latin American Review*, Vol. 10:2 (2001), pp. 251–71.

Gil-Bermejo García, Juana, 'La Casa de Contratación de Sevilla (algunos aspectos de su historia)', in *Anuario de Estudios Americanos XXX* (Seville: Escuela de Estudios Hispanoamericanos, 1973), pp. 679–761.

Grahn, Lance, 'Cartagena and its hinterland in the eighteenth century', in Franklin Knight and Peggy Liss (eds), *Atlantic Port Cities-Economy, Culture, and Society in the Atlantic World, 1650–1850* (Knoxville: University of Tennessee, 1991), pp. 168–95.

Gutiérrez Azopardo, Ildefonso, 'El comercio y mercado de negros esclavos en Cartagena de Indias (1533–1850)', *Quinto centenario*, No. 12 (Madrid 1987), pp. 187–210.

Hart, Francis, 'Spanish documents relating to the Scots settlement at Darien', *Proceedings of the Massachusetts Historical Society*, Vol. 63 (March 1930), pp. 3–17.

Hidalgo, Dennis, 'To get rich for our homeland: the Company of Scotland and the colonization of the Isthmus of Darien', *Colonial Latin American Historical Review*, Vol. 10:3 (Summer 2001), pp. 311–50.

Horton, Mark, *Caledonia Bay, Panama, 1979, a Preliminary Report on the Archaeological Project of Operation Drake* (London: Operation Drake, 1980).

Horton, Mark, 'To transmit to posterity the virtue, lustre and glory of their ancestors: Scottish pioneers in Darien, Panama', in Caroline Williams (ed), *Bridging the Early Modern Atlantic World: People, Products and Practices on the Move* (Farnham: Ashgate, 2009), pp. 131–50.

Jones, W. P., '"The bold adventurers": a quantitative analysis of the Darien subscription list (1696)', *Scottish Economic and Social History*, Vol. 21 (2001), pp. 22–42.

Karraker, Cyrus, 'The treasure expedition of Captain William Phips to the Bahama Banks', *The New England Quarterly, Inc.*, Vol. 5:4 (October 1932), pp. 731–52.

Karraker, Cyrus, 'Spanish treasure, casual revenue of the Crown', *The Journal of Modern History*, Vol. 5:3 (September 1933), pp. 310–18.

Landsman, Ned, 'Nation, migration and the province in the first British Empire: Scotland and the Americas 1600–1800', *The American Historical Review*, Vol. 104:2 (April 1999), pp. 463–75.

Langebaek, Carl, 'Cuna long distance journeys: the result of colonial interaction', *Ethnology*, Vol. 30:4 (October 1991), pp. 371–80.

Lockhart, Donald, ' The Scottish origins of Colonel John Anderson: commander of the *Unicorn* during the Darien expedition and president of His Majesty's Council for the Province of New Jersey', *The American Genealogist*, Vol. 83:1 (January–April 2008), pp. 1–3.

McPhail, Bridget, 'Through a glass, darkly; Scots and Indians converge at Darien', *Eighteenth Century Life*, Vol. 18 (1994), pp. 129–47.

Morgan, William, 'The expedition of Baron de Pointis against Cartagena', *The American Historical Review*, Vol. 37:2 (January 1932), pp. 237–54.

M'Robert, Patrick and Carl Bridenbaugh, 'Tour through part of the north provinces of America', *The Pennsylvania Magazine of History and Biography*, Vol. 59:2 (April 1935), pp. 134–80.

Munive, Moisés, 'Por el buen orden: El diario vivir en Cartagena y Mompox colonial', *Historia critica*, No. 28 (2004), pp. 177–200.

Nettels, Curtis, 'England and the Spanish–America trade, 1680–1715', *The Journal of Modern History*, Vol. III:1 (March 1931), pp. 1–32.

Oliva Melgar, José María, 'La Metrópoli sin territorio. ¿Crisis del comercio de Indias en el siglo XVII o perdida del control del monopolio?', in Carlos Martínez Shaw and José María Oliva Melgar (eds), *El Sistema atlántico español: (siglos XVII–XIX)* (Madrid: Marcial Pons, 2005), pp. 19–73.

Paul, Helen Julia, 'The Darien Scheme and Anglophobia in Scotland', *Discussion Papers in Economics and Econometrics*, No. 0925 (University of Southampton, 2009)

Pears, Thomas Jr, 'The design of Darien', *Journal of the Department of History of the Office of the General Assembly of the Presbyterian Church in the U.S.A.*, Vol. 17:1–2 (March–June 1936), pp. 5–108.

Pike, Ruth, 'Black rebels: the Cimarrons of sixteenth-century Panama', *The Americas*, Vol. 64:2 (October 2007), pp. 243–66.

Rodriguez, Frederick Marshal, *Cimarron Revolts and Pacification in New Spain, the Isthmus of Panama and Colonial Colombia, 1503–1800* (unpublished PhD thesis, Loyola University of Chicago, 1979).

Sanders, G. Earl, 'Counter-contraband in Spanish America; handicaps of the governors in the Indies', *The Americas*, Vol. 34:1 (July 1977), pp. 59–80.

Scelle, George, 'The slave trade in the Spanish colonies of America: the asiento', *The American Journal of International Law*, Vol. 4:3 (July 1910), pp. 612–61.

Service, Elman, 'Indian–European relations in colonial Latin America', *American Anthropologist*, Vol. 57:3, Part 1 (June 1955), pp. 411–25.

Smout, T. C., Ned Landsman and T. M. Devine, 'Scottish emigration in the seventeenth and eighteenth centuries', in Nicholas Canny (ed.), *Europeans on the Move – Studies on European Migration, 1500–1800* (Oxford: Clarendon Press, 1994), pp. 76–112.

Snyder, Holly, 'English markets, Jewish merchants and Atlantic endeavors – Jews and the making of British transatlantic commercial culture, 1650–1800', in Richard Kagan and Philip Morgan (eds), *Atlantic Diasporas: Jews, Conversos and Crypto-Jews in the Age of Mercantilism* (Baltimore, MD: Johns Hopkins University Press, 2009), pp. 50–74.

Spencer, J. J., 'Some Darien letters', *The Scottish Historical Review*, Vol. 11 (1914), pp. 404–8.

Steckley, George, 'Litigious mariners: wage cases in the seventeenth-century Admiralty Court', *The Historical Journal*, Vol. 42:2 (June 1999), pp. 315–45.

Storrs, Christopher, 'Disaster at Darien (1698–1700)? The persistence of Spanish imperial power on the eve of the demise of the

Spanish Habsburgs', *European History Quarterly*, Vol. 29:5 (1999), pp. 5–38.

Storrs, Christopher, 'Intelligence and the formulation of policy and strategy in early modern Europe: the Spanish monarchy in the reign of Charles II (1665–1700)', *Intelligence and National Security*, Vol. 21:4 (August 2006), pp. 493–519.

Strain, Issac, *A Paper on the History and Prospects of Interoceanic Communication by the American Isthmus, read by Lieut. I. C. Strain, U.S.N., before the New York Historical Society, June 17, 1856* (New York 1856).

Sullivan, John, *Report of Historical and Technical Information Relating to the Problem of Interoceanic Communication by Way of the American Isthmus* (Washington, DC: Government Printing Office, 1883).

Taylor, Benjamin, 'The Darien Expedition', (name of journal missing from copy available as Spencer 71, University of Glasgow Special Collections), (Paisley 1892).

Torres de Araúz, Reina, 'Datos etno-históricos cunas según documentos de la colonia escocesa en Darién', *Actas del II Simposium Nacional de Antropología, Arqueología y Etnohistoria de Panamá* (Panama 1971), pp. 93–111.

Torres de Araúz, Reina, 'Nuevo Edimburgo del Darién, Los Cunas: Anfitriones de Los Escoceses', *Lotería*, Vols 314–16 (May–July 1982), pp. 134–56.

Vásquez Pino, Daniela, 'Políticas Borbónicas en la frontera. El caso del Darién. 1760–1810', *historia 2.0*, Vol. 2:3 (2012), pp. 89–103.

Vaughan, G. E., 'Historia de la colonia escosesa en el Darién, 1698–1700, y su importancia en los Anales Britanicos', *Lotería*, Vol. VII:81 (August 1962), pp. 21–52.

Vaughan, G. E., 'The story of the Scottish settlement in the Darien (1698–1700) and its importance in British history (improved version of lecture given in Spanish at the University of Panama 15 June 1962, and published in Panama in *Loteria*, Volume VII, No. 81, August 1962)', (unpublished, undated).

Wassén, Henry (ed.), 'Anonymous Spanish manuscript from 1739 on the province Darien', *Etnologiska Studier*, Vol. 10 (1940), pp. 80–146.

Webb, Stephen, 'William Blathwayt, imperial fixer: from popish plot to glorious revolution', *The William and Mary Quarterly*, 3rd Series, Vol. 25:1 (January 1968), pp. 3–21.

Webb, Stephen, 'William Blathwayt, imperial fixer: muddling through to empire, 1689–1717', *The William and Mary Quarterly*, Vol. 26:3 (July 1969), pp. 373–415.

Young, John, 'The Scottish Parliament and the politics of empire: Parliament and the Darien Project, 1695–1707', *Parliament, Estates and Representations*, Vol. 27 (2007), pp. 786–804.

Index

Note: illustrations are indicated by page numbers in bold